Cross-Cultural Encounters in Modern World History

Jon Thares Davidann
Hawaii Pacific University

Marc Jason Gilbert
Hawaii Pacific University

PEARSON

Boston   Columbus   Indianapolis   New York   San Francisco   Upper Saddle River
Amsterdam   Cape Town   Dubai   London   Madrid   Milan   Munich   Paris   Montreal   Toronto
Delhi   Mexico City   São Paulo   Sydney   Hong Kong   Seoul   Singapore   Taipei   Tokyo

To Beth and Cathy

Executive Acquisitions Editor: Jeff Lasser
Editorial Assistant: Julia Feltus
Senior Marketing Manager: Maureen Prado Roberts
Marketing Coordinator: Samantha Bennett
Marketing Assistant: Diana Griffin
Production Editor: Meghan DeMaio
Creative Director: Jayne Conte
Cover Designer: Axell Design
Cover Image: © Gideon Mendel/In Pictures/Corbis
Editorial Production and Composition Service: Franklin Mathews,
    Integra Software Services Pvt. Ltd.
Printer/Binder/Cover Printer: R.R. Donnelley & Sons

On the cover: Playtime at Kingsmead School, London. Photograph by Gideon Mendel.

Credits and acknowledgments borrowed from other sources and reproduced, with permission, in this textbook appear on the appropriate page within text.

Library of Congress Cataloging-in-Publication Data
Davidann, Jon Thares
    Cross-cultural encounters in modern world history/Jon Thares Davidann
    Marc Jason Gilbert.—1st ed.
       p. cm.
    ISBN-13: 978-0-205-53266-7 (alk. paper)
    ISBN-10: 0-205-53266-7 (alk. paper)
    1. World history.   2. Intercultural communication—History.   3. Imperialism—History.
    4. Culture diffusion—History.   I. Gilbert, Marc Jason.   II. Title.
    D20.D384 2013
    909—dc23

                                                                        2011049728

10 9 8 7 6 5 4 3 2 1 RRD 13 12

ISBN-10: 0-205-53266-7
ISBN-13: 978-0-205-53266-7

CONTENTS

ACKNOWLEDGMENTS

The authors wish to thank the following reviewers for their helpful suggestions: John P. Boubel, Bethany Lutheran College; Daniel R. Headrick, Roosevelt University; L. Edward Hicks, Faulkner University; Theodore Kallman, San Joaquin Delta College; Mary Louise Loe, James Madison University; Timothy Schroer, University of West Georgia; and Rick Warner, Wabash College Christine Skwiot, Georgia State University, Jerry Bentley, University of Hawaii at Manoa, Peter Hoffenberg, University of Hawaii at Manoa.

Introduction: Cross-Cultural Encounters and Hybrid Culture

Introduction: Cross-Cultural Encounters and Hybrid Culture

One of the hallmarks of world history is the ever-increasing ability of humans to cross cultural boundaries. Yet, despite the growing frequency of these encounters over time, our understanding of these connections historically and in the contemporary world is rather limited. This volume is designed to address this key facet of the meeting of peoples around the globe from 1500 to the present. It examines the historical record of such contacts, distilling from those processes patterns of interaction, different peoples' perspectives, and the ways these encounters tended to subvert the commonly accepted assumptions about differences between peoples in terms of race, ethnicity, nationhood, or empire. A short review of the tools used to examine that record will demonstrate the need for and intended value of the present volume in modern world history.

The publication of Jerry H. Bentley's *Old World Encounters: Cross-Cultural Contacts and Exchanges in Pre-Modern Times* (1993) marked a watershed in the study of world history. Bentley was not the first to illustrate the primacy of cultural contact and exchange as an agent of historical change, nor was he the first to suggest that some of the more significant and lasting contacts between even antagonistic civilizations generated mutual respect. *Old World Encounters* was, however, the first to study the dynamics of encounter in a manner accessible to students by enhancing the traditional historical narrative through the use of brief but effective references to groundbreaking scholarship and applying throughout the text the illustrative power of the testimony of those involved in these encounters and exchanges, from Popes and Emperors to Christian Crusaders and Buddhist scholars.

However, instructors and students seeking to continue that discussion into more recent centuries have until now had to choose between using anthologies offering a host of primary sources or employing collections of essays by scholars. While useful, the primary sources approach usually asks beginning students to analyze documents produced by societies of which they then have only minimal knowledge, while edited scholarly collec- tions, such as the otherwise excellent *Implicit Understandings: Observing, Reporting and Reflecting on the Encounters between Europeans and Other Peoples in the Early Modern Era* (1994), edited by Stuart Schwartz, require graduate-level knowledge and reading comprehension.

Cross-Cultural Encounters in Modern World History seeks to provide a means to explore this subject suitable not only for more advanced students of world history but also for students at the secondary school as well as community college and the introductory undergraduate level. To do so, it employs very accessible language and closely connects scholarly discussion with expanded references to the voices of the participants.

The authors believe a user-friendly approach is necessary because of the complexities of encounters in the modern world. Studying encounters tends to be overly informed by the rise of world empires eventually domi- nated by the west, and thus casts modern history as a political struggle between dominant and subordinate cultures, of western imperialists against non-western indigenous peoples doomed to subordination, and inevitably lays stress on winners or losers. There is some value in this approach in that it can demonstrate, for example, that the rise of nationalism and imperialism often leads to limits on social tolerance and forces encounters into more nar- row categories of citizenship or noncitizen.

However, pursuit of that view to the exclusion of others can obscure the cross-cultural encounters that transformed both the supposed victor and the vanquished. Only an "encounters model" can begin to explain why for centuries Christians fought in the armies of the Muslim Ottoman Empire, why there are mosques on virtually every American military base today, even those in the Middle East, and why so many peoples in conflict seek a "mid- dle ground," as was so often the case among American Indians and European settlers in North America. Narratives which stress a single dominant culture obscure those aspects of encounter that suggest hybridity, syncretism, or cultural blending. Even modern colonial populations assumed to be strictly divided by race interacted in ways which altered the culture of the colo- nizer as well as the colonized, such as in the rise of chicken curry *masala* as the national dish of Britain, whose people once sought to impose their own culture on the people of India. The costs of ignoring such hybridity were recently revealed in an interview with British historian Niall Ferguson, who has been tasked with reforming history education in his country. When asked if he intended to promote knowledge of the world's civilizations in British schools, he replied that he would be happy to promote discussion of what western civilization got right and what non-western civilization got wrong, without conceding that what the non-west got right and shared with the west helped create the west as we know it—from its science to its music and, yes, even its foodways!

The encounters approach thus has the potential to open up history to a variety of different perspectives and experiences and reveal key patterns and transformations that are the chief subjects of world history. This approach often focuses on first encounters, and does so here, but these encounters are addressed so as to suggest their long term and often contemporary significance. These developments are as subtle yet as transformative as the rise of a belief in the appearance of the Virgin of Guadalupe (the Brown Virgin Mary) that followed the Spanish conquest of Latin America in the sixteenth century and the taking up of the wearing of the veil by Muslim women in post-colonial France in the twenty-first century. This work intends to illuminate both the large-scale (the "macro-historical") and the most intimate impacts of global encounters in the modern era. That dual goal is achieved through a focus on evidence and major themes together.

CONTENTS

The encounters studied in the first section of this volume include those associated with the Spanish conquest of the New World, the activities of Jesuit missionaries in East Asia, and the role of foreigners in the Ottoman Empire. These chapters focus on differences based upon religion and civilization. In Chapter 1, the expanding Spanish empire, which invaded the Caribbean and Mexico, brought with it the notion that the religion of Christianity and European civilization was superior to the religion and civilization of the Native Americans of the New World. This attitude was used to justify the Spanish conquest and also the virtual enslavement of Native Americans. Europeans, however, were not the only group to believe in the superiority of their own civilization. East Asians considered their civilization superior to the barbarism of Europeans, and therefore the Catholic missionaries of the Jesuit order sent to Asia from Europe were looked down upon and at times distrusted. Both Chinese and Japanese leaders severely circumscribed their interactions of their people with European missionaries, which included restrictions on their movement in the interior of their countries. By contrast, the Turkish Ottoman Empire, while it maintained that Islam was superior to other religions, interpreted Islam to allow Christians and Jews to live and work in its lands.

All empires discussed in this section, both western and non-western, possessed more military power than the other side in these encounters. At times, this disparity of power led these empires to force their will upon the other; violence thus often characterized these encounters. The Spaniards used the pretext of indigenous rebellion—the resistance of Native Americans to Spanish domination—to declare war on the peoples of Central America, conquer them, and enslave them. In addition, the Spaniards maintained that Native

Americans possessed no civilization or religion (neither of which is true) and believed that this gave them the right to force them to convert to Catholic Christianity. In sixteenth-century Japan, the political leadership allowed Jesuit missionaries to operate within severe constraints, but in a clash of cultural systems, the missionaries produced converts whose first loyalty was to the Christian god, not to their Japanese lords, and so these new Christians and by extension the missionaries became objects of suspicion. By 1640, the Japanese executed or banished all the missionaries and closed their borders to the west. In China, foreigners were generally banned from travel into the interior of the country, but Jesuits were eventually allowed to do so because they were considered useful for their knowledge of astronomy, map-making skills, and peculiar inventions, such as mechanical clocks. Even though the missionaries adopted Confucian ideas and dress to facilitate conversion to Christianity, the Chinese, who interpreted this as acknowledgment of the superiority of their civilization, embraced the missionaries not as one of their own but as ingenious westerners. Although some of the missionaries, such as Mateo Ricci, became well known and were respected in China for their writings, the missionary effort failed to produce a significant number of converts. However, the Ottoman Empire represents a significant departure from these scenarios. The Ottomans had tolerance built into their civilization and their interpretation of Islam. Ottoman laws provided protection for foreigners and sanction for people of different religions; for example, they encouraged communities of Sephardic Jews exiled from Spain by Christians to settle in their cities. Native Americans in the Caribbean also had a degree of tolerance of the "outsider" built into many of their cultures, but the power differential between them and the Spaniard conquistadors, who were exceedingly intolerant of others, was too great for them to successfully maintain their values and civilization in the face of military conquest and depopulation by disease.

In these cases, the outsiders, whether they were Spanish conquistadors, Jesuit missionaries, or Jewish merchants, impacted the societies they entered in important ways, although in East Asia the influence of outsiders was deliberately constrained by regimes that limited their movements. Spaniards imposed their religion and culture and today Catholicism and Spanish-influenced cultural patterns are dominant in Latin America, and Jews from Spain brought their language, religion, and trades to the Ottomans and helped the empire to flourish. A Castilian version of Spanish brought by the Jews became the language of business in parts of the Ottoman Empire.

However, the influence of outsiders must not be overstated since new evidence indicates that host societies treated outsiders as people useful to them, not as gods to be worshipped. They were perceived by the host cultures within the hosts' cultural context which should not surprise us but changes how we interpret these encounters, not just as stories of conquest or domination but as interactions where the perspective of the host was as important as that of the outsider. For instance, Chapter 1 sheds new light on the traditional historical narrative of the Aztecs falling down in awe of the Spaniards or prophesying their own doom; instead the evidence in this case shows the Aztecs saw the Spaniards as outsiders who needed to be overawed by Aztec greatness and eventually placed into subjection. Likewise, the power and influence of Jesuit missionary Matteo Ricci upon China, once exaggerated, is likely to have been much overstated. From the Chinese perspective, Ricci was not a true Chinese Confucian scholar, but rather an ingenious outsider whose ideas were intriguing but did not fundamentally change Confucianism in China.

Perhaps as important, the outsiders were changed as well through their encounters. So the changes were mutual, transforming both "insiders" and "outsiders" in the encounter. Some Jews in Ottoman lands converted to Islam and Jewish cultural habits fused with Muslim and Greek culture to form a common culture in many places. Jesuit missionaries were converted to East Asian culture and came to see China and Japan as their true homeland. And while Catholicism dominates in Latin America, it has become indigenized in significant ways. The celebration of the European Catholic "All Saints Day" as the indigenous-themed "Day of the Dead" is just one example.

Chapters 4–6 study a succeeding period when encounters were characterized by an openness which allowed the creation of middle ground alliances and moments of cultural hybridity between different tribes and nations in the Great Lakes region of North America between French and Native American tribes and sporadically in encounters between Europeans and Pacific Islanders in the Pacific and among Russians and steppe peoples on the Eurasian steppe. These middle ground encounters were mostly frontier encounters where territories and boundaries were not well defined and a relative parity of military and political power allowed for shifting alliances that were innovative and practical in nature. In these middle ground situations, both groups attempted to use the others' cultural frameworks in an appeal for peace and collaboration.

In Chapter 4, Native Americans in the Great Lakes region were particularly adept at negotiating the middle ground. Their traditional openness to outsiders allowed them to learn outsiders' cultural frameworks and in turn make appeals to these frameworks when needed. Threatened by the powerful Iroquois Confederacy, Algonquian peoples and French missionaries and military leaders in the region who were small in number and militarily very weak explored the middle ground, which was a metaphorical place where disparate cultures found common ground. Diplomatic alliances were negotiated, conflicts resolved, and cultural compromises made. In the Pacific Ocean, castaways from European ships in the Pacific were offered new identities and some were adopted into Polynesian society, as seen in Chapter 5. In addition, the British explorers who found peoples new to them were also presented with middle ground offers of sex and other gifts to welcome these newcomers into Polynesian society. However, the British officers sometimes refused these gifts and treated the islanders brusquely in which case the attempt to build a middle ground failed; at times these explorers so enraged the Polynesians that they were attacked and killed as in the case of Captain Cook in Hawaii. In Chapter 6, on the Eurasian steppe, a region located south of Russia and north of India, steppe khanates and Russian diplomats attempted to build a middle ground with mixed success. As in the other cases, neither side possessed a monopoly of power. In the early period of the encounter, the Russians were weaker and feared invasion and enslavement by the khanates. The Russians and Steppe peoples signed "sherts" or treaties of peace and cooperation. Even the word "shert" is significant because it was not a Russian term but Turko-Mongol term. This middle ground was less successful because the two sides interpreted the treaties and the roles of the Russian leader differently, the steppe peoples arguing that the Russian Tsar was just one among many princes and the treaties were simple alliances that could be broken at will, and the Russians arguing that the sherts were pledges of loyalty to the Tsar and gave them suzerainty over the steppe peoples who had signed. On the border between Russia and China, attempts at building a middle ground with Mongol factions there had purely diplomatic goals and created temporary stability that gave the Chinese the upper hand in the conquest of Mongols that followed.

These middle ground arrangements were easily broken and as Europeans in North America and the Pacific became more powerful and indigenous cultures transformed by their encounter with Europeans, indigenous dependency on Europeans resulted. In North America, as Europeans and then Americans in the new United States increasingly encroached upon Native American land and the viability of beaver-trading was destroyed, Native Americans became more and more dependent upon them to provide the basic necessities of life. In the Pacific, Polynesian cultural practices were banned by puritanical missionaries and they were reduced to poverty as Euro-Americans took control of their land and sovereignty through colonization. On the Eurasian steppe, Russian and Chinese domination produced similar results with poverty and dependence common among the steppe peoples.

Although these middle ground developments proved to be tenuous and temporary, they continued to influence events and identities long after their practical usefulness had disappeared. The encounter of Native Americans and the French produced Native American Christian converts among the Huron peoples and to this day, the Huron sing a Christmas carol called the "Huron Carol," which reflects their dual identity as Huron and French. In the Pacific Ocean, the encounter of Europeans and Polynesians and its impact on Europeans live on in Paul Gauguin's nostalgic and unfettered paintings of Polynesian women in their "natural state." In addition, Native Hawaiians, Europeans, and other immigrants in Hawaii developed a new language in the nineteenth century referred to as "pidgin" and its continuing use today is reminder of the encounter of westerners and Polynesians. This along with the renewal of the Hawaiian language and the Hawaiian cultural renaissance indicates strong cultural persistence. Finally, the continuing resistance of Caucasus Muslims to Russian rule in Chechnya and Ingushetia is a reminder of encounters past on the Eurasian steppe.

In the time period from the late eighteenth century, encounters were powerfully influenced by the growth of European empire and the rise of modern nationalism with its claims on identity and its definition of insiders and outsiders. The encounters in Chapters 7–9 focus attention on questions of resistance/acquiescence to dominant imperial powers in India, the Japanese Empire, and Africa. Although religion and civilization still played a role in the encounters, these issues were either overshadowed by or linked to nationalism in the march to build European empires. As much as nationalist ideologies in modern empires restricted the play and flexibility in these encounters, there was also room, especially early in each encounter, to redefine nation, religion, or civilization into moments where imperial overlords and subject peoples found common ground in the form of shared interest in indigenous civilizational roots, interracial marriage, and/or practical issues of power and governance. In addition, indigenous peoples who were being colonized cleverly used the encounters to gain knowledge of European political ideals of freedom and liberty and then turned these ideas upon the colonizers to spark independence movements.

The British expansion into India stimulated a reexamination of Indian values and practices through the work of British Orientalists (students of eastern culture) who saw some of the values and products of ancient Indian culture as superior to their own. This started an incipient cultural renaissance in India led by both Indian and British intellectuals who found universals applicable to all societies in Indian ideas. This atmosphere was squelched only when the British approach shifted to forced westernization in education and an increasing clampdown in the political arena. The British in India believed they were inculcating British national characteristics into the Indian elites but in fact they laid the groundwork for the independence movement in which Mohandas Gandhi took British and western ideas, fused them with Indian concepts, such as *satyagraha*, and used them against the British in his campaign for Indian independence.

In Africa, in spite of the European goals of hegemony, there arose considerable space for Africans to resist European imperialism in the process. In the southern part of Africa, the rise of indigenous Christianity and African-led churches that came from the initial encounter of missionaries and Africans expressed African independence in a time of European domination. Later, in Sudan, the encounter of Sudanese subjects and British overlords produced resistance to British rule. Sudan's independence movement, like India's, reversed the ideological flow of knowledge and embraced a modern western identity of the yet to be founded Sudanese nation as a unifying force against the British.

Finally the Japanese Empire, in a moment when modern nationalism reached its peak before World War II, ruthlessly stamped out resistance and forced its subject peoples in much of Asia to become Japanized in language, education, and religious and cultural practice. But even in Japan's rigidly controlled empire, there were examples of more open encounters with others such as interethnic marriages between Aboriginal Taiwanese and Japanese merchants in Taiwan's highlands that sealed economic alliances.

In the post–World War II period there is some evidence to suggest that nationalist ideologies which defined differences in encounters so strongly in the modern period have begun to weaken. Religion and civilization have reemerged in complicated ways to define differences while the middle ground space in which encounters can be redefined has expanded dramatically through intermarriage, economic exchanges, and flows of people across borders through global migration and travel. Chapter 10, which studies postwar immigration into Europe in the late twentieth and twenty-first centuries, has challenged Europeans' sense of identity and threatened their sense of security while creating a fierce debate about the meaning of immigration and its impact on European society. But immigrants themselves have described and defined a much more complicated process of cultural adaptation and change. Here there is ample evidence of new cultural forms and shared interests and vision arising from the encounter of Europeans and immigrants, from the coercive Danish marriage law, which has forced Muslims in Denmark to consider marrying non-Muslim citizens rather than selecting a Muslim partner who then immigrates into Denmark, to the rich multi-ethnic collage of cultures in today's Amsterdam, where for example Surinamese cultural forms from Latin America have influenced mainstream Dutch culture.

Conclusion

It has long been commonplace to argue that the more one learns about other cultures, the more one knows of ones own. Today, however, we live in a globalizing culture, which blurs the difference between "us" and the "other" each time we put on a shirt (most likely made in Southeast Asia), read an illustrated book (in most cases inspired by Japanese anime) or buy flowers for a loved one (in the United States, the flowers are most likely cultivated in Latin America). In such an interlinked world, it becomes of the first importance to master those processes that transcend human differences and enable us to negotiate the spaces in between cultures. The rising challenges posed by ecological degradation, population growth, commodity shortages, the spread of diseases, and the impact of mass migration across continents and from the countryside to the cities seem to be leaving humanity little choice but to do so. This volume is intended to serve to aid in that task by illuminating humanity's past successes, as well as its failures, in building such a future.

PART

B

Encounters
in the Age of
Exploration

Power and Unpredictability, Conquistadors, and Native Peoples: Conquest of the Americas

Generations of students know that the first encounter between Europeans and Native Americans took place when Christopher Columbus "set sail on the ocean blue" for the first of his voyages to what came in Europe to be called the New World in 1492. Few students, however, are aware of the significance of the early years of the Euro-American encounter or how controversial these early cross-cultural meetings proved to be.

The importance of these early encounters is suggested by the racial mixing of Spaniards and Native Americans that occurred during its initial stages. Hernán Cortés, a conquistador who came after Columbus and overthrew the Aztec Empire, had a male child with a Native American princess the Spaniards called Donna Marina. His birth marked the beginning of centuries of racial blending that gave shape to the largely mixed race (mestizo) population of Latin America today.

The early decades of the Euro-American encounter are controversial because people today debate whether Columbus was a hero or villain. Traditionally, Europeans and Euro-Americans celebrated Columbus's so-called discovery of the New World with a special day, Columbus Day. But Native Americans and others then and now see Columbus and his fellow conquistadors in a different light, as an evil force responsible for the enslavement and murder of their peoples. (In Native American history, Cortés's wife is called La

Malinche, "the evil one.") The five-hundredth anniversary of Columbus's voyage in 1993 became an opportunity for those who took the latter view to make their voices known by protesting the celebrations. Even the use of the term "discovery" in Columbus's arrival in the New World has been called into question. What does it mean to discover a place that already has millions of people living there?

Studying the actual face-to-face encounters between Columbus (and those that followed in his footsteps) and Native Americans can provide us with a more complete history of the Columbian encounter, while also providing us with a more complete picture of the making of the modern Americas. The Columbian encounter was characterized by an imbalance of political and military power. But because cultural power is less predictable and more ambiguous than military and political power, Euro-American cultural encounters often produced unexpected results. The Spaniards dominated the Native Americans politically and militarily. But the Spaniards themselves were changed by the encounter, as they mixed culturally as well as racially with the indigenous population. Similarly, Native Americans, who were once portrayed as going to their deaths in defense of their ancient cultures, now appear to have been more pragmatic in their relations with the Spaniards. The lines drawn between the roles of the colonizer and the colonized were thus complex: fraught with many moments of cross-cultural misunderstanding and role reversals.

"INDIOS"

Native Americans were labeled by Columbus as "Indios" because he believed he had arrived in Asia at an area referred to by Europeans as the Indies because of its proximity to India. However, the word and its cognate "Indian" do a poor job of representing Native Americans then and now, describing neither their home nor ethnicity. It is only because Europeans conquered the New World that the label stuck. The term "Native American" is much more descriptive of the place and origins of the indigenous peoples of the Americas.

Columbus's encounter set in motion a long-term decimation of the Native American population through warfare, virtual slavery, and disease. However, we must be careful in approaching the encounter in this way because the story of the depopulation of the New World and domination by Europeans suggests a tragic account of decline and disappearance. Native Americans did not disappear from the stage of history. Rather, their populations, after a dramatic decline, recovered and mixed with Spaniards and others. Their cultures survived, fused with Spanish culture to make a new hybrid culture that thrived in many parts of the Americas. Thus, Columbus's encounter with Native Americans is just the beginning of the story of New World encounters that continues today.

EUROPEAN AND NATIVE AMERICAN PERCEPTIONS

For several centuries before Columbus, Europeans knew little of the world beyond the Mediterranean. The book *Marco Polo's Travels*, published around 1300, the story of Marco Polo's travels from Europe to the seat of the Mongol

Empire in Mongolia and China and back to Europe via India, became for many Europeans the sole source of information about what to them was the "outside world." The book was well known and widely read and included assessments of the grandeur of Asian empires and the great value of the region's spices, but also included fantastic tales that much later raised questions as to whether Polo actually made the trip. In any event, Europeans saw a wealthy, if also strange and alien, world through Marco Polo's writing. These fantastical ideas of what lay beyond Europe included sea monsters and the mythical islands of Atlantis in the Atlantic, while to the east of Europe were great riches but also the dangers of the Mongols, the greatly feared warriors from Mongolia who conquered central Asia in the thirteenth century and threatened Europe. The Mongols were seen by some Europeans as a mythical race of human monsters—the Gog and Magog.

Few Europeans traveled outside of Europe because overland travel was very slow and arduous. It took European emissaries of the Pope more than a year to reach the seat of the Mongol Empire in Karakorum, Mongolia, from Italy, and Marco Polo's trip to China took three years. The earth was known to be round (almost no Europeans actually then believed that the world was flat) but much smaller than it really was. Because the world was actually larger than thought, estimates of sailing times to reach Asia were inaccurate. When Columbus proposed sailing west to reach the Far East, he believed it would take a few weeks. Of course, Columbus did not know that there was an entire continent in the way.

Europeans categorized some peoples from outside of Europe as barbarians. According to European thought, barbarians lacked an ordered existence, possessed no manufacturing, had no technological advancements, did not have agriculture, had no religion, and lived in forests, and therefore were fit only for conquest. While Europeans believed themselves more "civilized" and thus superior to these outsiders, many of their technological advances (such as gunpowder) and their most valuable trade came from China. Moreover, Europeans were rarely in a position of military or political superiority over any society in the post-classical world (500–1500 BCE). For instance, it was well recognized that if the "barbarian" Mongols chose to conquer all of Europe, they could easily destroy any European army, hence the great fear Europeans had of the Mongol "hordes."

Christianity marked another distinction between Europeans and outsiders. Christianity was an aggressive expansionist religion. The Crusades (1100–1300) inaugurated a campaign to convert outsiders to Christianity and conquer foreign lands for Christianity, especially Jerusalem, which was considered the home of Christianity. In addition, the reconquest of the Muslim kingdoms (Moors) in southern Spain, which took place shortly before Columbus sailed, created an entire class of warriors (conquistadors) looking for employment and primed to slaughter foes with non-Christian religious beliefs—which they were then already engaged in doing to heretical communities and Jews in Europe. European Christians believed that their religion was the one true faith. Christianity in Europe distinguished between infidels and pagans—infidels possessed false religion, but pagans had no religion. According to Catholic doctrine, conversion must be voluntary, unless the peoples were warlike, in which case forced conversion at the point of a sword was allowed.

Native American perceptions are more difficult to uncover. Most Native American cultures were oral cultures without written language. Thus, written descriptions of their ideas or their world are rare. The exception to this is the Mayan and the Aztec (Nahua) peoples, who both had writing systems. But the Spaniards destroyed much of their writing during conquest as their knowledge was considered pagan and thus dangerous. So we have precious little information on which to base such an assessment. Studies of Native American cultural practices can give us insights into their perceptions.

The Taino, sometimes referred to as Arawaks, were the first people Columbus met on the island of Hispaniola, home of Haiti and the Dominican Republic today. The Taino practiced extensive irrigation systems and used raised mound agriculture. They raised cassava and sweet potatoes, and also corn but this was less important. The Taino violated European norms by their nakedness. The men were naked except for an occasional loincloth and women wore skirts only. Europeans considered nakedness a sign of barbarism and primitivity so Columbus and other explorers concluded that the Taino had no civilization at all. The Taino also developed a ball game played in a public square similar to a game played in other areas of Central America. This evidence suggests long-range communication or migration of individuals who brought the game to the Taino. The Taino had extensive trade networks, though on a small scale, with other islands in the Caribbean. But they lacked the organizational structure to provide profitable long-range trade with Europeans.

The Taino were very welcoming of Columbus and his men until they saw or experienced the abuses arising from domination by the Spaniards. The Taino perspective on outsiders was framed by their religion, their family system, and their economic relations. The Taino religion had deities and icons for worship and small household shrines; their shamans or religious leaders were also the healers. The Taino religion was nonexclusive, unlike the Spaniards' Christianity. They were tolerant of others' concept of god, in part because their own religion had more than one god. They never attempted to impose their religion on the Spaniards. Of course there was little chance of this once the Spaniards began to conquer them and control them through slavery and forced labor. Their family or kinship system also encouraged an open attitude toward outsiders. Because trade, wealth, and economic activity were shared and distributed via families, finding outsiders who could be added to the family network as fictive kin would provide more resources and the potential for more trade for the clan, as in the case of a war captive who might be adopted by a family as in North America or Polynesia (Chapters 4 and 5). So outsiders represented a potential new source of wealth for the Taino. Thus it is quite understandable that the Europeans would have been welcomed.

That the Taino had no experience with Europeans, however, proved to be a grave disadvantage. They did not understand Europeans' exclusivist religious views, diplomatic methods, or warfare. They did have some experience with hostile outsiders. The Caribs, as the Spaniards labeled them, were a warlike rival people who would kidnap war brides from the Taino. So the idea that the Taino were a naïve innocent people can be discarded, but they and other Native Americans were unfamiliar with the Europeans' ease in resorting to violence and their implements of war. Their surprise at the use of the latter is documented in what accounts we do have of their responses when they witnessed Spaniard weapons being used.

> A thing like a ball of stone comes out of its entrails: it comes out shooting sparks and raining fire. The smoke that comes out with it has a pestilent odor, like that of rotten mud. If the cannon is aimed against a mountain, the mountain splits and cracks open. If it is aimed against a tree, it shatters the tree into splinters. This is a most unnatural sight, as if the tree had exploded from within.[1]

Native Americans were amazed at the sight of Spanish soldiers sheathed in metal. According to them, Spaniard horses, an animal not then present in the Americas, were magnificent, and seen as crushing the earth under their hooves. Native Americans described the Spaniard conquistadors and their war dogs in their own words.

> Their dogs are enormous, with flat ears and long, dangling tongues. The color of their eyes is a burning yellow; their eyes flash fire and throw off sparks. Their bellies are hollow, their flanks long and narrow. They are tireless and very powerful. They bound here and there, panting with their tongues hanging out.
> The stranger bodies are completely covered, so that only their faces can be seen. Their skin is white as if made of lime. They have yellow hair though some of them have black. Their beards are long and yellow, and their moustaches are also yellow. Their hair is curly, with fine very thin strands...[2]

Their surprise at Spaniards' weapons and appearance allowed Spaniards a significant advantage in battle because they could employ these weapons before Native Americans had much time to adjust and develop a successful strategy to confront these newcomers. Thus though wary of foreign visitors in general the peaceful Taino were no match for the aggressive warlike Spanish.

COLUMBUS AND THE ROUTE TO ASIA

The reason Columbus sailed west from Spain and encountered the Taino was the wealth of Asia. Asia was perceived as a place of great riches by Europeans, who traded for coveted luxury items from that region, such as silk, porcelains, tea, and spices for cooking and medicine. Of these, spices were most valued. One shipload of cloves or cinnamon could bring up to 400 percent profit to the merchant who sold it in Europe.

The Silk Road, which went through Mongolia across the central Eurasian steppe, had been established as the main trade route that brought spices and other goods to Europe from China through central Asia in ancient times. Though it had fallen into disuse with the collapse of the Roman Empire, the penetration of the Mongol Empire into central Asia in the 1200s revived the Silk Road and reconnected Europe and Asia to the profit of both the Mongols and Europeans. European traders from Venice, Florence, Genoa, and other cities picked up the goods on the Black Sea and brought them into Europe; the Venetians even had a trading post on the Black Sea. But the Silk Road was again disrupted by Ottoman conquests in central Asia in the 1400s.

The Ottoman Empire was a Turkish Islamic empire that began a rapid expansion by force in the 1300s to 1400s. The loss in 1453 of the capital of the long-lived and remaining eastern segment of the Roman Empire, Constantinople (modern-day Istanbul), to the Ottomans was a devastating blow for Europeans who traded with Asia. It was also a blow to European Christians, as not only was Constantinople important for trade, but it was also the last major outpost of Christianity in the East. Muslim traders assumed control over a large portion of the Silk Road trade, but their rates were high and they squeezed out European traders. As a result, Europeans began to look elsewhere for trade opportunities.

After the Ottoman conquest, some Italian merchants relocated to Spain and Portugal on the Iberian Peninsula, seeking to replace the loss of the Silk Route by trading with Africa. West Africa, long connected to the Mediterranean world, had quantities of gold and slaves to exchange with Europeans. An Africa–Europe gold and slave trade already existed by 1492, but like the Silk Road, it was controlled by Muslim middlemen, which made it very expensive for European merchants. Both Portugal and Spain sought to trade directly with African kingdoms for gold, and Portugal began exploration of Africa. Prince Henry of Portugal, who had a strong interest in exploration and became known as Henry the Navigator (1394–1460), sponsored expeditions down the coast of Africa, where Columbus later made a name for himself as a slave trader financed by merchants in Genoa. Those merchants, frustrated with Muslim and Portuguese control of much of Europe's trade, eventually bankrolled Columbus's successful appeal at the court of Castile to further fund his voyages to the west.

The House of Castile, which then ruled Spain, believed that by finding a new route to Asia, the competition with Portugal for African trade in gold would be overcome and the profits could be used to reenergize the expansion of Christianity at the expense of their economic and religious Muslim rivals, who had effectively come to monopolize the trade with Asia. A further motivation for such exploration came from the Renaissance inquiry into humankind and curiosity about the world outside of Europe. Columbus's own views even came into play. He was a millenarian who believed that the end of the world was approaching soon. Therefore, he wanted as much of the world as possible to be converted to Christianity before the end-time came.

Given all the obstacles to the riches of the East, it is not surprising that Europeans thought of attempting to sail west to find the Far East and its wealth. Columbus was not actually the first to think of it, but he was the first to find the route. The Portuguese had even dispatched ships eastward, but they had not found any evidence of land, such as land birds over the ocean. This deterred them, but not Columbus. He, like many Europeans interested in exploration, had attempted to calculate the size of the earth to better ascertain distances, estimating that the circumference of the earth was 17,000 miles (actual circumference is 25,000 miles). Columbus read books that gave this estimate and this boosted his confidence. He also studied maps such as Toscanelli's map on next page. He used these data in support of his calculation that the Indies could be reached in a matter of a few weeks. But the Americas were unknown to Europeans at the time and this explains the inaccuracy of Columbus's estimates.

COLUMBUS AND THE TAINO

When Columbus reached the island of Hispaniola, he was filled with antici-pation that he would see gold-roofed buildings and the silk gowns of the Mongol ruler called the Great Khan, and also those of his people as described by Marco Polo. Upon encountering the Taino and Caribs, it became clear to Columbus that the peoples he encountered were not from the realm of the Great Khan. Columbus had not yet found Asia by going west. After a few months of exploration, the realization sunk in. He revised his plan for trade with Asia concluding that he might be able to trade with the Native Americans he met like Portugal did with Africa. But Native American trade networks were small and local, so he was not able to use the African model. Therefore, Columbus decided upon another model of expansion known in Spain from the clashes with the Moors and on the Canary islands as well: conquest.

The Moors, as the Spanish called them, were Muslims from North Africa who had come north across the straits of Gibraltar and conquered large stretches of southern Spain by 800 BCE. They brought with them Islamic culture and learning and greatly enriched the lands of Spain with irrigated agriculture, great centers of learning, and grand architectural achievements. In an interesting coincidence, at the very same time that Columbus set sail in 1492, the Spanish had just succeeded in their reconquest of the Moorish lands, pushing the Moors back to North Africa. This became a potent example for the House of Castile and Columbus. The reconquest expanded the reach of Christianity and gave Columbus and the Spanish Crown the drive to con-vert areas of the world outside of Europe to Christianity. It also enriched the Spanish conquerors. Many conquistadors who fought against the Moors were given some of the newly conquered lands and the use of local labor for their service to the Crown. Others had not, and they were eager to seize the property and labor of non-Christian peoples.

Columbus continued to publicly state and write that he had discov-ered the route to Asia long after it was clear he had not. He knew he had

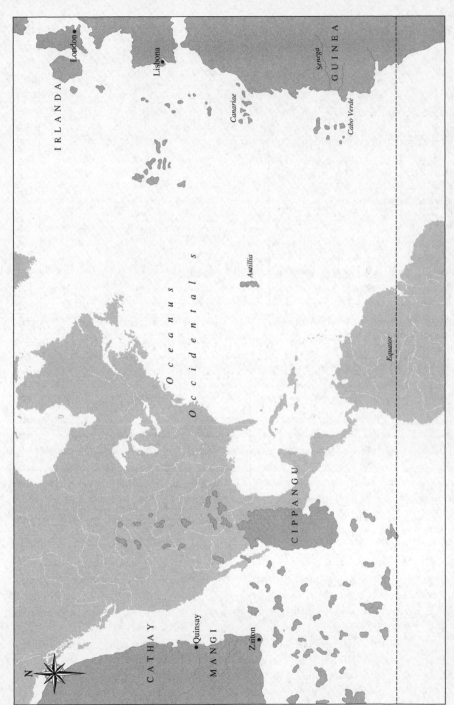

MAP 1.1 Columbus's Conception of Atlantic Ocean and Asia. Cippangu is Japan, Cathay is China   *Source:* Public Domain Map, Found on Wikicommons

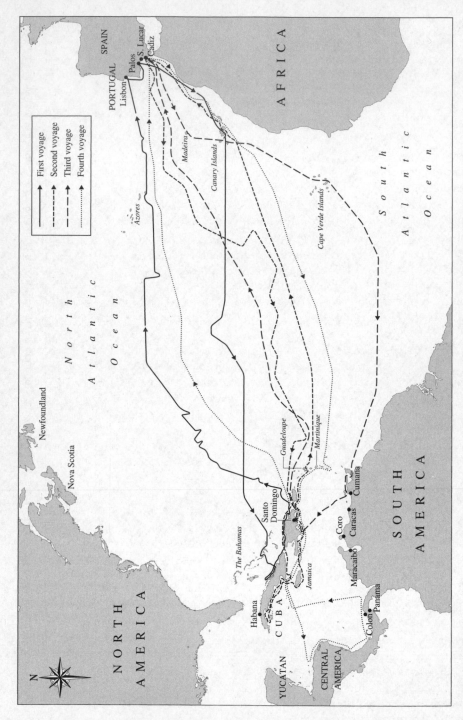

MAP 1.2 Columbus's Voyages to the Americas *Source:* GNU Free Documentation License, Creative Commons Attribute

raised expectations of discovery of a new route to the Far East and failure to find that route might damage his reputation. Columbus was a stubborn person and he refused to admit defeat or failure. He began a series of greatly exaggerated accounts about the New World that eventually destroyed his reputation. Columbus was also a poor administrator and his administrative failures combined with his exaggerations and unwillingness to admit that he had failed to find the riches of the Far East eventually forced the Crown to strip him of authority over the lands he found. It is a noteworthy comment on Spanish motivations in the New World that Columbus's poor treatment of Native Americans played very little role in his perceived failure, even though Queen Isabella knew of the abuses and disapproved of them. The Spanish were after wealth and power and the fate of the Native Americans they encountered was initially of relatively small concern.

The Native Americans (Taino) Columbus encountered were, according to his own description, friendly and innocent. Columbus saw them as noble savages—noble in their innocence and lack of malicious intentions, and savage in their supposed primitive way of life. Columbus believed they were completely pliable and submissive and claimed that 50 Europeans could dominate the whole island of Hispaniola, which he claimed for Spain. Columbus here illustrates the naïve and inaccurate concepts of superiority the Europeans maintained about themselves. His first words were:

> I, he says, in order that they would be friendly to us—because I recognized that they were people who would be better freed [from error] and converted to our Holy Faith by love than by force—to some of them I gave red caps, and glass beads which they put on their chests, and many other things of small value, in which they took so much pleasure and became so much our friends, it was a marvel… They should be good and intelligent servants, for I see that they say very quickly everything that is said to them; and I believe they would become Christians very easily, for it seemed to me that they had no religion.[3]

Columbus took with him to the New World European perceptions about others who Europeans regarded as having no religion or ordered way of life. He saw Native Americans as inferior and stated that they were "fit to be ordered about and made to work." Columbus's statement conforms to the European view that some people were natural slaves whose lot in life was to be under the control of others either as slaves or laboring in the equivalent of a modern-day labor gang, what the Spaniards called encomienda. In his public statements he continued to state that the Taino had no religion, likely because this allowed them to be defined as pagan and made their conquest easier to rationalize. However, on his second voyage, he commissioned a scholar to study the religion of the Taino, which indicated he had become convinced that they possessed religion and therefore needed to establish that theirs' was a false religion. A report by a religious scholar would accomplish this.

When Columbus explored the coasts of the island closest to Hispaniola, he took seven islanders captive to train them as interpreters. Eventually these seven and a few others were taken back to Castile. They were shown to the Crown as evidence of Columbus's discovery. Bartolome de Las Casas, who later became a powerful advocate for the Native Americans, witnessed these New World peoples among Columbus's assemblage in the Castilian city of Seville as a young man. Columbus had no qualms about taking these natives captive, since according to European thinking and the laws of the Catholic Church, they were barbarians, possessed no religion, and could therefore be compelled to do whatever Columbus wanted of them. This included his right to enslave them. One Native American stayed at the court of Castile and died soon after. Several others made their way back to the Caribbean. Another, named Diego Colon, became a loyal interpreter for Columbus. The Spanish Crown, needing the support of the Catholic Church and wary of conquistadors seizing people and lands without royal authority, took steps to protect the natives by issuing instructions to treat them well, and also to convert them to Christianity, although the first of these commands was largely ignored by Columbus and his men.

Though Columbus saw the Taino as innocents, he did not treat them with the same kind of tolerance they showed him. Columbus returned for three other trips to the New World. He still hoped to find Asia and the Great Khan of China. But he had to make the islands he had found pay. Trade hadn't worked out. So he proposed rounding up the natives and selling them as slaves. Columbus's soldiers eventually captured 1,600 Taino and made 500 of them into slaves. They forced 650 of them to serve Spanish settlers as forced laborers. The rest were freed. Soon, however, all Native Americans were forced to labor for the Spanish settlers.

Columbus also had to deal with increasing unrest among his soldiers and the rest of the Spanish settlers. Columbus was a poor administrator and shipments of supplies sometimes didn't arrive on time. Conditions were poor in the settlement and a rebellion resulted. Columbus quelled the rebellion by giving the settlers control of the labor of Native Americans. The House of Castile disapproved of enslaving of Native Americans. Isabelle even freed a cargo of enslaved Indians after she discovered they had been enslaved against her wishes. But because slavery was profitable, most Spaniards looked the other way or openly participated. A gold tribute system was also forced onto the Taino. They were forced to collect as much gold as they could from the rivers to deliver to Columbus and his men. Even the Crown could not resist the promise of more gold and though they offered protection to the Taino, they supported Columbus's gold tribute system.

By 1500, the relationship between Columbus and Native Americans—the gold tribute system, slavery, and the forced labor system—was codified. The labor and lives of the natives were controlled by the will of the Spaniards. This set in motion a pattern of abuse and control that continued well into the twentieth century under the Latin American hacienda system. Haciendas were huge privately owned plantations where Native American and mestizo (mixed race) peasants lived and worked. The owner of the hacienda believed he had the right to control the labor and the lives of the peasants who lived on his lands.

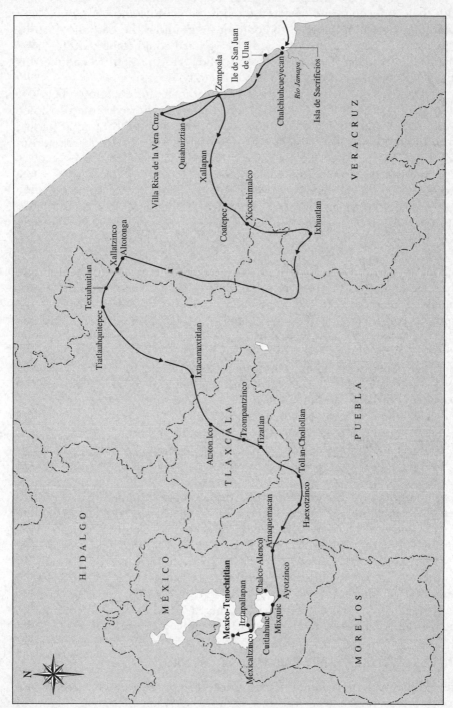

MAP 1.3 Map of Cortes Route to Tenochtitlan *Source:* GNU Free Documentation License, Creative Commons Attribute

Once the Taino started to resist this abuse, Columbus changed his mind about their innocence and declared them to be warlike and dangerous. This declaration gave him the right to conquer them under the Catholic doctrine of "just war." Whenever they resisted, the Spanish could claim that the Taino were making war on them and therefore they had the right to conquer the natives and forcibly convert them to Christianity.

There was much cross-cultural confusion in the encounter between Columbus and the Taino. Columbus and his men, who were unprincipled adventurers, made significant mistakes in understanding the Taino and other tribes. In addition to the mistaken assumption that they had no religion or civilization, his men became convinced that the Caribs, a rival tribe, participated in full-scale cannibalism, while there was little truth in this. Also, when Europeans saw the Caribs take females from the Taino, they assumed that the Caribs were taking them as slaves as Europeans might have done. In truth they were bride captives from the Taino, not slaves. While Europeans might have been appalled at bride capture, the Taino and the Caribs were more appalled at the European practice of slavery, forced labor, and forced conversion.

Columbus and others used indigenous peoples hostile to the Taino to help conquer them. They also moved to destroy the power of the Taino chiefs by making alliances with them and then turning against them. In 1503, the Spaniards convinced one of the chiefs to order a gathering of all the chiefs at his house. When the chiefs were duly gathered, the Spaniards barred the door and burned the house down, massacring the chiefs and eventually making the Native Americans submit. The forced labor system started by Columbus was institutionalized as the so-called encomienda system which consisted of royal grants of land and labor and the Taino died in great numbers because of it. Bartolome de Las Casas believed that up to 90 percent of the natives died in the gold fields after only three months.

The Spanish Crown, embarrassed by the open and great abuses to the encomienda labor system and by the widespread practice of taking the natives as slaves, asked a Spanish lawyer to evaluate whether the natives were being abused and deserved clemency. The lawyer determined that there had been abuse and only the peoples referred to as the Caribs could be made into slaves because they had made war against the Spaniards and were supposedly cannibals. But this ruling was too late to save the Taino from extinction. By 1524, there were more African slaves than Taino slaves on Hispaniola. In addition to Spanish abuses, European diseases killed up to 90 percent of Taino. By 1540, there were no Taino slaves left and by 1550 the Taino virtually disappeared. Today there are only a few mixed blood Taino who continue to practice Taino culture on the islands of Hispaniola and Puerto Rico.

CORTÉS, AZTECS, AND CONQUEST OF MEXICO

After Columbus, the islands of the Caribbean were quickly settled and the Spaniards began to scout and explore sections of the mainland of Mesoamerica. Hernán Cortés was a young impetuous Spaniard when he came to the Caribbean. Born into an aristocratic family in Castile, he rose in leadership in the New World and served as mayor of the capital of New Spain (Cuba) for several years. He became an encomendero (awarded an encomienda by the Crown) but was above all an adventurer and had become a strong leader when he was chosen to be captain of an expedition to explore the mainland in 1518.

Cortés first explored the fringes of the Yucatan Peninsula. Here he met the Mayans, a more powerful and sophisticated civilization than the Taino. The Mayans sent warriors and priests to meet them. They greatly outnumbered the Spaniards, and the Spaniards fled back to their ships. Later they attacked and decimated the Spaniard soldiers. Because the balance of power was against the Spaniards they were at least temporarily in a position of inferiority and it haunted them.

After this incident, the Spaniards sent reinforcements and the Mayans allowed them to peacefully enter their cities. There was much gold which attracted the Spaniards. During this expedition, the Spaniards were rejoined by Geronimo de Aguilar, a Spaniard who had survived a shipwreck and was spared by the Mayans, perhaps because of his skill with language. He had learned Mayan and when he joined the expedition, he became one of Cortés's most important interpreters.

A second Spaniard from the shipwreck, Gonzalo Guerrero, had a cultural conversion. He married a Mayan woman, had children with her, wore the tattoos and earplugs of a warrior, and became a war captain organizing attacks on Spanish ships. For some unknown reason he had turned violently against the Spanish. Possibly he felt betrayed when no one rescued him or he saw the abuses the Spaniards inflicted upon the Native Americans. Whatever the reason, he became a sworn enemy of the Spaniards. He continued to fight the Spanish and actually volunteered for a mission against them that was far from the Yucatan, in Honduras, where he was finally killed by the Spanish in 1534. Guerrero remained in the Spaniard consciousness, raising questions as to why he had turned against them and joined what they thought to be an inferior civilization. It struck "at the heart of their sense of self."[4]

During this expedition, Cortés, after winning a battle at Tabasco, was given several young native maidens including one known to the Spanish as La Malinche or by her later Spanish name, Donna Marina. Donna Marina became the mistress of Cortés and bore him a child, but most importantly for the future of Mexico, she also became his interpreter. She was from a tribe under the control of the Aztecs and knew their language, but also knew the Mayan language. She became Cortés's link to the subject tribes of the Aztecs. In the role of interpreter, she helped Cortés make crucial alliances with these tribes that resulted in the defeat of the Aztecs.

THE AZTECS

The Aztec Empire came into full form shortly before the arrival of the Spanish. The Aztec people, who were relative newcomers to the central valley of Mexico, came from the North American desert and were looked down upon by the other tribes. But they brought a powerful army and successfully conquered all of central Mexico. Outlying tribes conquered by the Aztec were then forced to pay tribute in the form of labor and humans for sacrifice in Aztec religious ceremonies.

The Aztecs have been portrayed traditionally by historians as a people steeped in ritual and mysticism. This view asserts that the Aztecs believed their conquest by the Spaniards was the work of one of the Aztec gods, the Aztec destroyer god Huitzilopochtli. This narrative of Spanish conquest tells a story of a submissive, fate-oriented people. However, James Lockhart, an anthropologist, rejects the premise that the Aztecs were primitives over-whelmed by Europeans and were paralyzed by long-held prophecies of their own doom. Rather, Lockhart sees them as self-interested and pragmatic people and he uses their own writings to bear this out.

The coming of the Spanish with their unknown ways and powerful weapons was an important event for the Aztecs and they recorded what they saw as the important moments of it. However, the overall impression given by the Aztec codices (books) written after their conquest is that the Aztecs were functioning much as they were before the arrival of the Spaniards. They recorded Spanish actions only when they impacted them in some way. In much of Mexico, the conquest did not impact native lives at all.

The codices demonstrate that the Aztecs interpreted Spanish actions through their own frame of reference. They read facial features and gestures and they assumed that these outward signs were enough to interpret the Spaniards' thoughts and actions. The description of their defeat by the Spaniards, described through dialogue, is an example of Aztec self-interest and pragmatism. The focus is also on internal rivalry among the various tribes ruled by the Aztecs, putting the Spaniards in the background. Primary interest focused on one's group and how the group fared. In the Aztec empire, the fundamental form of identity was the ethnically based set of villages or towns. Everyone else was an "other" including different towns or tribes and the Spanish, whom they considered to be just one more group of outsiders.

The first massacre by the Spanish at a Toxcatl festival was a surprise attack and this stuck in the minds of the Aztecs. But the Aztecs met the situation not with doom that their world would end, but with the pragmatic calculation that these outsiders had betrayed them and could not be trusted. Therefore, they decided to wage war against them. They acted in their self-interest, not out of some preordained myth that they were being punished or were to be destroyed. The Aztecs recounted the surprise attack at the ceremony and their response this way:

> When this had been done, the celebrants began to sing their songs. That is how they celebrated the first day of the fiesta. On the second day they began to sing again, but without warning they were all put to death.... They [the Spanish soldiers] ran in among the dancers, forcing their way to the place where the drums were played. Then they cut off his head, and it rolled across the floor.

They attacked the celebrants, stabbing them, spearing them striking them with their swords. They attacked some of them from behind.
And these fell instantly to the ground with their entrails hanging out…
Others they beheaded, they cut off their heads, or split their heads to
pieces…. The Sun [Don Pedro de Alvarado] treacherously murdered
our people on the twentieth day after the Captain [Cortés] left for the
coast. We allowed the Captain to return to the city in peace. But on
the following day we attacked him with all our might and that was the
beginning of the war[5]…

This new way of interpreting Aztec perceptions can help us reconsider
other parts of the traditional narrative. It has been argued that the Aztecs
saw Cortés with his helmet and feathered plume as the return of the
Aztec creator god Quetzalcoatl and therefore treated him with the greatest
adoration. Originally stated in Aztec codices, this story was taken up by
historians because it fit with their view that the Aztecs were fate-oriented
people. However, Lockhart suggests the argument that the Aztecs fawned
over Cortés is a misleading interpretation of events. He argues that the
custom of treating the newcomer royally was a matter of routine within
Aztec culture and was intended to overawe the outsider with the generosity
of the Aztec ruler and people. Lockhart thinks the claim that Cortés was a
god was created to explain the downfall of the city and empire after the
fact. The original Spanish account of the conquest contains no mention
of Moctezuma treating Cortés like a god. In fact, it states that there were
warnings told to the Spaniards in the towns along the way to the Aztec
capital Tenochtitlan that Moctezuma had invited them into the capital city
to trap them and kill them. It is unlikely that Moctezuma would have
planned this if he believed Cortés to be a god. The portrayal of Moctezuma
as weak and fawning in the Aztec codices, which were written many
years after Spanish conquest, makes it easier to explain why the conquest
happened, and it also created a scapegoat in Moctezuma himself among
the Aztecs. This account of Moctezuma was written by rival peoples who
wanted to blame Moctezuma for the Aztec downfall; they portrayed him
as weak in contrast to their leader Itzquauhtzin, who was portrayed as
virtuous and heroic.

Other evidence supports this version of the conquest. Moctezuma and
the Aztecs strove to understand the Spaniards and so he sent out skilled
painters to record what they saw when Cortés landed at the beach at Veracruz
to learn more about these new outsiders. Later, the Spanish were allowed
into the capital, Tenochtitlan, so that they could appreciate the greatness of
Moctezuma. The Spanish were given a lavish welcome. Food and housing
were made available to them. Moctezuma gave gold and silver objects to
show his generosity and the magnificence of the Aztecs. It was also a chance
for Moctezuma to observe the Spanish directly and to discern their weak-
nesses. None of these actions were those of a ruler who is resigned to his
peoples' destruction.

The great Aztec city-state of Tenochtitlan was established on an island in the midst of a large lake. Connected to the shores by causeways, supplied with fresh water by an aqueduct, it housed a population estimated to be over 150,000. Early Spanish observes compared its canals to Venice and were fascinated by its markets and gardens. To the Aztecs it was the center of political and spiritual power, or as they called it, "the foundation of heaven."   Schalkwijk/Art Resource, NY.

When Cortés and his soldiers entered Tenochtitlan, they were amazed by what they saw. The city was larger and more populous than most European cities of that time. Tenochtitlan had beautiful gardens and baths maintained by dozens of gardeners. The water for the gardens and baths was brought to Tenochtitlan through complex irrigation canals. Remarking on the canals, Cortés stated that they were greater than in Venice. And it held riches that the Spaniards had only dreamed of, with great rooms filled with gold objects inlaid with precious stones. They were impressed by the skill of the craftsmen and the massive buildings made of stone. The female weavers and seamstresses created beautiful cloth garments made from cotton and feathers that were worn by the royalty.

But the Aztec plan to overawe the Spaniards did not work. Shortly after their entrance into Tenochtitlan, Cortés turned the tables on the Aztecs and had Moctezuma kidnapped. Spanish actions here make sense if they believed a trap was being laid for them since they could use Moctezuma as a hostage to bargain their way out of the city or attempt to intimidate the Aztecs with this bold action. The new leaders who rose in his place made war on the Spaniards and were able to expel them from the city. Once expelled, according to Aztec rules of war, the Spaniards could no longer enter the city and the Aztecs believed the threat of further attack was over.

But the Spaniards had a number of advantages in the coming war with the Aztecs. The Aztec use of conquered peoples in their empire as sacrificial victims created deep hostility against them. Cortés exploited this antagonism, forging alliances with the Tlaxcalans, Totonacs, and the other outlying tribes, against the Aztecs, which expanded his army from a few hundred to many thousands. His relationship with Donna Marina and her abilities as an interpreter were crucial to Cortés's success in rallying these tribes against the Aztecs.

The Aztec approach to war itself favored the Spaniards. The Aztecs had heard rumors that Spanish warriors did not fight fairly, at least according to the Aztec definition of fair. Aztec warriors observed a highly ritualized form of warfare in which the taking of or being made captive could become an entrance to glory and the afterlife. Captor and captive were thus expected to cooperate in this ritual. It was therefore an honor to become a captive and to die properly. The Spaniards resisted capture and so time and again they were captured in battle and then released. This frustrated the Aztecs, who had no way to gain the spiritual power of the Spaniard if they did not cooperate.

In the midst of the war, there was an outbreak of smallpox. Smallpox was a European disease that was brought to the Aztecs by the conquistadors. It created open sores or pustules which were hideous to sight and left the sufferer racked with pain. Sometimes the pustules burst in the mouth of the victim or on his lips and led to bleeding. Well over 50 percent of Aztec sufferers died and it was indeed a very gruesome death. This very contagious disease spread rapidly and decimated Aztec warriors and the rest of the population. Later, it would reduce the Native American population in the New World by as much as 80–90 percent.

The Spaniards gained the upper hand in the war by shutting off trade and contact with the city. Then they joined with their allies to lay siege to the city and the allies of the Aztecs abandoned them. The Aztec leadership refused to negotiate with the Spaniards and the Spanish-led forces destroyed the city and its inhabitants. Then, the Spaniards took the Aztec leadership captive and later had them killed.

NATIVE AMERICAN RESPONSES

Columbus and Cortés's conquests initiated an encounter in which the power imbalance placed limits on the Native American response. Nonetheless they reacted in a variety of ways to Spanish intrusion. They openly rebelled against Spanish conquest, but rebellion eventually failed in almost every case, in part because European diseases spread so quickly that warriors fell from disease more often than from Spanish swords. The Spanish also possessed firearms which intimidated Native Americans and were more effective than arrows and spears. Perhaps most important were the alliances between the Spaniards and the tributary tribes. These alliances allowed the Spaniards to increase the numbers of soldiers and warriors fighting on their side dramatically.

Accommodation was perhaps the most widespread response to the Spanish. Many Native Americans eventually accepted Spanish rule and tried to make the best of it. For instance, the Spanish forced Native Americans to convert to Christianity. Instead of openly resisting Christianity, many Native Americans practiced syncretism, a method of combining aspects of Christianity with their own religious practices. They identified the Catholic saints with their native gods in some cases. The Mayans combined prayers to the Christian god with rituals to their agricultural deities. The Christian cross was sometimes covered with traditional religious cloth, the huipil, which allowed Mayans to practice both Christianity and their traditional religion.

This sixteenth-century print portrays Aztecs suffering from smallpox during the Cortés invasion (1518–1519).   Granger Collection, NY.

The Christian religious holiday "All Saints' Day" or "All Hollows Eve" (today the Western Halloween) became very important to Native Americans because they could celebrate the Catholic saints while also worshipping their ancestors by placing food offerings at their tombs. All Saints' Day is still celebrated following Mayan custom through the building of altars of remembrance in their homes and bringing food and/or flowers to the cemeteries where loved ones are buried, accompanied by parades in which celebrants often wear costumes ranging from traditional skeletons to SpongeBob SquarePants.

FIGHTING FOR THE NATIVE AMERICANS: LAS CASAS

The life and story of Bartolome de Las Casas runs counter to the misdeeds of the Spaniards in the Americas. Las Casas, who was born in Seville and saw the natives Columbus brought back from his first expedition there, knew Columbus and became editor of Columbus's journals. He went to the Indies in 1502, participated in several expeditions, and was given an encomienda over natives on the island of Hispaniola. After seeing firsthand the ill-treatment of the Taino in the encomienda, Las Casas began to have second thoughts about the actions of the Spanish.

Intensely religious, Las Casas began to evangelize the Indians under his encomienda. In 1511 he heard a sermon by Father Montesinos on the biblical subject "a voice crying in the wilderness," which was a condemnation

The contact between Europeans, Africans, and Native Americans eventually produced large numbers of castas, people considered to be of mixed racial origin. By the eighteenth century, especially in New Spain, a genre of painting flourished that depicted a husband and wife of different racial categories and their child who would fit one of the casta designations. The purpose and public for these paintings is unclear, but they illustrate domestic relations and material culture as well as racial ideology.   Museo Nacional del Virreinato, Tepotzotlan, Mexico. Schalkwijk/Art Resource, NY.

of the Spaniards' treatment of Native Americans in the New World. It was a transformational moment for Las Casas. He freed the Indians under his control and abandoned his encomienda.

From then on, Las Casas became the defender of the Indians. In 1512, he became the first priest to be ordained in the New World. Las Casas proposed to the Spanish King Charles that he be allowed to set up a self-supporting farm for freed Native Americans in Venezuela. This experiment failed when the neighboring encomenderos incited other Native Americans to continuously attack the farms. He wrote books exposing and decrying the abuses of the Spanish. In 1537 he convinced the Pope to issue a papal bull declaring that the Indians were rational beings so as to end the practices supported by the argument that because the New World Native Americans appeared to them to be without intellect, they needed to be enslaved under the will of the Spanish.

In 1550, Las Casas arranged for a debate between himself and Juan Gines de Sepulveda in Valladolid Spain over the enslavement of Native Americans. Sepulveda was an Aristotelian scholar who subscribed to Aristotle's arguments that there were two different kinds of men—educated men who were fit to become educated and to lead and natural men who were only fit to be slaves. Las Casas won the debate and the blessing of the Council of Vallalodid composed of theologians. King Charles, who wanted to reduce the power of the encomenderos and bring them under the control of the Crown, also supported Las Casas and declared enslavement of Native Americans illegal. In addition, the encomienda was eventually abolished. However, the abuse of Native Americans continued and the hacienda system which emerged in the late 1500s was yet another system that kept them under the control of Spanish overlords, who retained control of the land and developed great wealth and power. The hacienda system has disappeared today, but its legacy can be seen in the great disparity of wealth between the richest and the poorest in Latin America.

Conclusion

The Spaniards eventually conquered much of Latin America, although it took more than 100 years to quell the most stubborn resistance of Native Americans such as among the Maya in southern Mexico. Although the conquest was brutal and there was much suffering and death, the encounter also produced widespread mixing of peoples. The physical mixing that began with Native Americans intermarrying with Spaniards (whose offspring was labeled mixed, or mestizo) became over time a complex hybrid of European, Native American, and mestizo ethnicities to which was added African culture, after many of Africa's peoples were introduced to the region via the Atlantic slave trade. All contributed to the rich culture of today's Latin America. This cultural mix also helped shape western and global culture through contact with Latin American literature, music, art, and religion. Latin American literature's "magical realism," which is a product of its ethnic hybridity, is a theme that has been mined by authors globally. The Latin American contribution to the artistic school of muralism is an example of the use of European and Native American forms to produce innovative art. Some Latin American music uses a special flute that is indigenous to the New World, but beloved everywhere, while Salsa music, which has African influences, is appreciated the world over. Religious syncretism continues today among the Mayan populations of Mexico and Guatemala and in Brazil. The mixing of indigenous and European Catholic elements has produced unique religious institutions and symbols. For example, the Virgin of Guadalupe, the most popular religious icon in Latin America today, is a product of Spanish-indigenous syncretism. So the legacy of the encounter between Spaniards and Native Americans grew to be more than just conquest. It became a story of the survival of Native American culture and the fusion of indigenous Spanish and ultimately African culture in the Americas and the world.

Questions for Discussion

1. What were European perceptions of the world beyond Europe at the time of Columbus?
2. What were Native American perceptions of the Spaniards who arrived in the New World?
3. What motivated Columbus and the kingdom of Castile to make this voyage to the Americas? What did Columbus expect to find?
4. What were the different models available in Columbus's approach to forming an economic and political relationship with the Native Americans he encountered in the New World? Which of these did Columbus decide to pursue? Describe the Spanish treatment of Native Americans that resulted from this decision and from European assumptions about the nature of these New World peoples that influenced this decision.
5. Describe the culture of the Taino Columbus encountered. How did they respond to the Spanish intrusion?
6. What were the key elements in Cortés's conquest of the Aztecs?
7. How did the Aztecs respond to Cortés's intrusion?
8. Describe Las Casas's attempts to protect Native Americans from Spanish abuses.

Endnotes

1. Merry Wiesner, et al., *Discovering the Global Past* (New York: Wadsworth Publishing, 1997), pp. 47–48.
2. Ibid., p. 48.
3. Christopher Columbus, *The Diario of Christopher Columbus's First Voyage to America, 1492–1493* (Norman, OK: University of Oklahoma Press, 1989), pp. 65, 69.
4. Inga Clendinnen, *Ambivalent Conquests: Maya and Spaniard in Yucatan, 1517–1570* (Cambridge, MA: Cambridge University Press, 1987), p. 18.
5. Ibid., pp. 48–49.

Europeans on the Margin: Missionaries and Indigenous Response in East Asia

The year 1492 marked a dramatic moment in the history of global encounters. Five years later, another less dramatic but just as fateful event occurred: a Portuguese sea-captain, Vasco da Gama, seeking another route to the East rounded the Cape of Good Hope, marking the entrance of early modern Europeans into the maritime world of Asia. That sailor and his successors came with the same desire for domination—cultural and political—that accompanied the conquistadors of Spain in their voyages to the western hemisphere, but these ambitions were soon checked by the realities of Asian power. Whereas Europeans arrived in Latin America at a time when local regimes were in disarray and strangers to modern weaponry, the Asia of the fifteenth and sixteenth centuries witnessed the dawn of new empires—the Mughal in India and the Ming in China—which dwarfed European states not only in cultural achievement but also in military power. Europeans managed to wrest control over a few useful port cities and some valuable islands, but only those on the remote margins of or beyond the limits of these great empires. For the most part, Europeans were compelled to participate as equals or less than equals in the trade networks long utilized by Indians, and as less than equals with Chinese traders from the Indian Ocean to the East Sea. Indians and Chinese often heaped indignities upon them for their rude and unclean manners.

Westerners in Asia were initially from Portugal, who established their presence in Asia with da Gama's voyages. They were interested in the spice trade and other goods such as silks that could be obtained there and considered to be luxury items back in Europe. The Portuguese conquered the port of Malacca in Southeast Asia to gain control over the trade in spices such as pepper, cloves, and others. They also arrived in Macao, Indonesia, Taiwan, and Japan. Modern-day Sri Lanka was known as Spice Island by Europeans at this time for its fragrant cinnamon trees which could be smelled for miles offshore. There Portuguese traders landed and established a cinnamon monopoly in Sri Lanka that lasted for over a century. The Spaniards came to the Philippines in the later 1500s and were able to take control because the Philippines had no central authority armed with gunpowder weapons; they were merely a variety of communities who often engaged in divisive war, much like their counterparts in the Americas.

The Portuguese and Spaniards also brought Christian missionaries; others came from Italy. These missionaries became influential, meeting with emperors and shoguns and publicly representing the ways of the western world to China and Japan. Along the way, the missionaries remade their own religion and cultural habits to suit the needs of the Chinese and Japanese in the hopes that this would increase the number of East Asian converts. It is difficult to know if it worked. In China, where Jesuits from Italy and Portugal worked very carefully to emulate Chinese Confucian elite (scholars of the teachings of Confucius)—even dressing and wearing their hair in the Confucian style—there were few converts. A similar approach was taken in Japan, where there were many more converts, although we do not know if this was due to Jesuits dressing in Japanese kimonos and taking on the culture of Japan or to other factors, such as the cultural fit between the Japanese loyalty system of absolute loyalty to one's lord and the Christian ethos of loyalty to god.

It is very clear, however, that many Jesuit missionaries who came to convert the East were impacted as much if not more than the cultures they entered. They came to convert but were themselves converted to the host culture. In both China and Japan, several Jesuit missionaries came to identify with the culture and way of the life of their hosts. Matteo Ricci, the Jesuit who became a respected Confucianist, died in China and was buried as a Chinese Confucian scholar with a proper Confucian burial and grave site. In the case of Joao Rodrigues in Japan, even though he was exiled from Japan at the end of his life, he desperately wished to return to die there because he saw it as his true homeland. Indeed, some of the Jesuits, who had come as men of god, abandoned their religious calling in favor of managing the trade between the West and their adopted Asian home and thus were completely transformed by their encounter with the East. Moreover, those westerners who resolutely refused to be absorbed into the host culture also failed to transform their host cultures to any great degree as had the Spaniards in the Americas. Nor, as will be seen, did these encounters necessarily contribute to a better understanding of Asian cultures or of relations between European nations and China and Japan.

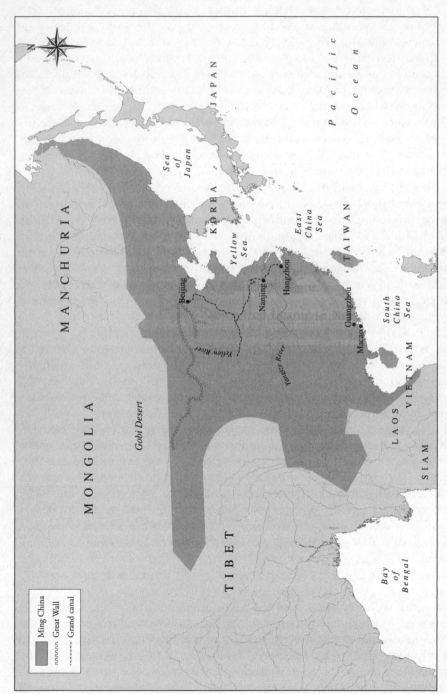

MAP 2.1 Ming China, 1368–1644 *Source:* Bentley Ziegler Traditions and Encounters, Third Edition, 2006

East Asians responded to this new European presence in a variety of ways. The political context in both China and Japan was crucial in shaping their responses. Japan was then governed by competing military warlords (daimyos) of the samurai class. The samurai were an elite class, the only educated class in Japan; they served in government positions, and were warriors, trained in martial arts. Only they could carry weapons, so they served in the regional armies that vied for power in Japan. Under their leadership, Japan became a warrior state and in the 1500s, the most powerful regional warlords competed for power over the nation. Even after the Tokugawa family prevailed over other regions and became the ruling clan of all Japan after 1600, political power continued to be decentralized, unlike the centrally ruled Chinese Empire. Each region had its own ruler and army and taxes were collected locally. This decentralized system created rivalry and suspicion between the regions. European missionaries sometimes became entangled in the tense political atmosphere of the time.

Unlike Japan, the Chinese Empire was a centrally governed state. Instead of warlords as in Japan, the emperor and a large number of civilian scholar-bureaucrats governed China. As a powerful intellectual and governing class, scholar-bureaucrats became important for the encounter with westerners because of their interaction with western missionaries and traders.

China developed a successful trade with the west in the 1500s to 1600s. At this time, China was the most powerful nation on earth in economic terms. The trade with the European nations profited China greatly. It was a trade that brought silk, tea, porcelain, and other goods from China to the west and great amounts of silver into China to pay for these goods. The Chinese had little interest in the goods that Europe had to offer. The silk industry was especially well organized in China, with workshops where the spinning and weaving took place. Chinese traders in the Philippines who had migrated from the mainland of China traded with the Spanish, sending Chinese goods to Acapulco, Mexico, by ship and then overland to the east coast of Mexico and onto Spain by ship. They received Spanish silver in return and sent it back to the mainland of China. A few western merchants were allowed to trade directly at Canton but this was tightly controlled and the merchants had to reside in Macao. While trade impacted the Chinese economy greatly, missionaries were most influential not in economic matters but in their impact upon the governing classes of China.

CULTURAL CONVERSION IN CHINA: MATTEO RICCI

In addition to its dominance in economic matters, China thought of itself in cultural and political terms as the "middle kingdom," superior to all others. Therefore, the Chinese did not have much interest in the western religion of Christianity. They also dictated the terms under which westerners were allowed into China. Western traders and missionaries were allowed to set up headquarters in Macao, which was nominally independent but in real terms under the control of China, but refused permanent residence within China.

During the trading season, traders and missionaries were allowed to visit Canton on the coast of south China to carry out the trade but at the end of the season had to leave.

Portuguese ships reached the south coast of China in 1513 and the interaction between Chinese and Jesuit missionaries began shortly thereafter. However, missionaries were unsuccessful in penetrating China until Alessandro Valignano, the leader of all Jesuit missions in Asia, decided in 1577 that missionaries to China should learn to use the Chinese language and learn the customs of China. One Jesuit Ruggiero learned Chinese at Macao but other missionaries criticized him saying it was a waste of time. Valignano, however, believed that in order to bring Chinese people to Christianity, the Jesuits had to become more like the Chinese, even dressing in robes similar to those of Chinese priests. Chinese officials also requested this and so Ruggiero wore a Chinese robe and shaved his head like a Chinese Buddhist priest. As Ruggiero later wrote, the Governor (Valignano) "wanted us to dress in the fashion of their priests which is a little different than ours; now we have done so, and in brief, have become Chinese in order to win China for Christ."[1] In Japan a few years earlier, Jesuit missionaries had similarly begun dressing in Zen Buddhist robes.

Given the prohibition on permanent residence in China for foreigners, the missionaries were at first only rarely allowed to enter the interior. This changed as Jesuits became more successful at making connections between Christianity and Confucianism that respected Confucian teachings, and they gradually earned the trust of the ruling class and the emperor. During the seventeenth century, Jesuit missionaries and the Chinese educated elite increasingly engaged in a prolonged period of mutually agreeable cross-cultural exchanges.

At that time, China had the most sophisticated leadership system in the world. Civil bureaucrats, not military warlords, ran the country. These scholar-bureaucrats had to pass a very difficult exam based upon the teachings of Confucius to gain their jobs; thus China had the first merit-based civil leadership system in the world. The scholar-bureaucrats that this system produced were, at their best, both sophisticated intellectuals and practical bureaucrats who practiced the Confucianist ideals of treating the people of China fairly. At their worst, they were deeply corrupt and cruel leaders. But the exam system laid the foundation for a brilliant civilization in China. The emperor ruled not as an absolute leader but was guided by a Grand Council, composed of scholar-bureaucrats.

The missionaries had to work within this system if they were to be successful. If a missionary won favor with a certain leader or Confucian scholar, he might be allowed to visit the great cities of China or even take up residence there. This would facilitate access to the scholar-bureaucrat population and, the missionaries hoped, create opportunities for effecting their conversion to Christianity. Thus the strategy of becoming more Chinese was for the Jesuits one of necessity as doing so created the favorable impression that would allow them access to the leadership of China and in turn the masses of China.

Jesuits in Chinese dress at the emperor's court. The Jesuits believed that the best way to convert a great civilization such as China was to adopt the dress, customs, language, and manners of its elite. They reasoned that once the scholar-gentry elite had been converted, they would bring the rest of China's vast population into the Christian fold.   Private Collection/Giraudon/The Bridgeman Art Library.

Matteo Ricci, a Jesuit missionary from Italy, was highly respected in China as a European who had mastered Confucianism. He and other Jesuit missionaries to China embraced aspects of elite Chinese Confucian culture, at first to gain converts, but later because they desired to become more Chinese. Ricci immediately took up the Chinese language and by 1585 he could converse in it and was beginning to read Chinese. A friend of Ricci's, Chu suggested that Ricci and other Jesuits ought to become Confucian instead of Buddhist in their dress and wear their hair long like a Confucian scholar. Up to that point the missionaries like Ruggiero had dressed like regular Buddhist priests and had been treated like Chinese Buddhists; however, Ricci learned that Buddhist priests were, in fact, not greatly respected by the Chinese government or literati. When Ricci and others began wearing the Confucian robes, which were in a beautiful purple color, they gained more respect. These beautiful but expensive robes were carried by the missionaries' servants along to market so that the robes could be donned if they met another Confucian official.

Ricci began a translation of the four books of Confucianism. He also wrote a book in Chinese presenting the Catholic faith in terms of natural reason, which he saw as active in Confucian philosophy as it was in some branches of European thinking. While Ricci was stationed in Kwantung, he and a colleague hosted banquets for local Chinese officials at the Buddhist temple where they were staying. These officials could visit him because the temple where he stayed was a public space not a private residence. Dozens of important officials came in their sedan chairs and boats and they were impressed by Ricci's knowledge of Confucianism. Later, Ricci engaged the literati of Nanjing and the surrounding area in 1695, and then moved to Nanchang to the west in Jiangxi province and bought a house. He held meetings of Confucian scholars there and gained respect from these literati not only for his knowledge of Confucianism, but for his powers of memory and techniques of memorization that he learned as a young Jesuit in training back in Rome. Ricci came to be seen as an exotic, but interesting species of European by the Chinese literati class who flocked to Nanchang and eventually the capital Peking to see him and read his writings on Confucianism.

Ricci and other missionaries to China used devices such as world maps, European mechanical clocks, or illustrations of the Bible to attract further attention to their cause. Later, the Jesuits became so well known for mapmaking and astronomy in China that the emperor appointed two of them, Fathers Verbiest and Schall, as heads of the Chinese Bureau of Astronomy. Ricci himself became a minor celebrity for his knowledge of Confucianism.

Ricci was greatly influenced by Chinese high culture and lived like a Chinese Mandarin. Assuming that his status as a respected Confucian scholar would bring converts, he stated at the time, "Thus, it was better now to proceed confidently as though we were in fact men of China."[2] Ricci's approach was this: He never started with the Christian gospel. Rather, he wrote a collection meant to appeal to Chinese scholars on the Confucian theme of friendship, annotated with references to the *Analects*, the gathered teachings of Confucius. "I make every effort to turn our way the leader of the literati sect, that is Confucius, by interpreting any ambiguities in his writing in our favor." He also assumed the pose of a writer who had come to China from far away to show respect for the cultural power of the "Son of Heaven," a reference to the Chinese Emperor.

Ricci began to see himself as a bridge between China and the West, translating Christianity into a Chinese context so the Chinese could understand it better. But in the process Ricci himself had changed irrevocably. By learning to speak, read, and write Chinese and by acting and dressing like a scholar-bureaucrat, he had become so Chinese that he used references to the Confucian analects in his writings about Christianity not just to lure Chinese into Christianity but because he saw legitimate connections between them. Ricci's attempt to appeal to a Chinese audience was probably a detriment to his mission of spreading the Christian gospel. Even though he continued to believe that he could bring Chinese to Christianity, he had become so thoroughly Chinese himself that he no longer truly represented the Christian missionary movement. A scholar of China stated, "The tactic of being more Chinese, started by Valignano, had no necessary stopping point."[3]

Ironically, Ricci himself was a testament to the failure of his mission. He initially thought he was offering Confucian scholars the choice of Christianity over Confucianism, but they really did not have an open choice as he assumed. One had to learn Confucianism to be successful in China, and Confucianism was a way of life, not merely a belief. Ricci himself became indoctrinated into Confucianism, much like a Confucian scholar. When he began to dress, behave, and write like a Confucian scholar, what began as a tactic became an identity. While he believed that becoming a Chinese scholar would simply facilitate conversion, Ricci became more Chinese and less western with every step he took. But he wasn't really Chinese either. Ricci occupied a space between western and Chinese culture and in so doing blurred the boundaries between China and the West.

Ricci ended his days in the Chinese capital, Peking, as an advisor to the Imperial Court, where he became the first foreigner to enter the Forbidden City. Upon his death, he was given an elaborate burial reserved for a Confucian scholar.

Ricci's example teaches us that it is difficult to adopt the culture of another people as a tactic without a deeper change in one's own identity. It also shows the complexity of these categories: Chinese, European, foreign, Christian, Confucian. Ricci became a Confucian scholar but he was not Chinese. He was a European foreigner but he did not dress or act like a stereotypical foreigner. He was a Christian missionary but did not act like typical missionary either. Ricci joined the literati but he did not become a Confucian scholar in a universal sense, but rather as a European who learned Confucianism.

Ricci's methods, though highly respected by an inner circle of Jesuits in China, became controversial among other missionaries. The missionary community in China began to debate the wisdom of this approach. The Jesuits were criticized for diluting Christianity and adding practices and symbols seen as heathen to it. Eventually the Catholic Church in Rome became concerned with the Jesuits's methods. After an investigation, in 1773 the Jesuit order was dissolved by Pope Clement XIV and thereafter its mission to China dwindled.

CHINESE-JESUIT DIALOGUE

The official Chinese history of the Jesuit missionaries stated that the missionaries were admirable because they were intelligent and talented and they came without need for profit. They were seen as a novelty because they and the things they demonstrated were new to the Chinese. However, the use of the word "novelty" suggests that Chinese officials did not see the Jesuits as particularly important or significant. The Chinese possessed a concept of China as the middle kingdom by which they meant the center of the world. They saw their civilization as superior to all others. Chinese maps from that time show China at the center with Europe depicted as a small island at the edge.

Li Chih, a Confucian scholar, commented that while Matteo Ricci was impressive, he still did not understand why Ricci was in China. When he considered that Ricci wanted to reinterpret the teachings of Confucius, he thought this was too foolish even to contemplate.

Another Jesuit missionary, Diego de Pantoja, was in China at the same time as Ricci. Pantoja wrote about China for a European audience and also wrote about Christianity for a Chinese audience; he stated that its philosophers reminded him of Plato but they were not as intelligent as western philosophers. Pantoja was a keen observer of Chinese customs although his views were sometimes quite superficial. He noted the dress of the lower classes in pants and shirt and the upper class preference for a robe or gown and he asked about the Chinese custom of foot-binding with the Chinese he met. One gentleman he talked to stated that foot-binding made women more beautiful and it made it difficult for women to leave the house and easier to control them. Apparently, though, Pantoja could get no one to tell him why bound feet were more beautiful (tiny feet were considered to be quite erotic by Chinese males and out of bounds for common conversation).

Pantoja also reflected on Chinese religious practice. He stated that the Chinese had no religion or beliefs, but then proceeded to describe a Chinese funeral in which it was clear that the Chinese possessed a belief in a spirit world. The Chinese possessed a sophisticated spirit world at that time. It is possible Pantoja might not have considered the religious practices of China to be "true" religion like Christianity. In another example, he discussed Chinese fortune tellers, pointing out what he believed to be Chinese superficiality in religious matters.

Pantoja noted that the Chinese had a fascination with cures for old age. Of course this is not unique to China. In the United States today there are many examples of attempts to stop the aging process. The Chinese believed the Jesuits themselves to be quite old. They also believed that celibacy among Jesuit priests was an attempt to extend their longevity. Pantoja reported that the Chinese also believed the Jesuits to be alchemists, able to mix metals and make silver from them, because their ships sometimes left China with mercury, an essential component in alchemy, and returned with silver. As Pantoja was in China for only one year when he wrote his account of China, his impressions of China and what Chinese thought of the Jesuits were fairly superficial and inaccurate in some respects.

Along with Ricci, Pantoja attracted a following in China through writings meant to appeal to Chinese elites. Pantoja chose to write a moral tract in Chinese to draw more Chinese to Christianity. Moral tracts were popular in China at that time. China was going through a period of social and political crisis that would end only with the overthrow by Manchurian tribes coming from the northeast in 1644. Moral tracts were an attempt to save China from the corruption into which it had fallen and the poor leadership of its governing officials. Pantoja's tract was called the "Seven Victories," an allusion to the seven deadly sins well known in the Catholic Church, and it went through three editions in China. He was helped in his writing by Yang Ting-Yun. Yang became very influential at that time for his writing on morality and published his own moral tract, "Family Rituals," which became one of the more important texts of the period. Even though there are echoes of Buddhism in Pantoja's tract, in general the Jesuits tried to stay away from Buddhism because they saw it as competing with Christianity. On the other hand, Confucianism was not seen as a religion and so it could be made compatible with Christianity.

There were seven prefaces to Pantoja's Seven Victories in all, the last three written quite close to the fall of China in 1644, long after the tract was originally published. The first Chinese preface writer of the text, Cheng I Wei, believed that Pantoja, rather than instructing the Chinese in morality, was exploring his own morality and true self. Another Confucian scholar wrote about the tract that Pantoja was a western sage different from but of the same order as a Chinese sage. A third commentator, Chen Liang-Tsai, argued in his own preface that the Seven Victories was Confucianist at its base. He, along with the other preface writers, believed that Christianity and its values could become a way to revitalize Confucianism by restoring moral rigor to China. Therefore, these Chinese read the text not as instruction in Christian morality but rather as ideas that could strengthen Confucianism. These interpretations put the tract within the Chinese context and made it useful to the Chinese, who were actively seeking ways to revitalize their society and government.

In later centuries, after western imperialists invaded China, Chinese scholars critiqued the "Seven Victories," arguing that while the text offered useful advice, the source of Pantoja's moralizing, western Christianity, because of its connection to western imperialism was questionable. One difference between the Chinese and the Christian moral systems was clear: Whereas Confucianists believed in the innate goodness of humans, western Christianity subscribed to the corrupted fallen nature of humanity. The Confucian concept of goodness was fragile and had to be cultivated. But it came from humanity, not the Christian god.

But mostly the response of Confucian scholars to Pantoja's work was cultural appropriation. It did not cause a radical reevaluation of Chinese concepts of themselves and their civilization. Pantoja's and Ricci's ideas were simply fitted within the Confucian system. Therefore, most Chinese scholars could admire the work of the Jesuits without feeling disloyal to Confucianism or feeling the need to convert to Christianity. This may help to explain the relatively small numbers of converts.

The missionaries in China had other problems in their dealings with the Chinese. Some priests among the more aggressive orders such as the Franciscans believed that China could not be properly Christianized without military conquest and advocated such a conquest. Because China was a large powerful nation, it is unlikely that military intervention in the 1600s would have succeeded. However, rumors regarding this led Chinese officials to become suspicious of the missionaries, who were also accused of sorcery and black magic. A few missionaries sexually abused their female adherents, which led to scandal and damaged their reputation, much as rumors of such behaviors had in the past been used to cripple Chinese Buddhist institutions.

Anti-Christian movements followed past anti-Buddhist feeling in other ways. In one instance in the 1620s, Christian missionaries were compared to the White Lotus Society, which was a peasant secret society that opposed government control, practiced a form of Buddhism, was accused of black magic, and was outlawed by the Chinese emperor. Later in 1664, Confucian scholar Yang Guangxian, who distrusted Christianity, accused Christian missionaries of causing the death of the emperor and his favorite mistress. Father Schall, who had been a close advisor to the emperor, and his Chinese assistants were sentenced to death after an initial investigation but later Schall's sentence was reversed. To these troubles was added a growing controversy about the Jesuits's use of Confucian ideas and symbols in attempting to spread Christianity in China.

Other Catholic orders such as the Franciscans objected to linking Confucianism with Christianity and accused the Jesuits of idolatry. A papal investigation into this issue condemned the Jesuit practice of adapting to Chinese culture and fusing Confucian ideas with Christianity. However, in the time of Matteo Ricci and succeeding generations of Jesuit missionaries, the Jesuits's willingness to find compromise in their encounter with the Chinese and the openness of Chinese ruling classes to their ideas reaped many benefits for them. They became respected and influential partners in China, serving several emperors. Ricci and Schall among others joined the ranks of Confucian scholars. They produced a few converts among the literati but more among the lower classes and this led to a permanent Chinese Catholic Church in China that exists even today. In comparison, the situation in Japan was quite different.

JAPAN AND THE JESUITS

While Francis Xavier founded the Jesuit mission to Japan in 1549 and is better known among historians, he died after only two years in Japan. Joao Rodrigues, however, spent several decades in Japan and became the most influential missionary there in the late 1500s. Rodrigues was from Portugal, who came to Japan as an adolescent.

Valignano, as he had in China, encouraged Jesuits priests to pursue a cultural adaptation approach in Japan. He encouraged Japanese language instruction and believed that the Jesuits needed to adopt the cultural habits of the Japanese. Valignano eventually wrote about the adaptation approach in his book on the history of the missionary movement in Asia. He placed special emphasis on dress, Japanese language acquisition, and the Japanese Tea Ceremony as a way of building cultural bridges with the Japanese and understanding them better. In addition, like in China, the Jesuits became close to the rulers of Japan. Joao Rodrigues became a close confidant of the Japanese leader Hideyoshi. Unlike China, however, there was less cultural appropriation on the part of the Japanese. Instead, the missionaries in Japan were met with suspicion and accusation and struggled to maintain their mission there.

Japan in the late 1500s was ruled by an individual warlord, sometimes called a shogun, who had won his power through military conquest, unlike China, where the civil bureaucracy dominated. While Japan had an emperor like in China, the Japanese emperor was a figurehead and possessed little real political power. The real power lay in the hands of the military leaders. In addition to the shogun, each region also had a top military leader, usually the eldest male of the leading clan of the region, known as a daimyo or lord. He held unquestioned power within his own region but had to answer to the shogun at the national level. Beneath the daimyo lay the basis for the military regime, the samurai warriors. The samurai class, from which all military leaders were chosen, represented a hereditary class which had unquestioned military, political, and social dominance in Japan. All other classes of people had to pay homage to the samurai or face execution by the sword.

Hideyoshi, the ruler of Japan in the 1580s to 1590s, had come to power through military conquest and intimidation, gaining the allegiance of other regional lords because they feared him. He understood the power of the sword and was capricious in his rule. In the cruelest of acts, he had his own son executed because he believed he represented a threat to his power. Hideyoshi's fearsome approach did not seem to bode well for civil relations between the Jesuits and the Japanese leadership.

The Jesuits established a training school and a college at Funai in Japan in 1580. These institutions were supported by the local lord, who had become a Christian. Japanese converts joined the training school and they took Portuguese first names as signs of their newfound faith (for example, Paulo Yoho and Vicente Hoin). Instruction at the school was designed to strengthen the ability of Japanese to keep to their Christian faith. There was a course for converts specifically designed to refute Buddhist tenets as well as Japanese language instruction for missionaries. In 1587 Hideyoshi signed a decree to expel the Jesuits from Japan. However, the decree was not enforced and the Jesuits stayed.

As in China, Jesuits in Japan spoke Japanese and dressed in Japanese costume. The Jesuit adaptation approach was more successful in its early stages in Japan than it had been in China at winning converts. There was then a great deal of disillusionment about Japanese Buddhism and disgust at the corruption of Buddhist priests, which was far worse than the way Chinese regarded the errors of Buddhists in China. The worship of the Christian god also appealed to Japanese cultural sensibilities, wherein one's lord or daimyo was to be worshipped with unquestioned loyalty. Many samurai and several lords as well as hundreds of thousands of peasants were converted to Christianity. The lord of Bungo, Otomo Yoshishige, was also very interested in Christianity. He was a young man of 15 when he met Francis Xavier, and Xavier and his religion made a deep impression on him. Even though he never converted to Christianity, he developed a deep respect for this foreign religion. He also protected foreigners from death, in one case preventing his father from killing European merchants and seizing their cargo.

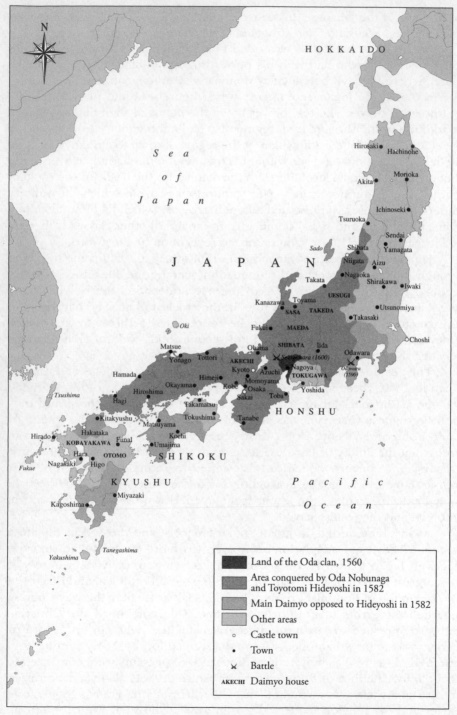

MAP 2.2   Japan in the time of Hideyoshi   *Source: Public Domain Map, Found on Wikicommons*

In this early period, the relationship between the Jesuits and the Japanese leadership was relatively positive. At the invitation of the Pope, an embassy of two Japanese nobles went to Rome in 1583 to attempt to parley the Japanese leadership's relationship with the Jesuits into enhanced influence in the West. However, the mission did not result in any major achievements for the Japanese.

The Jesuits likewise made official visits to the Japanese leadership, the most important taking place in 1591. Joao Rodrigues participated in the embassy as interpreter. The visit to Hideyoshi at his headquarters in Azuchi near Kyoto made a deep impression on him. Hideyoshi let the Jesuit embassy stay at a fancy palace before the ceremony. There was a solemn procession through the streets on the way to Hideyoshi's palace. Gifts were exchanged and a meeting was held. Hideyoshi expressed pleasure at the Jesuit embassy and the generous gifts that were given to him, including a beautiful Arabian horse and European weapons.

Rodrigues visited Hideyoshi several times after the embassy and Hideyoshi grew to like his company. With his knowledge of the West, his sophisticated sense of Japanese culture, and his excellent Japanese language skills, Rodrigues was very useful to Hideyoshi. However, shortly after the embassy, a rumor began to circulate that the Jesuits's friendly approach in the embassy had been subterfuge and they really intended to overthrow the Japanese government once its guard was down. Hideyoshi flew into a rage and turned against the Jesuits, writing a letter that threatened persecution against them. Later he was persuaded to revise the letter and tone it down. But he did not change his position that Christianity was a threat and could no longer be preached in Japan. The letter explained that Christianity produced divided loyalties between one's lord and the Christian god, therefore threatening the political system of Japan which was based upon absolute loyalty to one's lord. In spite of the letter, Rodrigues remained popular with Hideyoshi, likely convincing the ruler to not take further negative actions against the Jesuits even though Hideyoshi did have the buildings of the Jesuits in Nagasaki torn down.

Rodrigues continued to represent Christians and the Jesuits to Hideyoshi and other Japanese leaders. He became something of a lobbyist and was quite effective. He even met Tokugawa Ieyasu, who was later to become shogun, and discussed Christian theology and cosmology with him.

The embassy of 1591, even though it had raised Hideyoshi's suspicion, had also brought western culture to the attention of Hideyoshi's entourage. After the embassy, the western style of dress became popular as the officials of Hideyoshi's court began to dress in the Portuguese style and began to eat some European foods such as veal. The European trend was so strong that some Japanese non-Christians carried rosaries and learned the Ave Maria by heart. However, this temporary popularity of everything western did not run deep. It amounted to a fad among those trying to please Hideyoshi, lasting only as long as the missionaries were in his favor. Rodrigues continued to visit Hideyoshi in 1594 and 1595 and the leader continued to be benign toward Christianity, saying that it was a matter for the individual, not the state. Hideyoshi even entrusted Rodrigues with the buying of silk from China, but he still harbored the fear that Christianity would unify the lords who were suspected of being disloyal to him or possibly bring a foreign invasion against Japan.

When another Catholic order, the Franciscans, arrived in Japan in the early 1590s, they criticized the Jesuits as being too timid. They made the outlandish claim that the Jesuits were ashamed of Christianity or were afraid to show their faces in public. The Jesuits in return called the Franciscan friars "fraile idiota" or "idiot friars." The Jesuit approach of cultural adaptation came under fire and was eventually condemned by the Church. In defense of the Jesuits, it is quite likely that any other approach would have been met with violence and expulsion much earlier than happened. The Franciscan approach of boldness did not work well at all in the Japanese context where there was already growing suspicion that Christianity was a cover for a foreign attempt to take control of Japan or, just as serious, a means by which the lords who opposed Hideyoshi could become unified against him.

In 1596 a storm pushed the Spanish supply ship the *San Felipe* off course and resulted in a shipwreck on the Japanese island of Shikoku. Hideyoshi decided to confiscate its goods and found soldiers and munitions onboard. The ship had been bound for Mexico and so the supplies and soldiers had been intended to arrive there, not in Japan. But the suspicions of Hideyoshi were further inflamed. Earlier, he had been told that the Spanish sometimes used the missionaries to aid in their conquests. This fueled a fear that the soldiers and weapons were intended for conquest of Japan. Hideyoshi flew into another rage and ordered the execution by crucifixion of all western missionaries found in the capital Miyako. This was later reduced to just the Franciscans. Twenty-six missionaries in all were executed on crosses near Nagasaki.

This marked the beginning of the time of trial for the missionaries in Japan. The arbitrary decisions of Hideyoshi and the instabilities of the Japanese political system eventually made the western presence in Japan untenable. Hideyoshi's concern that the missionaries were storm troopers for Spanish conquest—while unrealistic given the strong military power of the Japanese, the lack of Spanish forces, and the long distance from Spain—reflected Spanish actions elsewhere and the fact that some Spaniards in Japan advocated conquest in Japan. For example, the Spanish Franciscans asserted that the Jesuits should have overthrown the Japanese regime. Speaking of the Jesuits, the Franciscan friar Martin de La Ascension stated,

> In Nagasaki alone they could have armed thirty thousand trustworthy musketeers, all of them Christians from the villages possessed by the fathers [Jesuit Priests]... And with these Christians and with the Spaniards they could with the help of God and with Spanish industry and military discipline, conquer and pacify all of Japan.[4]

Hideyoshi responded to the perceived threat of conquest with a letter sent to the Spanish government in the Philippines: "I have received information that in your Kingdoms the promulgation of the law (i.e. Christianity) is a trick and deceit by which you overcome other Kingdoms."[5]

Though his fears were clearly exaggerated, there was potential for trouble from the aggressive Franciscans and this prompted him to act against them.

In spite of Hideyoshi's fears, Jesuit missionaries were more concerned about Japanese converts' souls than about the overthrow of Japan. Japanese Christians, similar to Chinese Christians, interpreted Christianity through their

In this late sixteenth-century portrait, Hideyoshi (1536–1598) grasps the sword that catapulted him to power and exudes the discipline and self-confidence that made possible his campaigns to unify Japan. Although warrior skills were vital in his rise to power, he and othermembers of the samurai class were expected to be literate, well mannered by the conventions of the day, and attuned to the complex and refined aesthetics of rock gardens and tea ceremonies.   The Granger Collection, NY.

own cultural framework and this worried the missionaries. "The Japanese recruits were not given to prayer, they lacked zeal, they were not open to superiors." Even Valignano, the Jesuit missionary leader, admitted, "There always remains some indefinable difficulty in understanding the innermost thoughts of the Japanese."[6] Because the Europeans did not trust the Japanese converts completely and saw them as alien, they never received the highest positions within the Catholic Church in Japan. These were reserved for European priests. Michael Cooper, historian of this Jesuit-Japan encounter, notes the views of Japanese Christians although it is a stereotyped rendering of them. "Understandably they resented having to obey Europeans who, they thought, did not fully understand or appreciate the Japanese way of life. At times they felt a division of loyalties—loyalty towards their religion and Order on the one hand and towards their country and native fief on the other."[7]

After the crucifixion of the 26 Christians, the Jesuits were allowed to remain in Japan mostly because they were tasked with managing the trade with Portugal. Rodrigues became the official commercial agent and interpreter for the silk trade. It turns out that Rodrigues was a clever negotiator. This skill was due in part to the training he had received as a Jesuit about how to approach the Japanese in a culturally sensitive manner and his great skill with the Japanese language. However, his expertise in the worldly pursuit of money was upsetting to his Jesuit colleagues who thought this position was not befitting a man of god. It also put him in a dangerous position with the Japanese leadership. At one point the Japanese government accused Rodrigues of interfering in the governance of the city of Nagasaki. Later there were more serious charges. Rodrigues had created rivalries with the power he wielded as merchant, and now a prominent Japanese leader brought specious charges of unchastity against him. Murayama, a Japanese Christian who was a powerful leader in Nagasaki, was determined to destroy Rodrigues and he accomplished this by accusing him of consorting with his wife. Eventually the situation became so tense that a Portuguese ship was attacked in the harbor of Nagasaki and was sunk with its valuable cargo. This incident was the last straw and Rodrigues was forced to leave Japan. The encounter of missionaries with the Japanese in Japan was destroyed by politics, power, suspicion, and betrayal and ultimately ended in expulsion of the Jesuit community there.

Rodrigues was exiled to Macao and eventually became the procurator or governor of the community in 1624. He was involved in the governance of the western community there, was involved in trade with China, and served as chaplain as well. He became well respected in China and consulted with the Chinese on the issue of accurate maps. But he wanted to return to Japan and die there. After he was exiled, Rodrigues reflected upon his life. A lifelong wanderer, he still called the small town in Portugal where he was born his home. But his heart was in Japan, where he had formed his adult identity and spent most of his life. He also reflected on the mission he had left when he was exiled from Japan. By 1627 there were only 17 Jesuits left in Japan and the mission there was soon closed down.

Rodrigues believed that his generation of Jesuits had been solid and virtuous. But the younger generation of Portuguese was narrow-minded and not open to cross-cultural encounters. Referring to the governing of Jesuit communities in Asia, he stated, "the Portuguese act as if we were in Portugal ... They think it completely unreasonable for any foreigner, however much talent he may possess, to govern communities and they want only Portuguese."[8] Some Jesuits thought there was only one way of dealing with foreigners, according to Rodrigues. He responded with his own vision of cultural adaptation. "There is one way of dealing with the Camarins of India, another with the Christian Communities of black barbarians, and yet another with the Japanese, Chinese, and Koreans, for these people are so civilized and advanced in knowledge, government and other things that in this respect they are in no way inferior to Europeans."[9] While Rodrigues was not advocating the modern concept of cultural relativism and he clung to the notion of the superiority of European civilization over most other places, his experiences made him more sensitive to the position of others in cross-cultural encounters.

Toward the end of his life, Rodrigues became involved in the Chinese attempt to suppress a Manchu invasion of China in 1628. He accompanied a group of Portuguese officials delivering cannon to the capital city of Peking. They were even involved in a skirmish with the Manchu. In a narrow escape, the elderly Rodrigues was forced along with others to flee the city of Tengchow, which had been invaded by Manchu forces, by jumping from the parapets of the fort into deep snow. Rodrigues was even given an imperial audience in Peking and a commendation from the emperor after the incident. He was at the time 69 years old. Shortly thereafter he died and his remains were buried in Macao, his last resting place.

Conclusion

The Jesuit encounter with the Japanese ended quite differently from that with China, with expulsion and death rather than audiences with the emperor as in China. And the nature of the encounter was quite different. The missionaries in China were treated as celebrities, while in Japan they were treated with suspicion throughout their time there. While the Chinese appropriated freely from Jesuits's writings, little accommodation took place on the part of the Japanese, and their cultural appropriations such as wearing rosary beads at court were short-lived and superficial. Rather, the Japanese leadership responded negatively many times, in part because the Japanese political system was more unsettled than China's, and therefore the indigenous leadership felt that Christianity had the potential to overthrow it. But the approach of the Jesuits was the same in both places and though one was much more successful than the other, this accomodationist approach allowed some success in both countries, creating a bridge to Japanese and Chinese cultures.

Relations between westerners and these two nations continued to be strained into the modern period. Japan isolated itself from the west, officially closing Japan to westerners in 1640 thereby allowing only one ship of the

Dutch to enter the harbor at Nagasaki. The Japanese even created a man-made island called Deshima in the bay of Nagasaki for the ships to anchor so they would have no contact with Japanese other than the traders. Westerners who landed in Japan through shipwreck were liable to be executed under the law but this rarely happened. Isolation lasted until Japan was forcibly opened by the American Commodore Perry in 1853.

China continued to trade with the west on favorable terms until the introduction of British East India Company opium in the 1790s. The British in 1793 attempted to open up China to trade through the diplomatic mission of Lord George Macartney. Macartney met the emperor and requested more trade ports and fewer restrictions on trade. The emperor refused and condescendingly stated that China had no need for western trade goods. While Macartney's mission failed, the British began to illegally import opium into China and this caused the confrontation that led to the Opium Wars. In 1842, after a series of British incursions, the Chinese were forced to sign the unequal treaties. This incident began a time of western domination in China that ended only after World War II.

Questions for Discussion

1. Describe the approach of the Jesuit missionaries in China and Japan to convert these peoples to Christianity.
2. How successful were the Jesuit missionaries in making Christian converts in Japan and China?
3. How did the Chinese respond to Jesuit missionaries? To Matteo Ricci?
4. What purpose did Jesuit missionaries in Japan serve for the Japanese ruler Hideyoshi? How did this impact their stay in Japan?
5. What basic conflict of loyalties did the presence of missionaries in Japan engender? Why did this endanger their mission to Japan?

Endnotes

1. Stuart B. Schwartz, ed., *Implicit Understandings: Observing, Reporting, and Reflecting on the Encounters Between Europeans and Other Peoples in the Early Modern Era* (Cambridge, MA: Cambridge University Press, 1994), p. 409.
2. George Harris, "The Mission of Matteo Ricci, S. J.: A Case Study of an Effort at Guided Cultural Change in China in the Sixteenth Century," *Monumenta Serica*, Vol. 25 (1966), p. 70.
3. Willard J. Peterson, "What to Wear? Observation and Participation by Jesuit Missionaries in late Ming Society," in S. B. Schwartz (ed.), *Implicit Understandings*, p. 418.
4. Michael Cooper, *Rodrigues, the Interpreter: An Early Jesuit in Japan and China* (New York: Weatherhill, 1974), p. 160.
5. Ibid.
6. Ibid., p. 179.
7. Ibid., p. 180.
8. Ibid., p. 330.
9. Ibid.

Empires of Difference: The Ottoman Model of a Multicultural State

The long-lived Ottoman Empire, which lasted from 1299 to 1922, covered a wide swath of the Middle East, North Africa, and southeastern Europe. Led by Turkish leaders called sultans, the Ottoman Empire became the dominant force in this part of the world in the 1400s to 1600s and threatened central Europe until the failure of their siege of Vienna in 1683. The seat of this Islamic empire was Istanbul, formerly Constantinople, the capital of the Eastern Roman or Byzantine Empire until it was conquered by the Ottomans in 1453. By the nineteenth century the Ottoman Empire was in rapid decline until its collapse, under internal and foreign pressures after World War I.

The Ottoman Empire arose at a time when European society was dwarfed in power and cultural achievement by Islamic, Asian, and the Middle Eastern empires, such as the Safavid Empire in Iran and the Mughal Empire in India. During its heyday, the Ottoman Empire was admired for its innovations in architecture and art and its well-educated officials and well-trained bureaucrats, who conducted business while seated on beautiful upholstered raised platforms (hence the western term for a broad padded footstool of the same name). The Ottoman army inspired awe in its neighbors and fear in its enemies. Ottoman ruling elite—chiefly ethnic Turks, migrants from central Asia—often exploited the people they conquered, both Muslim and non-Muslim. However, the Ottoman Empire was and remains known as an "Empire of Difference," both for the way it respected and thus retained the loyalty of its scores of diverse religious and ethnic groups and for its generally welcoming and tolerant stance toward outsiders.

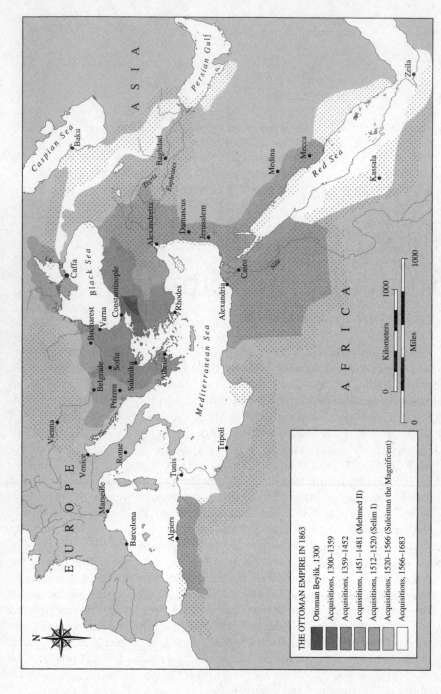

THE OTTOMAN EMPIRE IN 1863

- Ottoman Beylik, 1300
- Acquisitions, 1300–1359
- Acquisitions, 1359–1452
- Acquisitions, 1451–1481 (Mehmed II)
- Acquisitions, 1512–1520 (Selim I)
- Acquisitions, 1520–1566 (Suleiman the Magnificent)
- Acquisitions, 1566–1683

MAP 3.1 Map of Ottoman Empire—Constantinople is Istanbul   *Source:* Wikicommons Free Use Map

OUTSIDERS IN THE OTTOMAN EMPIRE

Western chroniclers traditionally characterized the rise of the Ottoman Empire as deeply hostile to non-Muslims. This portrayal is badly flawed. In fact, the Ottomans married their princes into Orthodox Christian families and used young Christian slaves from the Balkans to populate the Janissary corps, the elite Ottoman guard. In addition, the Ottomans took advantage of the expulsion of Jews from Spain and other areas of Western Europe to invite them into the Empire. Jewish merchants from Europe and North Africa brought expertise in trade, financing, and crafts, which were needed by the Ottomans and helped the Empire to prosper.

THE AMAN

The official Ottoman policy toward outsiders—called *aman*—was one of toleration and protection of outsiders within their territory. The foreigner requested this protection in return for promising to be peaceful and friendly toward the Ottomans. This policy was unlike policies toward foreigners pursued by the Japanese and Chinese, who limited the activities of foreigners greatly; they were deeply suspicious of foreigners and sometimes executed them on the slightest pretext. There were also exceptions to *aman*. The Janissaries, the elite Ottoman soldiers, could be quite cruel to outsiders if it served their personal interests. In one case they beat a Jewish merchant to death in the market square in the port city of Salonica, but they were cruel to their own people as well. The soldiers themselves were beaten often and trained in cruelty, which they could turn against others in defense of their personal as well as political interests.

People who were offered protection were usually merchants or diplomats. To them the Sultan gave special status and privileges called *capitulations.* For example, foreigners under protection who were accused of a crime had the right to representation, usually by someone from the foreigner's embassy or consulate. Foreign traders usually had to pay special tax in order to do business on Ottoman territory, but they often successfully negotiated their special status into tax exemptions. Tariffs paid by foreigners on goods were between 3 and 5 percent, which was always lower than what the Ottomans charged their own subjects. This advantage came to be resented by Ottoman subjects who could claim no such status. Despite such resentment, foreigners constituted an elite group within the Empire.

Legally, any foreigner who stayed in Ottoman lands more than one year automatically became a subject of the Sultan and renounced his allegiance to his homeland. In practice, the Ottomans did not enforce this policy and normally, as long as foreigners did not marry an Ottoman or buy real estate, they were able to retain their loyalty to the ruler of their home country. Even the rule on marriage was flexible; many foreigners kept their foreign identity after marrying an Ottoman subject and continued to live in Ottoman territory.

Travelers passing through Ottoman domains included traders and merchants, Christian missionaries, diplomats, people who wanted to learn more about Islamic empires, and people on pilgrimages. The Ottomans permitted

Interior of a Turkish Caffinet in Constantinople. The use of coffee and coffee houses promoted new forms of consumerism and socialization in several regions.   Private Collection/The Stapleton Collection/The Bridgeman Art Library International.

such foreigners to live and work in Istanbul and even hired some into the government. The Venetians and the French had embassies in the district of Galacia at the center of Istanbul. These diplomats and merchants were, for the Ottomans, a significant source of information on the state of European politics.

THE MILLET SYSTEM

Ottoman rulers also recognized the autonomy of various religious groups within their Empire through the concept of "millets," which may be rendered as "nation-alities," but refers to the recognition of the right of a community to live under its own laws. This arrangement allowed Jewish, Greek Orthodox, and Armenian Christian communities to keep their own religious practices and separate religious courts to regulate these practices. This enabled them to largely manage their own affairs, avoid persecution, and thus thrive under Ottoman rule.

TRADE AND COMMERCE

The Ottomans recognized that external trade was essential to strengthening the Empire and thus were not only tolerant of foreign merchants, but some-times invited them into the Empire to help the economy. Jews expelled from Spain during the Inquisition were invited to take up residence in Algiers, Salonica, Istanbul, and other places within the Empire because they were traders, merchants, and craftsmen and brought wealth to the Empire by plying their trade. As a French agent, Nicolas de Nicolay, explained:

> [The Jews] have among them workmen of all artes and handicrafts moste excellent, and specially of the Maranes [Marranos] of late banished and driven out of Spain and Portugal, who to the great detriment and damage of the Christnaitie, have taught the Turkes divers inventions, craftes and engines of warre, as to make artillerie, harquebuses, gunne powder, shot and other munitions; they have also there set up printing not before seen in those countries … [brackets and spellings in original][1]

Merchants from England, France, Venice, and later the Netherlands were allowed to travel freely in the capital and the provincial centers such as Ismir, Salonica, and elsewhere. Trade routes such as the Silk Road and others ran through the Empire and thereby invited many foreigners along these routes to travel through Ottoman lands. In some cases, these foreigners had little contact with the Muslim residents of these cities as they lived in their own quarters or sections of urban neighborhoods. In other cases however, especially in port cities, foreigners did business with Muslims and had daily interaction with them. Merchants from Italian cities such as Venice visited the Ottoman Empire and Muslim traders from the Ottoman Empire reciprocated by going to Venice to trade. Armenian traders loyal to the Sultan lived in Istanbul, but also as far away as Amsterdam. French traders lived and worked in Ismir and traded with Greek and Armenian traders. Iranian traders worked in some of the smaller Ottoman towns. A Venetian Doge's (ruler's) son worked in Istanbul for the Ottoman government and he kept his Catholic religion. Later he served as a high official in Ottoman Hungary, a conquered territory, but was assassinated there by anti-Ottoman Hungarians.

View of Istanbul from the Galata Bridge, c. 1890s.   Photochrom Prints/ Library of Congress.

IMPERIAL POWER, IMPERIAL DIVERSITY

Foreigners even became part of the ruling elite. The Ottomans possessed two types of rulers within the Empire: those who governed the House of Islam (Muslim lands) and those who governed the House of War (non-Muslim lands). House of Islam leaders were the Ottoman rulers themselves and other Sunni Muslim rulers. The House of War leaders were non-Muslim rulers of city-states and provinces within the Empire such as Dubrovnik, Hungary, Moldavia, Transylvania, and Walachia and the North African domains. For instance, Charles Gordon, a British subject, was the pasha or ruling governor over the Ottoman province of Sudan in North Africa in the 1870s. A German named Eduard Schnitzer, the so-called Emin Pasha, ruled over the province of Equatorial African Uganda, just south of Sudan, in the same period.

There was no neat division between Ottoman subjects and the outside world, in spite of clear legal distinctions between the two. In the Ottoman environment, even slaves and their masters could become friends in the realm of day-to-day life. Maps, books, and painted pictures showed the world beyond the Ottoman Empire to the Ottoman people, in spite of an official ban on outside images.

Because they felt secure in the Empire and religion, Ottoman rulers could be more flexible in their dealings with outsiders. The Ottoman government invited ambassadors from the major powers of Europe to reside in Istanbul at a time when this practice was only beginning to become commonplace within European capitals. Outsiders must have perceived Ottoman rule positively because they sent ambassadors and sometimes formed alliances. The estates of Bohemia received Ottoman support in their rebellion against the Hapsburgs in 1618.

The Ottoman government viewed alliances with Christian princes strategically. They had few foreign alliances before 1700, a period marked by territorial expansion, often at the expense of Christian peoples. However, with the Russian incursion into the Black Sea area and the Balkans in the late eighteenth century, the Ottomans aggressively sought alliances with Britain and France to counter the Russian threat.

Ottoman religious toleration in the 1500s allowed Jesuit and Franciscan missionaries to enter Ottoman domains to convert Orthodox Christians to Catholicism. These Catholic missionaries also attempted to gain control of religious holy sites in Ottoman territories, such as in Jerusalem, where the management of the Church of the Holy Sepulchre (marking the place where Christians believed Jesus was buried) was in dispute between Catholic and Orthodox believers, much to the disgust of Ottoman officials. Toleration of Orthodox Christians sometimes worked against the Ottomans in other ways.

The Eastern Orthodox Christian Church had been founded in Constantinople and this church, while Christian, had traditions that differed from Catholic Christianity. The Orthodox Church had spread throughout southeastern Europe and Russia, leading to the foundation of the Serbian

Orthodox Church. This church communicated with the Orthodox leadership in Russia, which had become a rival to the Ottomans. In effect, the Orthodox Church in Istanbul operated as a source of intelligence for the Russian Tsars. Orthodox nuns also helped Ottoman slaves escape to a convent in Athens.

OBSTACLES TO TOLERATION

The policy of toleration was, for other reasons, questionable in the eyes of some Ottomans. The Ottoman Turks were overwhelmingly Sunni (traditional) Muslims, but a minority took up Shiite Islam (just as old as Sunni, but taking a more mystical interpretation of Islam) and this became a source of friction, even though the form Shiite Islam sometimes took in the Ottoman Empire was Sufism, often one of the most peaceful of sects in the Muslim world. Shiite Sufis, referred to as "Dervishes," were quite open to other religions and embraced unorthodox religious practices such as the integration of expressive movement and dancing (hence westerners referred to them as "whirling dervishes"). The Sufis were criticized by Muslim leaders in the Empire for such unorthodox ideas and practices. Nonetheless, the Ottoman Empire continued to be tolerant of the Dervishes who were highly popular among the Janissaries. As a result, calls by leaders of Sunni Islam to ban the movement succeeded only in 1826 when the Janissary corps itself was abolished. But even then, the ban was short-lived as the Ottomans thereafter encouraged religious tolerance in their effort to align themselves with parallel growth of religious freedom in Europe.

Not long after the foundation of the Ottoman Empire, a rival Muslim state emerged in Iran, known as the Safavid Empire. In part to strengthen its internal cohesion, the Safavids committed themselves to Shiite Islam and used the differences between Sunni and Shia Islam as a weapon against the Ottoman Empire's efforts to expand into their territory. The Ottoman Empire thus found itself with a religious and political rival. Major wars were fought between the two in the sixteenth century. During the Ottoman wars with the Hapsburgs in Europe and the Safavids in the seventeenth century, foreigners of these warring powers were expected to leave the country. Also the merchants of the enemy were sometimes imprisoned and their wares confiscated as was the case with Iranian merchants during hostilities between the Ottomans and the Safavid ruler in 1512–1520.

Controlling the activities of foreigners especially at the frontiers of the Empire became more and more difficult as Ottoman control weakened. Ottoman notables and land owners worked directly with French traders without government regulation, especially on the Greek coast. The French exported olives, from which oil was extracted for the manufacture of Palmolive soap in Marseilles France.

The experience of foreigners at the northern frontier of the Ottoman Empire was the most problematic. This area was contested in wars between Russia and the Ottomans in the 1760s. These conflicts produced hostility among Ukrainian and other peoples toward Ottomans because the Ottomans could not protect the inhabitants of territory they controlled from the scourge of war.

TRADE

Muslim merchants from India entered the Ottoman Empire to trade high-value Indian cotton goods such as carpets and drapery. Iranian merchants also traded with Ottoman subjects, bringing Iranian silk. The Ottomans traded for Russian furs and in return sent valuable leather items such as horse saddles north to Russia. Most of the Iranian subjects in Ottoman territories in the early period were Armenians in the city of Djulfa, present-day Azerbaijan. They were very successful traders and sent caravans to Vienna, Venice, Amsterdam, Cairo, Moscow, St. Petersburg, Crimea, Astrakhan, and Manila and even traded by sea with the island of Java in present-day Indonesia. They controlled the trade in spices, garlic, and especially raw silk, some of which came from China via the Silk Road. The Armenians were crucial participants in the Silk Road trade and possessed such strong connections with Venetian trading houses that a street in Venice was named for them. In 1605 they were caught in warfare between the Ottoman Empire and Iran. They were then forcibly deported to the interior of Iran and their city of Djulfa was destroyed. Once the Armenians reestablished themselves in Iran in a city called New Djulfa, they once again became successful traders and brought the goods of Iran to the Ottomans and parts of Europe. There also existed an Armenian community in the Ottoman city of Ismir.

As mentioned above, commercial travelers from the west traveled to Istanbul, Aleppo, Bursa, Salonica, or Ismir. Venetians traded glassware, wool, silk, and books printed in Greek and in turn imported cotton into Venice. The Ottomans allowed Venetian traders to file claims against local merchants if they thought they had been treated unfairly. Ottoman goods also made their way into Poland especially in the period of the Polish-Lithuanian Commonwealth of 1569–1795. Carpets and pieces of clothing were favored. Armenian traders based in Lvov (in modern-day Moldavia) shipped goods back and forth between Poland and Istanbul. French traders from Marseilles traded wool produced in the region to the Ottoman Empire.

Europeans such as the Dutch and English attempted to compete with the French for the Ottoman market. English merchants who came to Ottoman domains brought wool. Silk made its way to Ottoman territory from East Asia through the efforts of Armenian traders from New Djulfa. In the seventeenth century, British woolen merchants became the dominant European force in the Ottoman Empire. Some Ottoman traders immigrated to Cairo, Egypt, which was a province of the Ottoman Empire until the mid-nineteenth century. They liked to trade at Cairo because there they could be more independent of the distant central government in Istanbul. The resultant high volume and tremendous variety of this trade enormously enriched the Ottoman domains and the Europeans who participated in it.

PRISONERS AND SLAVES

Because the Ottoman state was often at war, expanding or defending its frontiers, it accumulated many foreign prisoners of war from its enemies. Islamic law considered enslavement of these prisoners of war and many others legal. The Ottoman Empire's vast reach into the Middle East and North Africa meant the Ottomans controlled shipping lanes in the Mediterranean. With fast armed corsairs, they were able to attack trading ports and small islands as well as merchant vessels of their enemies. Normally the captives were ransomed for money. But if the families could not or refused to pay, prisoners were sold to private individuals within the Ottoman Empire as slaves. The enemies of Russia also sold thousands of Russian captives into the Ottoman slave markets in Kaffa on the Crimean Peninsula. Likewise, Ottoman soldiers, sailors, and merchants captured by European pirates were sold into the European slave market. In the sixteenth century there were literally tens of thousands of Ottoman slaves in the city-states of Italy and Sicily. In addition, slave captives from Russia and the Ukraine were introduced into the Ottoman slave markets by the Crimean Tatars (Turkish people living on the Crimean Peninsula), who raided Russia and the Ukraine, took captives, and sold them in Ottoman slave markets.

Conditions for slaves on both sides were sometimes severe. In one case, an Ottoman slave of Austrians was thrown out of the house and slept for six months on a dung heap to keep warm. Prisoners of European or Ottoman descent were sometimes forced to become rowers on galley ships. On the other hand, Ottoman laws considered slaves to be both human and property and therefore slaves in settled areas of the Empire were treated humanely and had recourse in Ottoman courts if treated unjustly. European slaves in Ottoman territory might receive help from the embassy of their home country or other Europeans, and in some cases Ottoman charities provided support such as food or clothing. And if they converted to Islam, they were freed.

PILGRIMS AND MISSIONARIES

Pilgrims of various religions traveled through Ottoman territory to sacred sites. Muslims from Morocco or India traveled through Ottoman domains to Mecca and those from Iran or elsewhere traveled to holy sites in Ottoman Iraq. Christians and Jews entered Ottoman territory on their way to the Holy Land (Palestine) and Jerusalem. European scholars came in search of Ottoman history and culture (and sometimes took artifacts home with them) and other Europeans came to Ottoman lands as part of a grand tour of the Middle East.

So many Iranians came to Ottoman Iraq on pilgrimage that Ottoman officials developed a policy to offer food and shelter to the pilgrims. The government assumed that the Iranians could live on their own resources for three days before allowing the Shah's officials to offer food and shelter. Ottoman officials became nervous when pilgrims to Mecca crossed their territory, fearing that Iranian pilgrims who were enemies of the Ottomans might actually be spies who took the opportunity while crossing the great deserts enroute to Mecca to form alliances with local Bedouins who were hostile to the Ottomans.

Christians entered Ottoman territory to make pilgrimages to Jerusalem. Muslim responses to Christian visitors varied. One Islamic visitor to the Ottoman-controlled holy sites in Jerusalem, Evliya Celebi, commented that "our Orthodox are a bunch of thick-headed and credulous men" who responded to images more than thoughtful preaching. Muslim visitors to Christian holy sites did not believe the story of Jesus's head crowned with thorns, and they were also skeptical of the so-called miracle of holy fire starting of its own accord inside the Church of the Holy Sepulchre. At times Christian pilgrims' encounters with Muslims were unfriendly. In 1601 a western Christian, Henry Timberlake, was arrested in Jerusalem because he announced that he was a Protestant from England. A Muslim friend intervened and he was released. In 1696, a Shiite village refused hospitality to a group of Christian pilgrims led by Henry Maundrell, who was chaplain to merchants in the Ottoman city Aleppo (in modern-day Syria). However, in most cases the Ottomans were quite hospitable to pilgrims, and Christian pilgrimages enhanced relations between western and eastern Christianity and the Ottoman Empire.

Catholic missionaries were very active on Ottoman lands in the 1600s, especially Jesuit and Franciscan from France. As missionaries traveled the Ottoman Empire they became acquainted with the food and culture of its inhabitants. One Jesuit missionary recounted being taught to prepare food in the Turkish manner with a rice pilaf and yogurt soup, demonstrating the intimacy of many encounters in the Ottoman Empire. The government demonstrated tolerance in policy, and the policy helped to shape individual encounters which in some cases became forums for positive exchanges.

COSMOPOLITAN PORTS OF CALL: SALONICA AND ALGIERS

While officially both Jews and Christians were considered to be inferior to Muslims, they had close interactions with both the ruling Ottomans and the diverse Muslim population they ruled. As historian Mark Mazower has observed, these relations were often quite fluid. "Boundaries were being constantly subverted by accident or design and in a bustling commercial port in particular, religious communities could not be impermeably sealed from one another." This was true of both Salonica and Algiers.

After their expulsion from Spain, many thousands of Spanish-speaking Jews joined other Jews fleeing persecution in Europe and settled in the Ottoman port city of Salonica (modern-day Thessaloniki in Greece). That the new arrivals felt grateful in their new environment is evidenced by the words of Samuel Usque, a Jewish poet from Spain who settled there. Europe had become "my hell on earth" according to Usque, and Salonica by contrast seemed like the Holy Land itself.

There is a city in the Turkish Kingdom which formerly belonged to the Greeks, and in our days is a true mother-city in Judaism. For it is established on the very deep foundations of the Law. And it is filled with the choicest plants and most fruitful trees, presently known anywhere on the face of the globe. These fruits are divine, because they are watered by an abundant stream of charities. The city's walls are made of holy deeds of greatest worth.[2]

And how did the residents of Salonica feel about this Jewish immigration? Again, Samuel Usque can be our guide. "The Jews of Europe and other countries, persecuted and banished, have come there to find a refuge, and this city has received them with love and affection, as if she were Jerusalem, that old and pious mother of ours."[3] The Jews of Salonica were given the responsibility of making the uniforms of the Ottoman's elite Janissary infantry corps. They also founded an important silver mine outside of the city and ran the mining business.

In Salonica a middle ground developed in which Jews, Greeks, and Muslims gathered together to do business, raise their families, and practice their faiths. A French commentator described the situation in Salonica as "a sort of fusion between different peoples who inhabit the place . . ."[4] Jews, Christians, and Muslims worked and lived together there. For example, a Castilian variant of Spanish brought to Salonica by Jews from Spain quickly became the preferred language of business, scholarship, science, and medicine.

There was also an underground folk religion in which Christians as well as Jews and Muslims all participated. One religious practice involved tying a knot in a rope and, after dripping some lamp oil on it, using it to cure illness. Another common element was the belief that someone with an evil eye could put a jinx or a hex on another person. A wide variety of items, from a boar's tusk to an ostrich egg, were used to undo the curse of the evil eye. A Turkish woman might grab a few hairs from a Jewish man's beard; Christian children might receive a blessing from a Muslim holy man which would include spitting on them, which was a Greek Orthodox custom.

At times Jews converted to Islam while still claiming to practice Judaism, while at other times Muslims secretly practiced Judaism. The most famous example of such syncretism or cultural blending occurred after a popular Messianic Jewish preacher, Sabbatai Zevi, declared in Salonica that he was the redeemer of the Jewish people destined to usher in a new age which would sweep away the Ottoman state. When the Ottomans arrested him and offered him a choice of conversion or death, he agreed to convert to Islam, and was allowed to continue teaching so long as he used his charismatic skills to convert Jews to the Muslim faith. Instead, while practicing forms of Islamic worship such as keeping the fast of Ramadan and publicly professing the Islamic faith, he used this freedom to win many Muslims over to Judaism throughout the Ottoman Empire and persuaded many others to observe Jewish laws. These thousands of nominally Muslim followers of Zevi, known as *Ma'min*, joined with many other Muslims, nominal and otherwise, who sought to promote secular knowledge and political reform within the empire. According to Mark Mazower, the Muslim followers of this would-be

Jewish messiah helped turn late-nineteenth-century Salonica into the most progressive city in the Empire.

Of course, there were also moments of tension and violence. The Greeks who had dominated the city until it fell to the Ottomans quickly became a minority, a situation that fueled inter-religious tension. Feeling liberated by the protections of Turkish rule, some Jewish victims of past Christian persecution threw garbage into the grounds of Salonica's Orthodox Cathedrals and mocked Orthodox religious festivals. But on the whole, the history of Salonica offers remarkable stories of toleration, cultural fusion, and hybridity.

Algiers also had a large Jewish population which wielded strong influence. Algiers became the center of Ottoman authority in northwest Africa after 1516 and quickly became the bulwark of the Islamic world in the struggle between the West and the Ottoman Empire over control of the western Mediterranean. Algiers was the center of corsair activity in which Muslims attacked shipping from Christian states; the island of Malta served Christian corsairs in the same manner. Both sought to acquire slaves to sell in their marketplaces and also captives to hold for ransom. Miguel De Cervantes, author of *Don Quixote*, was captured by a Muslim corsair in one such attack. As he carried papers marking him as a friend of the Spanish government, he spent half a decade in Algiers as a slave awaiting payment by his family of the large price demanded to secure his release because of his presumed status (though he would have been freed immediately upon converting to Islam). He translated that difficult experience into the "Captives Tale" in his masterwork, *Don Quixote*. However, as Cervantes historian Michael McGaha notes, Algiers was by no means a simple society, nor was Cervantes' experience there one of unalloyed frustration and pain.

> Algiers in Cervantes' day was one of the largest, wealthiest, and most cosmopolitan cities in the world. Especially in comparison with Cervantes' native Spain, Algiers was home to an amazingly free and tolerant society... Most notably, it was a society in which any man, regardless of race or ethnicity, could rise to the very pinnacle of power by dint of intelligence and hard work. A former slave could, and did, become king there. Cervantes, who hated Spain's rigid class system based on ancestry rather than merit, cannot have helped admiring this aspect of life in Algiers. During the five years he spent there, Cervantes became acquainted with all sorts of Moors and renegades, ranging from noble, generous, enlightened men such as Hajji Murad (Agi Morato) to amoral and cruel ones like his master Hasan Pasha (Azán Agá).[5]

Unlike Cervantes, many Christians in Algiers, ranging from Greeks to Slavs and from corsair captains' to slaves, converted to Islam. They blended easily into the local population of mixed Arab and Berber descent. A female Christian captive who converted to Islam was given the status of a member of the Turkish elite. Because they could speak a variety of languages, some of these converts served the Ottomans as translators throughout the empire, thereby acting as significant agents of cross-cultural contact, as did Algiers' Jews.

Since Roman times, Jews occupied a significant place in the region, part of which was ruled for a time by a Jewish Queen of a Judeo-Berber tribe. A historian of the Jews of North African Jewry, David Corus, records that Jewish-Muslim relations in Algiers were, "on the whole, good. It was only occasionally that outbursts of fanaticism gave rise to local persecutions [and even then in] certain towns it was accepted that at such times the mosques, although forbidden to infidels, should serve as a refuge to the Jews." Just prior to Ottoman rule, the Jewish community in Algiers grew due to the expulsion of Jews from Spain in 1492, similar to the situation in Salonica, and continued to grow with an influx of Jews from elsewhere in Europe. Relations between the Muslims and Jews in Algiers were among the most cordial of any in the Islamic world. Jews paid the *jizya*, the tax levied on all non-Muslims, but rabbis were exempted from the tax; so were Jewish merchants, as they paid customs on their imports. It was usually well-off Jews originally from Leghorn, Italy, who brokered the release of Christian captives seized by Algerian corsairs and who performed other key diplomatic assignments at the request of the Dey, or the Ottoman's designated ruler of the city. Unfortunately, the Janissaries in Algiers resented this expression of trust in non-Muslims as they did elsewhere in the Empire and this resentment led in 1805 to a massacre of Jews in Algiers, the only one of its kind. The success and status of the Jewish community in Algiers were so high that it figured in the fall of Algeria to the French. In 1830, the Dey of Algiers insisted that the French pay off their large outstanding debt to two Jewish merchant families, who for decades had supplied France with grain. In response, the French invaded the province, thereby voiding the Dey's demands and fulfilling their rising desire for an empire in North Africa.

The new French colonial regime sought to give the Jewish community of Algeria social and political advantages over Muslims there and even freed them from the requirement of the Ottomans that Jews, like all other minority ethnic groups, wear distinctive clothing. However, the Jews of Algiers were not eager to abandon these symbols of their traditional place in Algerian society, nor would they reject its cosmopolitan values. The bonds of that society were reinforced by refusal of Muslim Algerians to join in French anti-Semitic attacks on Jews in the later nineteenth century. Not long thereafter, a member of an old Andalusian Jewish family named Edemon Yafil spearheaded the development of a multicultural association to preserve and propagate the music of Zarieb, an Iraqi Muslim in Spain whose music was appreciated by both Jews and Muslims. Yafil was pleased to hand the reigns of this movement to a member of the Turkish elite, who ultimately came to be guided by an advisory board evenly divided between Jews and Muslims. A historian of Algiers, Omar Claier, notes that due to Yafil's effort, for more than a generation thereafter Jews and Muslims were to practice their art together in brotherly harmony, pursuing a common passion for a mixed musical tradition which they continually asserted.

THE OTTOMAN ENCOUNTER WITH "ORIENTALISM"

At its height, the Ottoman Empire was feared by Europeans as the scourge of Christendom, but also admired for its great wealth and magnificent court from which Ottoman sultans ruled over three continents with an ever victorious army. However, the early success of its political and military institutions, its ability to generate wealth via the conquest of new lands, and its role as leader of the Muslim world blinded Ottoman rulers to the inherent weakness of its monarchial structure; to the potential for corruption inherent in a privileged military elite (the Janissaries); and to the dangers arising from holding aloof from the industrializing trends in the West. Ottoman confidence in their continued superiority undermined their ability to see how quickly the west was overcoming some of these same obstacles to growth—steps the West, to some extent, was forced to undertake to meet the challenge of Ottoman expansion.

The first phase of industrialization in Europe and Tzarist Russia enabled its armies to win battles against the Ottomans and push the Ottomans out of much of Eastern Europe. These victories emboldened western writers to define their own rising civilization in terms of what they perceived as the failings of the premier government in global Islamic society. The once admired Ottoman military machine was dismissed as the product of militarism; the brilliance of the Ottoman court was demonized as place of tyranny and of sexual excess; and the old Empire's failure to rapidly industrialize was regarded as a clear indication of the Ottoman's, and by extension, the Muslim world's, imagined static nature and imperviousness to change. Of course, European states themselves were as militaristic, their own court life at least as licentious and their industrialization slow and fraught with disastrous human consequences, such as the clearance of poor farmers from their lands to promote commercial agriculture, a step the Ottomans strove to avoid due to their belief in the moral right even tenants had to the lands they tilled for others. Such realities had little impact on the growing western propensity to see the Ottoman society negatively, as an exotic and inferior "other," a process called Orientalism as it was applied to all the peoples of the "Orient" or East, including Indians, Chinese, Japanese, and the peoples of Southeast Asia.

The Ottoman court may have been slow to see this change in the attitudes of Europeans, as well as the shift in relative power between them, but to its credit it eventually attempted to address them through a politically costly process which historians call "defensive modernization" (which in this case compelled the Ottoman Sultan to destroy the Janissary corps). University education on the western model was introduced, land was privatized (permitting the removal of indebted tenants in the western fashion), the means of public communication were expanded, and western political freedoms were introduced, such as the granting of formal equality of Muslim and non-Muslim subjects within the Empire. However, the turmoil created by these changes undermined confidence in the regime, especially among restive non-Turkish minorities within the Empire. In the late nineteenth century, groups like the Ma'min sought to preserve the unity in diversity that was in Ottoman states, but these were soon overwhelmed by minorities who saw in Ottoman disarray the chance to carve out states of their own.

Salonica in 1913 during Greek Occupation.   Library of
Congress

Conclusion

By the opening salvos of World War I, many would-be reformers of the
Ottoman Empire among the ruling Turkish population envisioned the creation
of a Turkish state out of what they could take from Arab, Berber, Greek, and
Kurdish areas of the Empire. This nation-building impulse, with its emphasis
on Turkish ethnicity and language, pushed the Turks away from traditional
Ottoman tolerance of its minority communities. In the midst of the war itself,
many Turks also came to view these peoples as potential threats to their security,
with horrific consequences, particularly for the Empire's Armenian population.

In such an atmosphere, it is not surprising that the Ottoman defeat in the
war, and its ultimate dissolution by Allied treaty in 1922, was accompanied by
an explosion of ethnic tensions. Representatives of Arab communities met in
Damascus, Syria, to explore the creation of an Arab homeland, though they
could not agree on whether it should be only for Muslim Arabs, or for all Arabs,
including Arabic-speaking Christians and other minorities. An overwhelmingly Muslim but modern nation was founded by Turks, which attempted to
carry on the Ottoman tradition of openness and toleration by adopting the
secular and progressive program favored by groups such as Ma'min (whose
origin and vision are subject to criticism by anti-secularist Muslims in Turkey
today). But even there intolerance triumphed. Turks expelled Greeks from
their Mediterranean coast, if in part because Greeks had seized Salonica as a
prize of war and cleansed the city of its Turkish Muslim population.

Salonica's Jews suffered the same fate. A wartime fire which razed much
of the old section of Salonica offered an opportunity to remove unwanted
groups and rebuild the city according to the wishes of Salonica's resurgent
Greek community. At their hands the Jewish section of the city was almost
completely destroyed, including 37 synagogues. In the postwar atmosphere

of rising ethnic nationalism and anti-Semitism, Salonica's multi-ethnic heritage was so thoroughly destroyed as to have passed from the memory of its current inhabitants. The Jewish community in Algiers survived longer but was ultimately trapped between the anti-Semitism of the French and rising Muslim nationalist sentiment in North Africa. The creation of Israel led to persecutions of Jews by Muslims in Algiers that resulted in the slower but ultimately complete end to that community via emigration.

With its breakup in the aftermath of World War I, the Ottoman Empire disappeared into the mists of history. A loose-knit empire that allowed different ethnic groups to define their experiences with one another, the Ottoman Empire could not survive in an age where nations were rising and defining themselves on the basis of a common language, religion, or ethnicity. While western writers had once admired the relative peace and tranquility its diverse population long enjoyed, they eventually buried the history of Ottoman open-mindedness and prosperity under charges of Oriental brutality and stasis. Such revisionism is now at work in Muslim intellectual quarters. Today, some within radical Islamic movements advocate a revival of an Islamic world empire, but they reject the hybridity and toleration which accounted for the Ottoman state's longevity and much of its grandeur.

Questions for Discussion

1. What principles did the Ottoman Empire espouse in dealing with outsiders?
2. Describe the different kinds of outsiders who crossed into the Ottoman Empire? What were the different reasons they came into the Empire?
3. How did slavery operate within the Ottoman domains? Who became slaves?
4. What was the state of relations between the Ottoman Empire and the Safavid Empire of Persia (modern-day Iran)? How did tensions between the two Empires impact outsiders in Ottoman domains and how did the presence of outsiders influence the relations between the two empires?
5. Why did Jews come to live and work in the Ottoman Empire? Describe the evolving situation of Jews, Greeks, and Muslims in Salonica and Algiers.

Endnotes

1. Avigdor Levy, *The Sephardim in the Ottoman Empire* (Princeton, NJ: Princeton University Press, 1992), p. 26.
2. Samuel Usque, *Samuel Usque's Consolation for the Tribulations of Israel* (New York: The Jewish Publication Society, 1977), trans. Martin A. Cohen, 2nd ed., p. 211.
3. Ibid., p. 212.
4. Basil Nicolaides, *Les Turcs et la Turquise Contemporaine* (Paris, 1859), ii, p. 45 cited in Mark Mazower, *Salonica, City of Ghosts: Christians, Muslims and Jews, 1430–1950* (New York: Alfred A. Knopf, 2005), p. 65.
5. Michael McGaha, review of María Antonia Garcés, *Cervantes in Algiers: A Captive's Tale*, *Cervantes*, Vol. 23 (Fall 2003), pp. 437–442.

Encounters—Middle Ground Successes and Failures

Cultures in Competition: Native American Encounters with Europeans

In North America there were no great indigenous empires, as the great urban center of Cahokia on the Mississippi River had collapsed shortly before the arrival of Europeans. As a result, the circumstances of the encounter between Native Americans and European settlers in North America were quite different than the encounter between Europeans and the societies of Latin America, East Asia, or the Ottoman Empire. Since the indigenous peoples of North America were gathered in relatively small communities, diversity reigned: there were dozens of different states, 500 different languages were spoken, and each community practiced their own cultural forms.

The British who first met Native Americans upon their arrival in Roanoke Island, North Carolina, and Jamestown, Virginia, were soldiers of fortune like the Spaniards in Latin America. Britain's goal was to establish colonies in North America before the Spanish expanded northward from their outpost in Florida. However, the Roanoke Island settlement completely disappeared, generating a genuine historical mystery as to why it vanished. And the Jamestown settlement was barely more successful, relying heavily upon the assistance of neighboring Native Americans for its survival. The more successful settlements were the groups of religious dissenters who landed farther north in modern-day Massachusetts: the Pilgrims and later Puritans. These settlers were not conquerors, although like the Spanish conquistadors they were intent on controlling land in the new world and expanding their holdings. In addition, the French came to ply the fur trade in

N

Beaufort Sea

Baffin Bay

ARCTIC

Labrador Sea

Tlingit

Inuit

Hudson Bay

SUBARCTIC

Inuit

NORTH WEST COAST

Tshimshian

Montagnais

Kwakiutls   Shuswap

Cree

Nootka   Kootenay
Makah   Colville   Blackfeet
Skagit
Salish   PLATEAU   Assiniboine   Chippewa
Chinook   Walla   Cheyenne   Sioux   Micmac
Walla   Penobscot
Umatilla   Nez   Flathead   Hidatsa   Sioux   Algonquin
Tillamook   Cayuse   Perce   Mandan   Chippewa
Klamath   Crow   Arapaho   Menominee   Ottawa   Huron   Mohegan   Wampanoag
Pomo   Modoc   Northern   Kiowa   Winnebago   Neutral   Iroquois   Pequot
Maidu   Paiute   Apachean   Pawnee   Iowa   Fox   Erie   Susquehannock
Costano   Shoshone   Sauk   Potawatomi   Lenni   Narraganset
Shoshone   Goshute   PRAIRIE   Kickapoo   Lenape
GREAT   Illinois   Shawnee   Mosopelea
Chemehuevi   GREAT BASIN   PLAINS   Kaskaskia
Chumash   Southern Ute   EAST WOODLAND
Serrano   Paiute   Pamlico
Luiseno   Cahuilla   Apachean   Wichita   Cherokee   Tuscarora
Diegueno   Hopi   Zuni   Chicksaw   Catawba
CALIFORNIA   SOUTHWEST   Pueblo   Apachean   Caddo   Creek   Catawba
Pima   Choctaw   Yamasee   Timucua
Jano   Natchez   Apalachee
Coneho
Yaqui   Karankawa   Calusa
Lagunero   *Gulf of*   CARIBBEAN
Coahuiltec   *Mexico*   Arawak
NORTHEAST
MEXICO

Pacific Ocean

AZTEC EMPIRE   Maya   *Caribbean Sea*

MAIN SUBSISTENCE MODE
Agriculture
Hunting and gathering
Fishing

0   Kilometers   1000

0   Miles   1000

MAP 4.1 From Experience History: Interpreting America's Past, 7/e, by James West Davidson, Brian DeLay, Christine Leigh Heyrman, Mark H. Lytle, Michael B. Stoff. Copyright ©2010 by The McGraw-Hill Companies, Inc. Reprinted by permission of the publisher.

the northernmost reaches of the Americas, the area of the Great Lakes, and to convert Native Americans to Catholicism.

Encounters between the Native Americans and the Puritans and Pilgrims have traditionally been portrayed as friendly and constructive. While Native Americans did help supply the settlers in their early years when food was in short supply, this friendliness has been overstated. Relations between the two became quite hostile within a few years of contact when after European traders disrupted local Pequot trade networks, the Pequot killed a well-known European trader, John Oldham. The Puritans exacted revenge by burning a Pequot village to the ground and the Pequot war of 1636 began. In retribution, the Pequot attacked Puritan towns and the Puritans responded by burning the main Pequot village to the ground, massacring almost all its inhabitants including women and children. Their action was so vicious they nearly exterminated the Pequot as a people.

Because there were no Native American empires controlling large swaths of land, conquest and control by Europeans took place not as the result of the rapid destruction of a great centralized state by European soldiery as in Mexico, though the indigenous people of North America were, as were the peoples of Latin America and the Caribbean, decimated by European diseases such as cholera and smallpox. Instead, it was a piecemeal affair over a much longer time, during which the encounter between Native Americans and colonists involved periodic clashes between a variety of peoples, with "middle ground" alliances and environmental forces playing a large role. For example, there were moments when groups of Native Americans and settlers of competing European states joined together for survival or to fight a common enemy.

EUROPEAN AND NATIVE AMERICAN PERCEPTIONS

When they sailed across the Atlantic in the early 1600s, the Europeans saw the new world through their own cultural lens. They saw a wilderness that was filled with seemingly infinite abundance, but untamed, having no plowed fields, fences, or farm houses. The Native Americans they met were considered to be savage peoples, with none of the characteristics of European civilization, nor did they possess true religion according to this view. Lacking civilization, however, they lived closer to the natural world, and some Europeans believed this gave them a simple nobility that Europeans themselves lacked. Thus they coined the term "noble savage" to describe Native Americans.

Native Americans thought about Europeans simply as new outsiders. They welcomed the Europeans into their villages and tribes, not because they were very friendly people but because outsiders in the Native American view could be quite useful to them. Outsiders brought resources such as tools and other items which had the potential to strengthen the Native American economy, and they brought the promise of population increase which strengthened Native American sustenance. However, Native Americans understood through long experience with rival tribes that outsiders could also bring war, death, and destruction. So Native Americans had to judge the intentions of outsiders and might adopt outsiders they came to trust or might

JOHN ELIOT PREACHING TO THE INDIANS.

English Presbyterian missionary John Eliot addresses a gathering of Algonquians. Known as "the Apostle of the Indians," Eliot established the first church for Native Americans in Massachusetts. Missionary efforts of this sort formed a key element in shaping societies in the Americas.   Corbis.

execute the outsiders if they believed they had evil intentions. This approach had allowed Native Americans to survive for centuries in North America and cope with the expanding settlement of Europeans in the time before the American Revolution. However, by then, the relationship between the two peoples had changed fundamentally. The encounter began when Native Americans gave the Europeans food and expertise to help them survive and adjust to the new world, but by the end of the eighteenth century, Native American survival was at stake as they lost much of their land to colonists and they became dependent upon them for food and other goods.

NEW ENGLAND NATIVE AMERICANS AND LAND

Native Americans used the land differently than British colonists. The New England tribes were semi-nomadic so after the summer months when they would stay in an area where their crops were planted and wait for harvest, they carried the harvested food with them as they moved to hunting grounds in the forests. With the coming of snow and the winter months, these tribes moved again to places giving access to open water and resources. Trapping animals was their means of obtaining food in this time of year. By early spring they moved back to the fields; by late spring they began to plant crops again. The land became a circle of seasonal changes for these tribes. Historian William Cronon states,

> The relationship of New England Indians to their environment, whether in the north or south, revolved around the wheel of the seasons: throughout New England, Indians held their demands on the ecosystem to a minimum by moving their settlements from habitat to habitat. As one of the earliest European visitors noted, 'They move from one place to another according to the richness of the site and the season.'[1]

During the summer months Native Americans also selectively burned forest areas, clearing the forest of the underbrush without destroying the large trees, which created clearer paths for animals that the tribes hunted. The burning also enriched the soil encouraging the growth of flowers and berries that Native Americans used for food and medicine.

The first British to arrive in New England came as settlers and farmers, not as soldiers and conquistadors. To be successful farmers in the new world, they believed they had to take possession of and control land. According to the laws and customs of England, land there was held in private possession through a fee-simple arrangement. The buyer paid a fee and received title to the property. However, the situation in North America was quite different. There Native American tribes had no concept of private property ownership. Instead, tribes controlled large pieces of land and could grant the right of the use of the land to others, a concept that under European law was called usufruct. The Native American concept of usufruct and British colonial concept of private property land ownership came into conflict when Native American tribes made agreements for land use that the British colonists interpreted as granting them private property possession over the land. In turn, the colonists fenced the land and built their farmhouses on it. Native Americans became unhappy with this situation and sometimes protested by moving back onto the piece of land they still considered to be theirs to use. At other times, they attacked the cattle of the colonists as a means of protest. This situation led to further conflicts and sometimes to war between the settlers and the Native Americans. Property in animals also became an issue; colonists assumed they owned their livestock whether or not it was on their property. Indians assumed ownership of an animal only at the point when it was killed. Whoever killed the animal had the right to own it. Native Americans sometimes killed the livestock of the colonists and took the dead animal as theirs, under their assumptions of ownership. Colonists were outraged and tried to get payment for their dead animals under their assumption of ownership. In one instance, colonists accused a Native

American of shooting one of their pigs in 1631. A colonial court investigated and found him guilty. Chickatabot, the local chieftain in charge, grudgingly paid the fine of one beaver skin. Eventually Indians became accustomed to European assumptions of animal ownership, but incidents such as this one bedeviled the colonist–Native American encounter for decades.

Europeans and Native Americans also differed on who should labor on the land. Colonists believed that Native American men were lazy because they did not work in the fields. They also thought Native American men were cruel to their wives because under their division of labor, women worked in the fields raising the crops. In turn, Native American men called European husbands foolish because they did not take advantage of their wives as field laborers. "Lazy Squaws" is how they referred to European women, who actually labored mightily around the European home and hearth. Each merely judged the other on the basis of their own cultural assumptions. Both utilized labor efficiently; Native American women farmed while their husbands were gone for long periods of hunting, and European women did household jobs that were essential such as sewing, spinning cloth, making clothes, and cooking. Some Europeans judged Native American women to be "slaves" of their husbands. But as a perceptive European commentator observed, Native American women had the freedom to choose their lives (more than European women who were bound by law and custom to their fathers or husbands) and therefore could not be called slaves in any sense.

> There are many persons who believe, from the labour that they see the Indian women perform, that they are in a manner treated as slaves. These labours, indeed, are hard, compared with the tasks that are imposed upon females in civilised society; but they are no more than their fair share, under every consideration and due allowance, of the hardships attendant upon savage life. Therefore they are not only voluntarily, but cheerfully submitted to; and as women are not obliged to live with their husbands any longer that suits their pleasure or convenience, it cannot be supposed that they would submit to be loaded with unjust or unequal burdens ...[2]

Though the ethnocentrism of the commentator is obvious in his reference to "civilized" society, he reveals a deep understanding of the freedom and power of females in Native American society.

Differences in the way the two settled the land also became a source of conflict. When Europeans came to the new world, they preferred fixed sites of land settlement to the Native American approach of movable settlements. English colonists assumed that Native Americans' annual cyclical migration patterns were a sign of poverty and criticized Native Americans for living like paupers in the midst of the abundance of the new world. Another commentator, Thomas Morton, pointed out that the Indians fed and clothed themselves successfully and could be considered not paupers at all, but quite wealthy.

If our beggars of England should, with so much ease as they, furnish themselves with food at all seasons, there would not be so many starved in the streets … Now since it is but foode and rayment that men that live needeth (though not all alike,) why should not the Natives of New England be sayd [sic] to live richly, having no want of either?[3]

According to many Europeans, Native Americans were poor because they had not improved the land. By improvement, Europeans meant cutting down trees and bounding the land with fences, the development of towns, and permanent settlements. John Locke used Native American behavior to make this very point about land as capital and improvements adding to that capital. The American tribes, he wrote, were a people,

whom nature furnished as liberally as any other people with the materials of Plenty, i.e. A fruitful soil, apt to produce in abundance, what might serve for food rayment, and delight; yet for want of improving it by labour, have not one hundreth part of the conveniences we enjoy: And a King of a large fruitful territory there feeds, lodges and is clad worse than a day Labourer in England.[4]

But Locke did not recognize that the Indians did not see themselves as poor. They met their needs, lived lightly on the land, and were quite content with the fruits of their labor.

We have seen that the New England Indian way of life fit with the ecology of New England and the needs of Native Americans. However, the charge of the supposed poverty or laziness of Native Americans heralded the determination of European colonists to replace the Indian collective use, kin-based economic system with their own evolving market economy and capitalist mentality. Europeans argued that since Native Americans had squandered their resources by possessing no concept of land as capital the way Europeans did, they had forfeited their right to it. The charge of Native American laziness, which arose out of culturally differing conceptions of how wealth was defined, would thus become the primary justification for the colonists' seizure of Indian lands.

The problem for Native Americans was not merely how the colonists justified the seizure of their lands through an unsupportable "lazy Indian" stereotype, but with its results: the Europeans' aggressive settlement of land used by Native Americans damaged the ability of Indians to sustain themselves. A Narragansett leader in New England made this plain in 1642.

Our fathers had plenty of deer and skins, our plains were full of deer, as also our woods and of turkies, and our coves full of fish and fowl. But these English having gotten our land, they with the scythes cut down the grass, and with axes fell the trees; their cows and horses eat the grass, and their hogs spoil our clam banks, and we shall all be starved.[5]

IMPACT OF THE FUR TRADE

Despite the growing tension over land use, Native Americans and colonists engaged in a lively trade in goods. New England tribes hunted beaver before British colonists came, but with the arrival of Europeans and the demand for beaver felting to create hats for the European upper classes, Native Americans became enmeshed in a global trade in beaver skins. In return for beaver skins, they received copper pots, clothing, and firearms. These items gave them more power and raised their standard of living. Since they did not possess coins or other forms of money, they also sought "wampum" from European merchants, which was considered to be a source of social prestige. The more wampum possessed, the higher one's status in Native American society. Europeans gladly traded wampum because it was not considered valuable by them. Wampum was made by drilling a hole in a colorful sea shell and shaping it to make a bead. The trade in fur and wampum brought Native Americans into an economic exchange system completely unfamiliar to them: market capitalism. Native Americans practiced a very different system of exchange referred to as kinship trade. Kinship trade was based upon kin or extended family relations. Many villages, especially small ones, were populated entirely by extended families referred to as clans or kin. The family would trade within and beyond the village but their trade and other economic exchanges were mostly with their kin. So they saw trade as one part of kinship or family responsibility, not as an economic transaction. Higher status clan members who possessed more goods such as the chief of the village would be obligated to occasionally give away goods. Because they had no concept of profit, they hunted and farmed enough for their survival only and gave any extra away. Therefore, in the Indians' kin-based system over-hunting was never an issue. The Indians took what they needed and there was plenty to go around.

Initially the fur trade gave Native Americans more power. They had something the Europeans wanted but could not get on their own. They knew the lands where the beaver lived and used their skills to trap the beaver, skills and knowledge the Europeans lacked. These advantages gave them bargaining power against the colonists. This fact was especially true with the Iroquois Confederacy, which was a large group of six tribes that formed a political union in upper New York state. The Confederacy possessed the power of great numbers of hunters and warriors and began to monopolize the fur trade, in the process negotiating with both the British and the French and playing one off against the other. However, the fur trade enmeshed Native Americans in an international capitalist system of exchange that over time destroyed their initial advantages and eventually left them dependent upon Europeans for survival.

In the new capitalist exchange the demand was global, and as Indians traded more and more beaver skins, the beaver began to be over-hunted. By the eighteenth century when Indians had become dependent on beaver trapping and the fur trade for their living, the disappearance of the beaver and other species important to Native American sustenance had serious consequences. Native Americans had become dependent upon the trade goods of Europeans, but they had less to trade with the colonists. The hunt for scarce beaver drove the tribes west of New England into the Great Lakes region and created a domino effect on Native American nations all the way to plains area, pushing tribes westward and changing their economies and cultures in the process.

But later on the beaver became even more scarce, even in the Great Lakes region. As a result, Native Americans lost their bargaining power. They became dependent upon the British and French for the items they had traditionally received in the fur trade. They needed firearms and had become accustomed to cooking in copper pots and using European woolen blankets. Once they became dependent, Europeans and eventually the American government after independence used their dependency to force them to sign treaties giving away their land. In the process, the boundaries of the world the Native Americans had inhabited in North America changed. They now lived in a larger, more interconnected world brought about by the global fur trade. As land expansion overwhelmed Native Americans on the eastern seaboard, they were forced to migrate inland not just to seek out precious beaver fur, but also because their culture and way of life had become marginalized by European intrusion.

THE MIDDLE GROUND

The Iroquois Confederacy initiated this westward shift. As the dominant military force in North America, they could field as many as 2,500 warriors. They moved westward in search of beaver, spreading into the western Great Lakes area and the Ohio River valley, and encountered Algonquian tribes including the Fox, Sac (Sauk), Menominee, Ottawa, Winnebago, Chippewa, and Huron. There the Iroquois initiated the "beaver wars," a campaign of terror against these smaller tribes, which unsettled the entire region and forced the westward migration of Algonquians to the Wisconsin area. Agriculture was impossible and even hunting and gathering were made more difficult by the migration, while cultural habits were disrupted. The Algonquian tribes also were gripped by the terror the Seneca and other Iroquois tribes instilled.

This crisis over the Iroquois intrusion led the Algonquian tribes to search for allies. French fur traders were very active in the Great Lakes area, but French settlements there were small in population and they had also been attacked by the Iroquois, so they were a natural choice for an ally. As the French and Algonquian Indian tribes worked together to fend off the Iroquois, they created what historian Richard White has referred to as the "middle ground." The middle ground was a geographical and cultural place where Indians and whites compromised and made appeals to the others' cultural assumptions to cement diplomatic alliances, bridge cultural gaps, and punish violence.

In one instance, the middle ground alliance between the French and the Algonquians was tested by diplomatic maneuvering and story-telling. The French had undertaken negotiations with the Iroquois to stop their attacks. They feared that the Algonquians had done the same and they would be left in a poor diplomatic position if the Algonquians struck a separate peace with the Iroquois. Sieur de Cadillac, the French commander of the fort at Michilimackinac (in present-day Mackinaw City, Michigan) in an attempt to derail negotiations between the Iroquois and the Algonquians, sent a message to the Algonquians urging them to start war parties against the Iroquois. In return, a Huron chief named the Baron convened a council of the French and the Algonquian tribes. The Baron told a story at the council of a wise man who knew of the beaver wars and understood the antagonism between the Iroquois and the Algonquians. First the old man exhorted the Algonquians to pay attention to the French missionaries and to the great three in one, the Christian god, because those who did not would be punished. He then encouraged the French and Algonquians to pursue a truce with the Iroquois because he believed that those who did not and instead pursued the path of war would lose. The Baron used the old man's story to buttress his argument that the Algonquians should pursue peace with the Iroquois. However, the French leader Cadillac remained unconvinced and refused the gift that the Baron offered at the end of the story, thereby symbolically rejecting the story and the path of peace with the Iroquois. But this refusal was made more difficult for Cadillac because the story contained elements very appealing to him. It encouraged worship of the Christian religion and respect for French missionaries. The story was intended to offer to the French a concession on religion in return for French consideration of peace talks with the Iroquois. The Baron used the story to try to create a middle ground by appealing to French religious sensibilities in order to try to persuade them to accept his idea of peace with the Iroquois. The story of the wise man was cleverly constructed so that however the French responded they would have to pay a price. If they agreed with the story, it meant they endorsed negotiations with the Iroquois and they risked weakening their alliance with Algonquian peoples. If they rejected the story, they risked looking foolish because they were in essence rejecting their own religion. Ultimately, the French leader Cadillac, in refusing to accept the gift and thereby rejecting the story, forced the Indians to abandon peace talks with the Iroquois in favor of continuing the French alliance.

Beyond diplomacy, the French and the Algonquians developed a cultural middle ground around their sexual relationships. Young unmarried Indian women had complete control over their bodies and could choose to be with whomever they wanted. Sometimes they went with the French fur traders, called the *Coureurs de bois* (literally runners of the woods), who many times traded without proper licenses from the French authorities. They traveled with the traders, worked for them, and became their sexual partners. Because sex ratios among the tribes favored females heavily, this practice allowed women who could not find a marriage partner in the tribes to reproduce and add to the tribes' population in a time when disease and warfare had depleted their population. In addition, the French traders would sometimes marry these young women in order to facilitate their trade with the tribe. The French opposed the marriages initially, but later came to support them because it made the relationships acceptable to French missionaries and helped to populate French settlements. The tribes were enthusiastic about it because it strengthened their alliance with the French and brought greater population and outside resources to them.

Murder and blood revenge were also at play in the middle ground. Violence was a part of the commerce between the French and the Algonquians. The French accused the tribes of stealing their goods and canoes. Because Native Americans had no concept of private property rights, only use rights, they did not consider taking and using French goods as stealing. This was a source of conflict that sometimes ended in murder. When one of their own was murdered, Native Americans had two choices. The first was to kill the murderer or someone from his group, a step referred to as blood revenge. The second option involved accepting a gift or a person as replacement for the murdered tribe member who would become a part of the clan of the murdered person and might eventually be adopted by the clan with full clan rights and obligations. For the French, the act of murder was an individual act and they considered execution of the killer or killers an appropriate response; they were not accustomed to negotiating over it.

In one particular case, two Frenchmen were murdered by some Algonquian (Chippewa) warriors near modern-day Green Bay, Wisconsin. French authorities discovered that one family had done the killing. The French leader first captured the murderers and threatened to execute the whole family but later backed down after it became apparent that this act would cause war between the French and the Algonquians. The tribes offered the French two of their own people to replace and "resurrect" the dead Frenchmen. The French leader Dulhut refused them saying, "a hundred slaves and a hundred packages of beaver could not make him traffic in the blood of his brothers."[6] Once again a council was convened. The French turned the council into a trial of the family and the tribes played along, believing that once the trial ended, the negotiations over how to settle the matter would begin. After the trial, the French agreed to execute just two of the family members for the two murdered Frenchmen, which constituted blood revenge and was acceptable to Algonquians. Then, because the Algonquians had the right under their customs to seek compensation for the execution of the family members, the French leader Dulhut compensated the family of the executed with a feast and other gifts. Tensions subsided and the alliance was restored. The resolution of this incident reveals the effectiveness of the middle ground appeals to the others' cultural practice.

Finally, farther north in modern-day Canada, a cultural middle ground was reached between another Algonquian tribe, the Huron, and a Jesuit priest named Father Jean de Brebeuf. De Brebeuf served the Huron who had built their longhouses close to de Brebeuf's mission in Fort Sainte Marie to protect themselves from attacks by the Iroquois. De Brebeuf proved to be an adept intercultural interpreter, translating many European books into Huron. He is best known for taking the Christian story of the birth of Jesus Christ and remaking it into a Huron Christmas carol. Similar to what Jesuit priests in East Asia did before him, he reinterpreted Christianity into the local context. De Brebeuf was eventually killed by the Iroquois in 1649 and the French had to abandon the mission and retreat to Quebec City under pressure from them. The Huron scattered, some going west, some south to what is today Oklahoma, and the rest with the French to Quebec City, where today the Huron have a flourishing tribal life. Notably, the Huron continue to sing the Huron Christmas carol and consider a part of Huron culture today. With de Brebeuf's help, they took the Christmas story from French culture and made it their own. More recently, the Huron carol was translated into English and has become a popular Christmas tune, recorded by singer Burl Ives in the United States in 1952, and later by Bruce Cockburn in Canada. The song exemplifies the ease of cultural appropriation in the Native American context, with all of these different versions in different languages.[7]

THE CATAWBA

The Catawba, a tribe that was created out of remnants of other Native American tribes in modern-day South Carolina, also formed a middle ground alliance with European colonists. The original tribes, separate until they encountered European diseases through trade with English colonists in the late 1600s, were the Succa, Suttirie, Charra, and Nassaw. Disease was an equal-opportunity killer, taking down chiefs and shaman, village elders, young, and old alike. Smallpox in particular ravaged these villages, killing up to 80 percent of the inhabitants in highly contagious outbreaks which left the sufferers' bodies covered with painful boils before death occurred. Warfare with colonists also took a toll. The number of Native Americans from each of these tribes who survived the outbreak was so small they no longer constituted a tribe. The functions of leadership, decision making, food-gathering and farming, and the rituals of society were severely damaged, leaving the tribe vulnerable. In order to regain these functions, remnants of various tribes combined to form the Catawba, a new Native American tribe along the Catawba River.

This union was forged, tested, and expanded in warfare. In the aftermath of the Yamasee War, fought in the Carolinas and Virginia from 1717 to 1720 between Europeans and Native Americans, the negotiations for peace with the colonists revealed a new order among the peoples of the Catawba River. They collectively took a prominent place in the negotiations even, to the extent that they destroyed a group of Indians who refused to negotiate, the Waxhaws. The loss of population occasioned by the war and the memory of their joint action against the Waxhaws drew the Catawba peoples together in a common identity. Since the region's population was further reduced by the Yamasee War, the Catawba pragmatically invited the war's refugees to join them and become one tribe; even former enemies were invited to join them, sometimes under the implicit threat that if they did not join, the Catawba would destroy them. They also offered protection to escaped slaves who nonetheless needed no such threat to bind them to this new community. This new nation developed myths and rituals that pulled

Father Saint Jean de Brebeuf (1593–1649). The
French Jesuit missionary preaches to an Indian
Council. Bettmann/Corbis.

them together more forcefully into single people. For example, because of
their exposure to whites, they developed a religion that had some aspects
of Christianity such as one supreme god, and an afterlife characterized by
either a realm of bliss or one of misery which was similar to the Christian
concepts of heaven and hell. War dances and the communal sweat lodge
also became commonplace among the Catawba. Their reputation as fierce
warriors helped keep away rival Native American peoples and united them
as well. Another source of strength was the usage of English names such as
George Chicken or Captain Peter among many mixed blood Catawba. And
they at times donned European clothing.

The Catawba nonetheless fell on hard times. First, disease continued
to reduce their population as colonial settlers moved closer to their villages.
A smallpox outbreak in l738 was particularly devastating. Second, the food
sources of the Catawba dried up because they over-hunted deer and other
game for pelts to sell to European traders, while their crops burned up in the
severe droughts of the 1750s. Third, their enemies increased in number and
variety as their reputation as ruthless warriors spread. In addition to having

many Native American enemies, the Catawba made enemies of the French when they refused a French offer of alliance with them. Thereafter the French encouraged the surrounding tribes to make war against the Catawba.

To stem the tide of decline, the Catawba negotiated settlements with the colonists in South Carolina and Virginia. Skillful diplomacy allowed them to turn the British need for allies against the French into concrete gains such as meat products and other useful goods the British delivered in return for their loyalty. However, this alliance was not enough to prevent settler invasion of the Catawba River valley in the 1750s, which forced the Catawba to identify and codify their land boundaries. This involved further cooperation with and dependence upon colonial officials, and their traditional economy of hunting disappeared. As a result of this loss of economic habitat, many of their people perished, but the Catawba people ultimately survived these catastrophes and live on to this today.

A tribal leader accurately described the changes contact with Europeans had brought to Native Americans by the time of the American Revolution. "The times are exceedingly Alter'd, Yea the times have turn'd everything upside down, or rather we have Chang'd the good times, Chiefly by the help of the White People, for in Times past, our Fore Fathers lived in Peace, Love, and great harmony, and had everything in Great plenty … But alas, it is not so now, all the Fishing, Hunting and Fowling is entirely gone."[8] Although European contact had driven the changes, Native Americans were partner to them. They had become enmeshed in economic and social systems that were damaging to their way of life as their environment became depleted of valuable resources. This encounter had an increasingly negative impact on the traditional Native American way of life.

NATIVE AMERICANS AND THE U.S. GOVERNMENT

As Native Americans became increasingly impoverished in the late colonial period, their encounter with colonists changed dramatically in the American Revolution and early national period. Some Native American tribes chose to fight on the side of the British in the Revolutionary War and afterward the American government punished these tribes. No longer powerful enough to negotiate from a position of strength, some Native American tribes were forced to sign humiliating treaties that took away land in exchange for promises of money and education for Native American children. These promises were almost always broken, with less money going to Native Americans than promised and more land taken than allowed for in the treaty. Sometimes the American government chose to negotiate with minority chiefs who had very little legitimacy among the nations themselves because these chiefs were more amenable to sign treaties after being bribed. A minority chief named Corn Planter of the once proud Seneca of the Iroquis Confederacy did just this, negotiating away a large chunk of Seneca land in return for alcohol and firearms. After the turn of the century, the American government settled on a civilization policy for Native Americans that combined treaty-making with education, teaching the cultural norms of Euro-Americans. The men were expected to become farmers and the women to run households on small plots of land. Most commonly, Christian missionaries who went out to live on their reservations became the educators of the tribes and attempted to convert them to Christianity as well. These encounters did not go very well because missionaries judged Native American culture to be heathen and Native Americans wanted missionaries to become part of their community and share their resources. Missionaries shared their resources only grudgingly and openly resisted entreaties by Native Americans to integrate them into their culture, rejecting their dances and the smoking of the peace pipe as the work of the devil.

The story of the rise of the Cherokee nation demonstrates that the civilization policy of the federal government in the 1800s was less about civilization than the taking of Native American land. The Cherokee were a large nation of Native Americans in the American southeast. Under the influence of missionaries and the pressure the U.S. federal government, the Cherokee chose a course of civilization in the early 1800s. They became successful farmers and eventually owned slaves like their white neighbors. They developed a written language and published a national newspaper and eventually embraced American political forms by adopting a republican constitution. But none of this prevented whites from encroaching on Cherokee territory in the 1820s when gold was discovered there. Pressures mounted within the state of Georgia and the federal government to remove the Cherokee to the western United States. The Cherokee sued to keep their land and in a U.S. Supreme Court decision, the Cherokee were recognized as a sovereign nation with rights to its land and customs. But President Andrew Jackson, a renowned Indian fighter, ignored the decision and Congress passed the Indian Removal Act in 1835. The result was the tragic "Trail of Tears," a forced removal to Oklahoma by the U.S. Army in which more than 1,000 Cherokee perished. The Cherokee plight illustrates once again the deleterious impact of the encounter upon Native Americans.

Conclusion

The cross-cultural encounters between European colonists and Native Americans were wide-ranging and complex. In some cases, a cultural clash of values developed between Europeans and Native Americans in their social, economic, and political practices and in others, where they needed one another, middle ground approaches flourished. But even when Native Americans adopted white values, economic practices, and political institutions, as in the case of the Cherokee, whites still took an aggressive expansionist approach which forced them off their land. Some encounters were productive and successful at resolving these conflicts at least for a time, as in the case of the Algonquian and French and the Catawba and the colonial government of the Carolinas. Others were filled with conflict and boded ill for Native Americans. Many New England tribes were in this situation after a short initial period of good will.

Whereas at the beginning of this encounter, Europeans were dependent upon Native Americans for basic necessities, Indians began to become more dependent upon Europeans for their basic necessities as time went on. As Native Americans signed treaties selling land in exchange for food and other necessities, the American government took advantage of this situation by breaking treaty after treaty. Native American territory was taken and they were forced onto small reservations of the poorest quality land. The end result was depopulation because of European diseases, and starvation and poverty for Native Americans. But Native Americans have survived. Today, casinos permitted on federal lands have provided Native Americans with a source of income, have raised their standard of living, and have given them greater access to education, making them less dependent upon the U.S. government. In some instances, Native Americans have used casino money to strengthen their autonomy by suing the federal government to gain back land and rights they lost in a long history of broken treaties. However, some have argued that casino culture comes at a high price in terms of the stress its profits pose for Native American leaders and the detachment from traditional values it can promote. It seems that the Native American future looks brighter than its past, though the past still extracts a high cost in terms of land and culture lost.

Questions for Discussion

1. Describe New England Native American migration patterns and explain why this worked so well for these Indians?
2. Explain the root of the "Lazy Indian" stereotype. How did Europeans use this stereotype to rationalize their settlement in the new world?
3. What was the impact of the expanding fur trade upon Native American life in the northeast woodlands in both the short term and long term?
4. How did Algonquians and French respond to the encroachment of the powerful Iroquois Confederacy into their territory? How successful were they in this enterprise?
5. How did the rise of the Catawba Indian tribe come about? What did the Catawba do to stem their decline in the period leading up to the American Revolution?
6. In what ways did the Catawba response to European colonization in North America resemble Ottoman defensive modernization.

Endnotes

1. William Cronon, *Changes in the Land* (New York: Hill and Wang, 1983), p. 53.
2. Reverend John Heckenwelder, *History, Manners and Customs of the Indian Nations Who Once Inhabited Pennsylvania and the Neighboring States*, rev. ed. by Reverend William Reichel (Philadelphia, PA: Historical Society of Pennsylvania, 1876), pp. 154–158.

3. Thomas Morton, *New English Canaan* (Amsterdam: Jacob Frederick Stam, 1632), 132–136; Charles F. Adams (ed.), *Publications of the Prince Society* (Boston, MA: The Prince Society, 1883), chap. XIV, p. 177.
4. John Locke, *Two Treatises of Government*, rev. ed. by Peter Laslett (ed.) (New York: New American Library, 1963), pp. 338–339.
5. "Leift Lion Gardner His Relations of the Pequot Warres," *Massachusetts Historical Society Collections*, 1st Ser., Vol. 3 (1833), pp. 154–155.
6. Dulhut Letter, April 12, 1684, quoted in Richard White, *The Middle Ground: Indians, Empires, and Republics in the Great Lakes Region, 1650–1815* (Cambridge, MA: Cambridge University Press, 1991), p. 78.
7. Father Jean de Brebeuf, *The Huron Carol*, illustrations by Frances Tyrrell (New York: Dutton Children's Books, 1990), postscript.
8. Mohegan Indians Describe Effects of White Settlement, 1789, Harry Quaduaquid and Robert Ashpo to the most honorable Assembly of the State of Connecticut, May 14, 1789, quoted in William Cronon, *Changes in the Land*, p. 107.

From First Contact to Entanglement: Polynesian Encounters with Euro-Americans

Many world historians generally regard the earliest encounters between the "Old World" of Europe and the "New World" of the Americas as the true beginning of global civilization, as it heralded the creation of a single world system, in terms of both ideas and material exchanges. Historians of Polynesia would beg to differ. In their view, it was not until the completion of the first phase of European contact with this region—centuries after the West's conquest of the "New World" that global integration can be said to have been achieved. They argue that despite Polynesia's relatively small land mass and population, its initial encounter with the West tells us a great deal about how the West as well as the Polynesians constructed their views of the world. Also, European and Polynesian destinies were linked together at the moment of the first encounter. Polynesia is thus of special significance when seeking to understand the pattern of modern cross-cultural encounters.

In some respects, the modern West's engagement with Polynesians was typical of its past and future encounters with the rest of the world. The West's initial fascination with what they perceived as an exotic world culture quickly gave way to conceptions of European superiority backed by missionary zeal and military conquest. This contact culminated in Western assaults on indigenous culture and the loss of indigenous sovereignty, whose

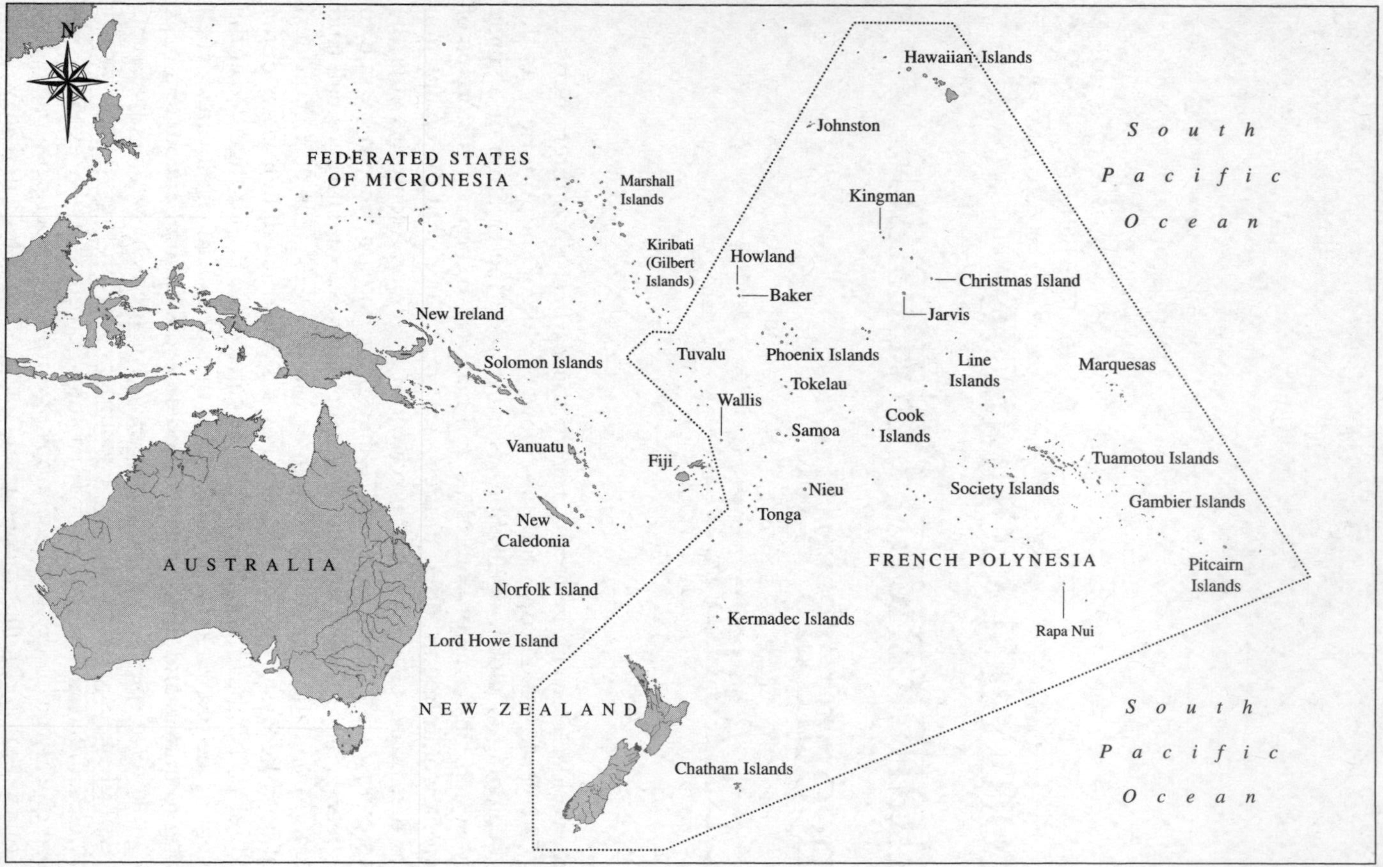

MAP 5.1 Map of Polynesia

impacts were all the more severe due to the West's introduction of diseases for which Polynesians had no immunity.

However, in important ways, Polynesia's encounter with the West, and the cultural exchange that followed in its wake, was unique. While most of those traditional societies confronting American, European, and Japanese expansionists had been in decline, Polynesia was then witnessing the rise of new state systems and experiencing political expansion that was as powerful as that then taking place in Europe. The European conquest thus did not hasten the fall of a declining polity, but threatened to bring an abrupt end to the independent evolution of Polynesian politics and society. Such a "fatal impact" suited the West, which sought to legitimize its conquests by projecting images of Polynesian culture first as unspoiled, but unsophisticated, and later as unchanging and barbaric. In time, this "fatal impact" model became a popular means by which the West acknowledged the devastation their imperialism wrought upon the peoples of the Pacific, an acknowledgment they hoped would advance the course of forgiveness and healing.

However, while the intrusion of the West did mark the end of independent cultural and political evolution in Polynesia, it did could not dim its peoples' social energy and momentum. Some Polynesian societies creatively borrowed from the West to build polities and nations that endured. This was certainly the case of Hawaii up to the close of the nineteenth century. Other societies, such as the Marquesans and Tahitians, proved more adept at converting at least some early missionaries to their way of life rather than the other way around or proved so unreceptive to early missionary activities so as to frustrate the latter's conversion efforts. Both examples speak to the vibrant, tenacious, and flexible responses of Polynesians in adapting to often rapid and difficult changes that came so swiftly upon them in the late eighteenth century.

The Western encounter approached a "fatal" outcome in the sense that the diseases Westerners brought from Afro-Eurasia drove some Polynesian populations to the brink of extinction, while Western political domination marked the death knell for full indigenous sovereignty. Yet, a Polynesian identity survived. Most of its peoples are acting to recover or repair much of the traditional sciences, customs, and languages damaged by Western contact, while others are striving to recover their political sovereignty. For that reason, it is probably best to follow anthropologist Nicolas Thomas' conception of this encounter as an entanglement, rather than one of annihilation or erasure.[1]

POLYNESIA AT THE TIME OF ITS CONTACT WITH THE WEST

The settling of the southwest Pacific by Polynesian people in 500–1550 AD is one of the greatest stories of human migration in world history. Waves of people descended from earlier arrivals in the South Seas (Austronesians and Melanesians) struck out into the western Pacific Ocean in canoes carrying with them not merely an ark's worth of animals and plants, but well-honed skills of navigation by stars, currents, and winds. They were formerly thought to have traveled from one island group to another, with little contact with their past homes, but the evidence of stone adzes (axes) in Hawaii obtainable only in the central Pacific and the spread of sweet potatoes (known only in South America) suggest that there was some, even if limited, contact between island groups. Polynesians also believed in one practice that, in one form or another, was present throughout Southeast Asia from whence they had come: it was customary to join (via marriage, contract, or ritual) a visiting chief or trader with a young girl to cement political and/or commercial relations.

Also of recent discovery was that, from the middle 1600s, monarchial states capable of exercising considerable power arose and sought to incorporate neighboring chiefdoms into their domains. This process was marked by the relatively sudden appearance of new architecture. The age-old small, low natural coral stone platforms of Polynesia called *heiau* were surpassed by cut-block temples "reaching ever higher toward the heavens...that was clearly an important part of the strategy of chiefly elite to gain favor with the gods and to assert their power and prestige over their people."[2] These may have arisen first in Tonga in the western Pacific. In the late 1700s and early 1800s, an equally impressive ritual complex was built in Hawaii by King Kamehameha I, who united the Hawaii Islands through military action and diplomacy effectively backed by both the threat of force and the promise of abundance with the coming of peace.

Polynesian communities large and small lived, as in most traditional social systems, including those of the pre-modern west, by laws both secular and divine. Secular law operated under royal and/or priestly authority. Secular law included property rights (*ahui*), while divine law was often expressed through rights and prohibitions, some of which were called *tapu* or *kapu* (the source of the English word *taboo*). As this social system and its human regulators were equally bound by tradition and custom to seek the common good, there was little serious crime, which was reduced as much by the abundance of the material necessities of life as by the communal values of the people. These collective values are those that might be expected from a society that had its roots in a fleet of ocean-going canoes which faced a common fate and whose voyagers were organized by often related lineages.

These collective values were reinforced by the view that the people (*kanaka*) owned nothing, but were part of a spiritual environment which could be expressed in the divinity of the chief or king, but reached down through the nobility to the commoners to the land itself, which in turn was divided so as to provide for all, from the hunters of indigenized pigs in the uplands, to the farmers of taro patches of the well-watered valleys, to the keepers of fishponds by the sea, which used tidal gates to extract only those fish of adequate size, while preserving the rest for future harvest. Their holistic and eminently sustainable use of their environment was expressed in every craft, especially the making of canoes and also ritual cloth (*tapa*), which was made from pounding mulberry bark. It was also expressed in their poetry, which did not suffer from a lack of writing. It flourished as oral tradition expressed in song and dance as well as speech.

Yet, this social system was not an idyllic tropical paradise for all. Some of the larger and expanding Polynesian societies—Hawaii, Tahiti, and Tonga—were highly stratified, with vast ritual gulfs separating the nobility and priesthood from the commoners. Some lineages (*kikino*) held so low a status as to fall beneath that of a commoner, so low as to be outside the *tapu* system. Most Polynesian communities engaged in warfare that was often large in scale—with hundreds of war canoes and thousands of men comprising an assault force which could be dispatched not merely to settle local quarrels, but to extend the power of their community over others. As in most warrior states from Sparta to the Ashanti, Polynesian social hierarchy may have been harsh and rigid, but never casual. The execution of violators of certain *tapu* and the sacrificial burnt offering of enemies taken in battle were solemnly carried out in sacred precincts where the divine spirits—metaphysical as well as connected with stages of life and material necessities—were honored. Infanticide was employed as a means of population control: violation of local limits placed on the population or on special priestly groups could result in the strangulation or burying alive of a new-born child. Also as in most warrior societies, patriarchy generally ruled supreme, with women forbidden to directly participate in religious rituals. However, also as in other patriarchal societies, Polynesian women still often exercised substantial and autonomous power in social, political, and occasionally military realms, as well as in matters of genealogy and succession.

In sexual matters, monogamy was the general rule. Young, unmarried boys and girls (*ka'oi*) were released from many *tapu* and expected to devote themselves to playful games and the arts. They were also given a certain degree of sexual freedom, but any pregnancy arising from youthful sex-play usually led to marriage. Even the lowest of the low could expect justice as reflected in Hawaii's "Law of the Splintered Paddle," which expressed the idea of human rights in terms that bound even the hands of the King himself.

Law of the Splintered Paddle:

O my people,
Honor thy god;
respect alike [the rights of] men great and humble;
See to it that our aged, our women, and our children
Lie down to sleep by the roadside
Without fear of harm.
Disobey, and die.[3]

In sum, Polynesian society was complex, moral, and deeply spiritual, with strong collective values. Warfare was no more or less endemic than in Europe and, as then in Europe, was accompanied by evolving forms of government and political expression. It functioned to the satisfaction of most of its members, though, as was the case in early modern Europe, most lived as social inferiors.

What is most remarkable about the contact between Westerners and Polynesians is that the lives of Polynesians quickly disappeared beneath a set of shifting and often contradictory Western perceptions of their existence which were based more on European cultural needs than Polynesian reality. Indeed, European and later American self-serving misrepresentations of Polynesians became so dominant and pervasive that historians, anthropologists, and even

Polynesians themselves are unsure about many major aspects of the traditional Polynesian society.

THE WEST AT THE TIME OF THE FIRST CONTACT WITH POLYNESIA

Though some Europeans had previously ventured into the Pacific— enough for the Spanish who were trading from Acapulco to Manila to call it "the Spanish Lake"—the first prolonged contact between Westerners and Polynesians occurred at Tahiti, which was visited by Captain Samuel Wallis of Britain (1728–1795), the French Captain Louis-Antoine de Bougainville, and the British Captain and later commander James Cook. Cook would visit Tahiti on each of his three voyages to the Pacific between 1768 and 1779.

All had entered the Pacific on what were publically viewed as missions in the service of science. The so-called Age of Enlightenment had spurred a desire in Europe to gain a greater knowledge and command of the natural world, whose rationality and orderliness might serve as a model and cure for all of mankind's ills, material and political, moral and philosophical. Earlier adventures during what is now known as the Age of Exploration had not provided answers to these questions as they were not even asked. European voyaging around Africa, to South America, and from the Arctic Ocean to Eastern Asia had revealed a larger world, but those encounters were not driven by the great questions raised in the eighteenth century, such as were men and women born good or evil, or born good, with human evil the mere product of poor upbringing or environment? Was the idea of progress on the side of the angels or the devils of man's nature? Did the observation of nature reveal natural laws perceptible by human reason?

The latter question lay behind Captain Samuel Wallis' dispatch to the South Seas. He was to find evidence of a major continent which European scientists theorized had to be there on the basis of what they called "geographical symmetry." In other words, the shape and placement of other continents suggested a large land mass, a "Great Southern Continent," would be found in the South Seas. The French Captain Louis-Antoine de Bougainville was given a similar mission, as was the British Captain James Cook, who was able to explore much of the coast of Australia, though it fell short of the scientists' expectations in both size and placement, being judged but a large island among smaller ones in Southeast Asia. But Cook's first voyage had an additional mission. Wallis' discovery of Tahiti, where he spent a few weeks in the spring of 1767, had identified an ideal place in the southern hemisphere for Cook to set up one of more than a hundred stations worldwide where accurate observations could be taken of a rare transit of the plant Venus across the surface of the Sun, the measurement of which was expected to enable humanity to test Isaac Newton's cosmological theories and accurately gauge the distance of the Earth from the Sun.

None of these missions were free of larger political agendas. Each seafaring European government sought new venues for trade within Oceania or means of gaining leverage in the trans-Pacific commerce established earlier by Spain. For this reason, Wallis' mission was kept secret and upon his arrival, he laid claim to Tahiti for the British crown. Bougainville, who registered the same claim for the King of France, specifically referenced the advantages his voyage might gain for France in terms of commerce with China and Japan. Cook's officers saw themselves as "kings" of the islands and the people as their servants as soon as they arrived; Cook not only claimed Tahiti for Britain, but erased a marker left by a passing Spanish ship claiming the island for their king.

That conquest would become as much a part of the initial European voyages as science was inevitable given the then current state of European affairs. For decades prior to Wallis' voyage out and for decades thereafter, Europe was in the throes of incessant warfare over the ownership of territories within Europe and overseas. As early as the 1740s, these wars reached truly global proportions. Wallis' voyage was immediately preceded by the Seven Years' War (1756–1763), which saw fighting spread not only to the Americas (where it is known as the French and Indian Wars) but also to India. These wars ravaged Europe, with their impact deepened by the bitter cold of a Little Ice Age (1738–1742), which darkened skies, froze combatants, cut food supplies, and encouraged disease. To be sure, this was an age in which electricity was demonstrated, and revolutionary political theories, such as Montesquieu's separation of the powers of government, were advanced. It was, however, also an era where commoners could still be executed for stealing a rabbit off a nobleman's estate, and the chaos arising from the revolutions in America and France undermined social cohesion in Europe to the extent of eroding the evolving faith in rational science as well as traditional belief in a loving God.

Bougainville, Wallis, and Cook were fully aware of what we now look back upon as the birth pangs of a new world order we call "modern." As the first generation of men to judge others by their level of technological achievement, they had no doubt that their own civilization was superior to any other, but they were under no illusion that European behavior met the high moral standard expected of a society that made such claims. As a result, both Bougainville, a romantic, and the more pragmatic Wallis and Cook took their scientific curiosity and sense of superiority with a grain of salt. In that sense, they were all well suited to seek new worlds and make contact with other civilizations. Upon their first contact with Polynesians, they all registered concern that contact between the two cultures might prove injurious to the Polynesians and took steps to prevent it. However, they also believed that there was little they could do to stop the European encounter with Polynesian society from destroying it or bringing out the very worst impulses of their own tortured civilization.

Wallis' approach to the island of Tahiti in late June 1767 appeared so aggressive to the Tahitians that they met him with stones thrown from a fleet of canoes, which Wallis drove off with canon fire. Having learned the dangers of running afoul of men with gunpowder weapons, the Tahitians tried a more pacific approach. After identifying the visitors' need for food and supplies for their large ships and the desperate state of British sailors, they brought gifts of food, cloth, and their friendship. Once they realized Wallis possessed iron implements—of which they had none—they made no attempt to restrict the access of Wallis' crew to their unmarried young women who could not break any sexual taboos. For their part, *kakino* women needed no encouragement to do so. They could actually gain status by intimate contact with (and knowledge of) European sailors by trading sexual favors to sailors for the iron implements their people sought, particularly hatchets and nails. Wallis made little official mention of women offering their attention and/or favors to sailors for these items of value. He was, however, worried about the impact of sexual relations between his men and Tahitians. The common British sailor was often recruited or drafted from the lowest rungs of society. He consorted with prostitutes in his home port and was often the carrier of venereal disease. As a result, Wallis took the precaution of having his men checked for signs of syphilis and sought to restrict contact between his men and the Polynesian women, who must have held enormous attraction for men who had seen hard service at sea for many months.

Bougainville arrived in Tahiti in April 1868 for what proved to be a stay of 19 days. He had no knowledge of Wallis' visit, but the Tahitians built on that experience to greet him warmly and to convert their lessons learned from Wallis into more formalized behavior. They sent a single young girl to swim to his ship, who dropped her clothing upon arriving on deck and seemingly offered herself as a sexual present. When Bougainville failed to grasp the meaning of this gesture of commercial alliance—a marriage serving to seal commercial relations between two peoples—the Tahitians prepared a highly ritualized form of public greeting which was attended by Tahitians attired in ceremonial clothing and accompanied by Tahitian music. With great pomp, a woven mat was placed before Bougainville. A virginal girl was then brought forward by elders and clear indication was given to the French captain that he should have sex with her. Lacking any recent European context for such behavior, Bougainville could not perform as expected and, despite the girl's clear distress, he entirely misunderstood the Polynesian political and commercial implications of the ritual—which was to be repeatedly conducted, and misunderstood, by Europeans elsewhere in Polynesia.

Bougainville concluded that this ceremony and the behavior of *kakino* who subsequently sought to engage in sex with his men were representative of a guiltless attitude toward nudity, seduction, and the sex act itself, behavior which he assumed to be universal, constant, and knew no bounds. Bougainville was steeped in the ideas of French Enlightenment thinker Jean Jacques Rousseau and those of Bougainville' close friend, the French philosopher Dennis Diderot, who believed human beings in a "state of nature" were by their very nature kind, good, and innocent, but that they had permitted themselves to become wedded to artificial institutions of government and society that led to greed, hatred, and shame even with regard to biological necessities, such as procreation. Bougainville thought Polynesian society was proof that these philosophers were right. Bougainville saw men and women in a setting of great natural beauty unmarked by war or human despoliation or hard labor, enjoying perfect peace and innocence, indulging in sex without guilt or limit—as the living embodiment of what Rousseau and

Diderot called a "natural state" uncorrupted by civilization. This was an inaccurate picture arising from too short an acquaintance with the realities of Tahitian life, but, as Alan Moorehead has written, it was in fact quite natural that Bougainville, "with his recent memories of the destitution caused by the Seven Years War in Europe…compared [Tahiti] to the Garden of Eden and had it renamed New Cythera after the Peloponnesian island where Aphrodite (or Venus, the Goddess of Love) had first emerged from the sea."[4]

Bougainville greatly feared that Europeans drawn to this "land of love" would quickly pollute it and made this fear known in his published reports of his journey. Diderot and many other rationalist thinkers produced by the French Enlightenment were deeply moved by Bougainville's plea that Europe should keep clear of the region. Diderot, who wrote a commentary on Bougainville's report, was drawn to the testimony of a Tahitian chief who may himself have feared that "the arrival of a new race of men would trouble those happy days which he had spent in peace." Diderot reimaged this chief and his people as weeping at the departure of the European visitors over lost friendships, when, according to Diderot, they should have wept at the coming sequel, when further contact would lead to the erasure of Polynesian customs "wiser and better" than those of the West, to an end to dying principally of old age, and to "staining their blood [Syphilis]." Europeans, Diderot declared with some accuracy, would soon come "with a crucifix in one hand and a dagger in the other."[5]

AN OFFERING BEFORE CAPTAIN COOK IN THE SANDWICH ISLANDS.

This European painting shows Captain Cook and his officers participating in a Hawaiian ceremony. Note the stereotyped way in which the Hawaiians are represented.   Library of Congress.

Captain James Cook arrived in Tahiti less than a year after Bougainville's visit. He initially was impressed by the Tahitian's paradisiacal lifestyle, but was too much a realist to give in to Bougainville's romantic fantasies. Moreover, his long initial stay and three subsequent visits (during 1773, 1774, and 1777) exposed him to the Polynesian version of human sacrifice, ritual cannibalism, and the devastating effects on the land and population of a major war between chiefs. His more lengthy experience enabled him to grasp the fact that the women who sought relations with sailors were of the lowest social orders, and that most of these women had material gain, not romance, in view. Cook also began to see Polynesian chiefs, priests, and commoners as individuals, who had personal ambitions and demons like any other, rather than as mere objects of Western philosophical exploration.

Cook was too much the efficient and responsible ship's captain to ever fully understand the amusement with which Polynesians sought to "steal" iron implements and other equipment vital to his ship's functions, and his impatience with that kind of behavior eventually led to his death. He was killed in Hawaii while attempting to take a friendly chief as a hostage against the return of a stolen ship's boat. That chief's supporters, on hearing that nearby gunfire associated with the effort to recover the boat had led to another chief's death, attacked Cook out of fear that their leader was about to meet the same fate. However, no European voyager more accurately gauged the potential impact of contact between Europeans and Polynesians. Whereas Bougainville and Diderot sought to preserve what they fancifully regarded as a means of resolving philosophical issues about human nature, Cook believed it was already too late for the Tahitians themselves to wish to preserve all of their traditional way of life. Writing only eight years after he and Bougainville had first visited Tahiti, Cook was of the opinion that "it would have been far better for these poor people to have never known our superiority in accommodations and arts [labor-saving devices] that make life more comfortable, than after once knowing it, to be again left and abandoned to their original incapacity for improvement." But they had been exposed to them and they now "cannot be restored to the happy mediocrity in which they had lived before we discovered them." Cook saw this as no reason to increase European presence in the region, but:

It seems to me that it has become...incumbent on the Europeans to visit them once in three or four years, in order to supply them with those conveniences which we have introduced among them, and have given them a predilection for. The want of such occasional supplies, will probably be felt very heavily by them, when it may be too late to go back to their old less perfect contrivances, which they may now despise, and have discontinued since the introduction of ours. For by the time [our] iron tools, of which they are now possessed, are worn out, they will have almost lost the knowledge of their own. A stone hatchet is, at present, as rare as a thing amongst them, as an iron one was eight years ago and a chisel of bone or stone is not to be seen.[6]

Cook's more sober and somber reports should have given more accuracy and weight to Bougainville's and Diderot's arguments, but they did not. While Cook carefully prepared his report for publication, John Hawkesworth published an edited official version of Cook's journal which preferred the false exotic to the real. Cook's ship's artists produced accurate images of tattooed Polynesian chiefs and other aspects of Polynesian life, but most chose to mass produce engravings that greatly departed from reality. These ultimately misleading but very popular images literally reflected Bougainville's vision that Polynesia was of heavenly paradise as dreamed of by the Greeks and Romans and in popular Christianity. These engravings often portrayed Polynesians with light skin and long Roman noses, wearing Greek togas, carrying bow and arrows, and either running across verdant grass lawns like Cupids in search of lovers or arranged as if at a picnic in Tuscany. Cook's last report included an eyewitness account of a human sacrifice, but Europeans literally out in the cold sought not the harsher realities of Polynesian life, but the tropical fantasy it could be made to represent. This escapist desire led to instant celebrity status afforded to the small number of Polynesians who Cook and others had brought back to Europe, and to lavish European theatrical productions with Polynesian themes; one such production featured an on-stage volcano.

This fantasy was slowly undermined by subsequent reports of European ships seized and crews killed by Polynesians who either did not welcome their intrusion or felt their hospitality had been abused. These reports included more realistic physical images of Polynesians and offered more graphic accounts of ritual cannibalism, making it increasingly harder to see Polynesians as confirming Rousseau's vision of a "noble savage." Rousseau himself was confronted by a junior French naval officer who brought his ship back from New Zealand. That officer had witnessed his captain and all the senior officers being killed and cooked-up by previously friendly Māori warriors in New Zealand. These Polynesians had grown angry with frequent French requests for food that were draining their own supplies. That officer understood that growing anger—he even warned his fellows of this danger—but he was so furious at the death of his companions that upon his return he confronted Rousseau, declaring, "Your noble savage ate my Captain!" However, even this incident could not deter the continuing search by European intellectuals to find in the South Seas examples of their theories. Thomas Malthus sought support for his influential ideas about the benefits of low population by citing the practice of Polynesian priests who limited their numbers by infanticide. Defenders of western civilization's presumed gentility came to view the killing of Cook as an original sin for which Polynesians had to be made to atone. Such discourse could not but further undermine the image of the noble savage.

The most dramatic change in European attitudes toward Polynesia occurred after a major shift in European society. In the wake of the disturbances of the status quo wrought by the French Revolution, European elites turned against Enlightenment ideas such as the expansion of individual liberties. They also abandoned Rousseau's idea of religion as little more than a civic duty necessary for social cohesion. They also returned to fervent Christian evangelicalism. By 1813, even the British East India Company, whose commercial relations with the people of South Asia depended to a great degree on noninterference in local religions, was forced to admit missionaries into the subcontinent. Converting the heathen became a unifying political as well as a social force at home.

To garner support for the evangelical outreach to Polynesia, Christian leaders denounced as sins of promiscuity the imagined guilt-free sex of its people. They so exaggerated European reports of Polynesian human sacrifice that the region appeared home to rampant cannibalism. Funding followed for the Western education of Polynesians as well as the eradication their customs: Even the most modest of dances within the *hula* tradition were banned as licentious. By the 1850s, Polynesia became an early testing ground for the "White Man's Burden" as Western interests exploited Polynesian land and labor in return for the blessings of Western civilization, such as literacy and Christianity. The West also introduced their way of war: Dozens of Polynesians, a seafaring people, ultimately took to crewing Western whaling and other commercial vessels, only to find themselves pressed into Western military service as early as the Napoleonic Wars and American Civil War (some Hawaiians fought on both sides of the latter conflict long before Hawaii's annexation by the United States).

By then, much of Polynesian society was already in decline as a result of its contact earlier with the West which undermined ancient crafts and institutions within which Polynesian customs and beliefs were rooted. As Cook predicted, iron adzes (axes) quickly replaced stone adzes and with the adzes went their heavily ornamented hafts or handles and the occasions in which they were ceremonially employed. In the face of readily available Western whaleboats, canoe-building faded away along with the fine skills and important social rituals and spiritual meanings that were embedded in that activity. Cheap imported cloth eroded *tapa*-making, one of the social functions of women. The status of women further suffered as gifts of *tapa*, which long served as an essential element of many ceremonies, were no longer valued. Muskets and their ammunition, more an item of curiosity than trade prior to 1813, thereafter became the principal currency of the islands, one which was obtained without the ritual of exchange feasts. Without such exchanges, chiefs might more easily get guns, but they lost the legitimacy these exchanges provided, and thus suffered the erosion of their authority.

These developments undermined the *tapu* system itself, leading to the lifting of many proscriptions that had acted as social restraints that might have proved useful in resisting the impact of European culture. Anthropologist Greg Denning notes that the decline of these restraints had at least two effects: As *ka'oi* in the Marquessas learned about shipping seasons, one of their forms of play became the making of mock ship-decks on which to practice enticing behaviors, while husbands began offering wives as a form of commerce.

CASTAWAYS

Often accelerating this process were a wide range of individual contacts between Polynesians and Euro-Americans. Whalers and sandalwood traders spread disease, while "blackbirders" kidnapped Polynesians and sold them as slaves: South American blackbirders virtually denuded Easter Island of its Polynesian population. Standing somewhat apart from these agents of negative change were European shipwreck survivors, deserters, and mutineers (such as from the HMS *Bounty*) who are often placed within a separate category of "castaways," and "beachcombers." A few castaways not only avoided aiding in the destruction of Polynesian culture, but helped make what little record we have of Polynesian society that exists outside of European official reports. Others, including some ship captains, well-educated adventurers, and traveling writers, cast their lot with Polynesian peoples and attempted to act as bulwarks against Western influence. Still others fell somewhere in between, instructing local rulers in the ways of using the muskets the rulers had seized or salvaged from European ships and serving as gun crews for the captured cannon used by Polynesian rulers seeking to expand their domains.

One such crew was formed out of the survivors of the seizure and plunder of the merchant ship *Port-Au-Prince* by King Fīnau 'Ulukālala of Ha'apai of the central island group of the Tongan islands during his campaign to conquer the entire archipelago. A survivor of that wreck, then 16-year-old William Mariner, produced an account of his four years living as Fīnau 'Ulukālala's adopted son (Mariner apparently reminded him of his own son who had been lost to illness). Mariner was renamed Toki, or Iron Axe, after the principle trading commodity of European voyagers. In recalling those years, Mariner conveyed the impression that though Tongan life was no paradise and he was glad to return to home in England, there was much in that way of life that deeply impressed him. He once had a conversation with Fīnau 'Ulukālala about the Tongan ruler's puzzlement over the coins that were found among the *Port-au-Prince*'s treasure. Mariner then explained the function of money in European society, but found that the King far surpassed him in insight into such things:

> If money were made of iron and could be converted into knives, axes and chisels there would be some sense in placing a value on it; but as it is, I see none. If a man has more yams than he wants, let him exchange some of them away for pork…Certainly money is much handier and more convenient but then, as it will not spoil by being kept, people will store it up instead of sharing it out as a chief ought to do, and thus become selfish…I understand now very well what it is that makes the papālangi [white men] so selfish—it is this money![7]

Like many castaways, Mariner served as the initial source of knowledge of the written word. He advised the King that the writing was elsewhere used to send messages across great distances. The King agreed that this was no doubt true and acknowledged writing "to be a most noble invention." According to Mariner, Fīnau 'Ulukālala then remarked:

> It would not do at all for the Tongan islands; that there would be nothing but disturbances and conspiracies, and he would not be sure to live, perhaps even for another month. He said, however, that he would like to know it himself and for all the women to know it, so that he might make love [by arranging meetings] without discovery, and not so much chance of incurring the vengeance of their husbands.[8]

Some castaway Europeans lived among the Māori as either slaves or equals; some of those treated as equals had their faces tattooed in Māori fashion. While some returned to the European fold as the settler population expanded, others fought along side their adopted Māori communities against British soldiers and settlers in defense of their adopted culture. Like his contemporary, William Mariner, Frederick Edward Manning left an account of his life among Māoris that acknowledged the rougher edges of Polynesian life, but also evinced considerable nostalgia:

> Ah! those good old times, when first I came to New Zealand, we shall never see their like again...before Governors were invented, and law, and justice, and all that...Who cared then whether he owned a coat? Or believed in shoes or stockings? Little did I think in those days that I should ever see here towns and villages, banks and insurance offices, prime ministers and bishops; and hear sermons preached, and see men hung, and all the other plagues of civilization. I am a melancholy man.[9]

Polynesian rulers, such as Fīnau 'Ulukālala and Hawaii's kings, who survived the initial impact of the West generally strove to control further Western impact through a process that in Japan's encounter with the West was called "self-strengthening." Polynesian elites often came to agreements with foreign powers that preserved their status, but often at the expense of disenfranchising commoners in favor of white traders, settlers, or those colonial administrators content to rule through them. Some rulers used the taxes paid by traders and planters to build European palaces with modern conveniences such as electric lights that they hoped would project enough Western-style material progress and political power to preserve their sovereignty. They also often converted to Christianity, an act which further served to preserve their status (it was harder for Western powers to overthrow a Christian monarch than a heathen ruler), but which also (as the missionaries taught them) put their souls in the hands of a god who would forgive their past "idolatry." For that reason, the masses loyally followed their chiefs into the new religion, despite the slow deprivation of their political rights which they did not immediately perceive due to their faith in their leaders. Bound by both traditional and Christian morality to be worthy of that faith, Polynesian rulers did their best to balance the needs of preserving their states with the interests of commoners. Hawaiian rulers, and ultimately even the kings of Tonga, led the way in embracing Western writing and also the coinage of money as a new technology that could aid in the self-strengthening process and enable Hawaiians to constitute themselves as a member of the world family of nations. Hawaiian king David Kalākaua (1836–1891) undertook a world tour designed to secure treaties recognizing him a ruler of a sovereign state and thus securing its independence. As demonstrated by scholar Stacy Kamehiro, King Kalākaua and his people also participated in international exhibitions where they presented material intended both to undermine foreign conceptions of their islands as a society of unworthy "others" and to demonstrate their own modernity through visual presentations of "culture," "history," and "nation."[10] Unfortunately, neither religious conversion nor treaties protected Polynesian elites and commoners alike from the self-interest and venality of Westerners, particularly in the largest Polynesian lands, not; Aotearoa (New Zealand) and Hawaii. Tongan and Samoan kings were able to retain a semblance of their traditional royal status, but Tonga came under British control and Samoa

Image of King Kalākaua, who brought back the Hula and other traditional Hawaiian practices in the 1880s.   Library of Congress.

was partitioned and annexed by Germany and the United States. Both Hawaii and New Zealand became colonies of white settlement as disease and loss of traditional livelihoods reduced their indigenous peoples to a tiny minority and mired them in poverty in which many still live as low-wage workers where once they were warriors. In both of those instances, Western-style treaties (such as the Anglo-Māori Treaty of Waitangi in 1840) and constitutional arrangements signed by indigenous leaders in good faith to avoid war with their Western "teachers" (the Hawaiian "Bayonet" Constitution in 1887) were interpreted by Western colonizers so as to permit them to violate the Polynesians' own under-standing of these agreements (which did not directly threaten their sovereignty). These agreements were also used as cover for illegal land seizures (in Aotearoa) or to lay the groundwork for annexation (in Hawaii's case, to the United States).

Even under such pressure, Polynesians never quite abandoned their traditional values or even many customs. Hawaiian King Kalākaua defied missionaries by summoning the surviving masters of *hula* to perform the

Queen Lili'uokalani in later life. She was a prolific composer and performer and used traditional Hawaiian styles in her compositions.   Library of Congress.

banned dancing and Queen Lili'uokalani composed and performed music that used the Hawaiian language and musical styles so that these traditions could not only be saved for posterity, but be placed into the service of revitalizing the people and the nation. Missionaries to Polynesia may have thought that the adoption of the game of cricket would help accomplish their goal of Westernization, but "*Kilikiti*," as the game is known in Samoa, was entirely indigenized:

> There is no limit to team size, and teams are made up of whoever turns up regardless of gender or age…A kilikiti game is a multi-day community event full of singing, dancing, and feasting. Entire villages will compete and everyone will be involved, whether as player, cook, or spectator…the only universal rule is that the host team forfeits if it cannot provide enough food.[11]

Polynesians are very proud of a language the missionaries failed to eradicate. It is generically called *pidgin*, which is designed and employed between two peoples joined by trade who have no other language in common. Because it uses elements of the languages of the colonizer and the colonized, and thus does not entirely exclude the language of the colonized, Polynesian variations of *pidgin* became not only an honorable means of communication, but developed into a full blown literature now taught in Pacific and Pacific Rim universities.

Some scholars have argued that such hybridization merely disguises a virtually complete surrender to Western culture.[12] Others, such as Nicolas Thomas, reject a simple "us/them" dichotomy between the cultures of Westerners and Pacific Islanders. Thomas stresses that all colonial history is shared or entangled. He draws attention to examples of how visitors and islanders "have fashioned identities for themselves and each other by appropriating each others roles, ideas and exchange of goods." After all, whereas Hawaiian converts were among the first missionaries who brought Christianity to the Marquesas, some European missionaries to Polynesia "went native." Few Polynesians or Westerners know that the Portuguese introduced an instrument that became closely associated with Polynesia: the ukulele. For decades Māori taught in their schools that they had come to New Zealand in 1350 in a "great fleet" of seven canoes from the Tahitian region. This proud conception—fully shared by other islanders who built memorials to what they believed was the true point of departure—was, in the opinion of some scholars, not based on a story told over the generations, but the creation of two Western writers whose analysis of Māori oral traditions was later rejected by Western anthropologists who faulted their poor use of the oral history record and its creators' insufficient knowledge of Māori traditions. The gift of modern scientific analysis thus helped create a Māori past, only to seemingly take it away, though the story's power still has a hold on many Māori hearts.

It is somewhat ironic that two of the greatest ideals of the Age of Enlightenment that spurred the West into its initial encounter with Polynesia—freedom and equality—were long denied to Pacific Islanders. That irony lies in the fact that only after the final triumph of colonialism, with indigenous peoples reduced by as much as 90 percent by European introduced diseases, overwhelmed by European and Asian migrants associated with the recruitment of plantation labor (first sandalwood, then sugar and other commodities), and suffering the near universal loss of political sovereignty, did Western intruders formally recognize how far they had departed from these ideals. In 2002, the Prime Minister of New Zealand extended an apology to the people of Samoa for the suppression of a Samoan nationalist movement which led to the killing of nine Samoans and to the banishment of several Samoan leaders who were also stripped of their chiefly titles. They also apologized for the deaths arising from an avoidable influenza epidemic arising from colonial rule, both events occurring when the islands were under New Zealand's administration. Authorities in New Zealand have since engaged in negotiations with Māori leaders to redress violations of the guarantees set out in the Treaty of Waitangi in 1840. Moreover, as of 2006, large tracts of land have been returned to Māori control. Legislation is currently before the U.S. Congress intended to secure the interests of the indigenous people of Hawaii who lack rights long afforded to American "Indians."

Conclusion

Many Polynesians today see little profit in such efforts beyond the achievement of political equality and self-sovereignty as commonly enjoyed in the West. In Hawaii, a few insist that a restoration of a traditional Polynesian monarchy, with its attendant spiritual values, is as important as sovereignty. Most Polynesians believe that it is better to find ways to preserve the past while adapting to the present, with the ultimate goal of finding a place for their culture in the modern world. That hope is expressed in the *Hōkūleʻa*, a double-hulled canoe, built by Hawaiians using ancient techniques so as to preserve their traditional canoe-building skills. Since 1978, it has voyaged from Hawaii to other Pacific Islands in an effort to reconnect Polynesians with each other and to their common past. The *Hōkūleʻa* invariably arrives at its destination using traditional navigation arts: It carries no modern navigation aids or even a radio. Yet, over the horizon, a modern ship tracks its journey in case any of the crew need urgent medical attention or the craft suffers a catastrophic loss of seaworthiness. At the beginning of an attempt to retrace the route of Polynesian migration between the Hawaiian and the Tahitian islands, when there was no such support-ship, one of the *Hōkūleʻa*'s two hulls was breached, the canoe capsized, and, despite tide and distance and growing darkness, one of the crew members, a 31-year-old much respected lifeguard and surfer, Edward Ryan

Makua Hanai Aikau, volunteered to paddle on a board back more than 12 miles to the nearest land to get help. The crew was later rescued by the U.S. Coast Guard, but Aikau was lost, despite a massive air and sea search of the surrounding waters. To this day, Hawaiians facing a challenge tell themselves, "Eddie would go." This brave and adventurous spirit helped fuel the Polynesian migrations, saw them through their epic encounter with the West, from noble savage to servant underclass, and still nurtures the people of Polynesia in the age of increasing modernity and globalization.

Questions for Discussion

1. What were some characteristics of Polynesian society at the time of its encounter with Europe?
2. What developments within European society shaped the West's changing views of Polynesia?
3. What roles did castaways play in the European-Polynesian encounter?
4. What are some of the results of early contact between Polynesian and non-Polynesian peoples? Why are these called "entanglements?"
5. What obstacles do Polynesians face when attempting to access their own pasts?

Endnotes

1. Nicolas Thomas, *Entangled Objects: Exchange, Material Culture, and Colonialism in the Pacific* (Cambridge, MA: Harvard, 1991).
2. "Polynesian Temple History by Dating Coral," *Archeology Daily News* at http://www.archaeologydaily.com/news/201008174817/Polynesian-temple-history-by-dating-coral.html. Accessed October 28, 2010.
3. King Kamehaha I, "The Law of the Splintered Paddle," found at http://www.hawaii.edu/uhelp/files/LawOfTheSplinteredPaddle.pdf, created by Hawaii Legal Auxiliary. Accessed May 21, 2011.
4. Alan Moorehead, *The Fatal Impact* (Honolulu, HI: Mutual Publishing Paperback Series, Tales of the Pacific), p. 8.
5. Ibid., p. 43.
6. James Cook, *The Voyages of Captain James Cook Round the World*, Vol. 2 (London: William Smith, 1842), p. 211.
7. http://en.wikipedia.org/wiki/Tongan_pa%CA%BBanga. Accessed September 25, 2010.
8. John Martin, M.D., *An Account of the Natives of the Tonga Islands, in the South Pacific Ocean. Complied and Arranged from the Extensive Communications of William Mariner, Several Years Resident in Those Islands* (Boston, MA: Charles Ewer, first American edition, 1820), pp. 94–97.
9. A Pakeha Maori [Frederick Edward Maning], *Old New Zealand: Being Incidents of Native Customs and Character in the Old Times* (London: Smith, Elder, and Company, 1843), p. 1.
10. Stacy L. Kamehiro, "Hawai'i at the World Fairs, 1867–1893," *World History Connected*, Vol. 8, No. 3 (October 2011) at http://worldhistoryconnected.press.illinois.edu/8.3/forum_kamehiro.html. Accessed October 4, 2011.

11. See http://en.wikipedia.org/wiki/Kilikiti. Accessed September 15, 2010.

12. See *Trobriand Cricket: An Ingenious Response to Colonialism* by Jerry Leach, and G. Kildea (United States: University of California at Berkeley Extension Center for Media, 1976). This film makes the argument that the style of cricket played among Trobriand islanders in Melanesia reflected indigenous not European culture. It interprets cricket matches serving as a surrogate for "tribal" battles of old. The film makers argue that the pre-match rituals (chants, face painting, etc.) mirror those that warriors traditionally performed before battle. These rituals include chants similar to ancient legends and histories. R. Stewart Geiger at Georgetown University notes that from this film "the assumption can easily be made that Trobriand cricket is a positive cultural activity." He begs to disagree. "If a deeper analysis is performed, it is clear that Trobriand cricket detaches the tribes from their history and military forces, leaving them powerless and open to domination. While the first generation of Trobriand cricket players most certainly remembered the historical and military context of the ceremonial acts, those who grow up in a post-cricket world are likely to see the rituals as nothing more than game play. There is no context for children to place the rituals in, as cricket has rendered war obsolete." R. Stuart Geiger, Trobriand Cricket: An Ingenious Response by Colonialism. at http://www.stuartgeiger.com/portfolio/papers/trobriand.pdf. Accessed September 21, 2010.

6

On the Frontiers of Central Asia: Russia, China and Steppe Empires in Eurasia

Russia and China both built great empires in the period between 1600 and 1800. This empire-building, however, was not a simple matter of conquest and expansion. And the conquests themselves do not tell the whole story of these two nations. Instead, both states had to deal with peoples of the Eurasian steppe, who were spread across a huge expanse of central and north Asia and southeastern Europe. Great numbers and varieties of people moved across this frontier like a flowing river. Today the area consists of Ukraine, Crimea, and many former steppe kingdoms or khanates including Kazakhstan, Uzbekistan, Kyrgyzstan, Turkmenistan, Tajikistan, and the Mongolian steppe to the east. To the north, the vast lands of modern-day Siberia were sparsely populated by communities with whom the Chinese to the south and the Russians in the northwest of Eurasia traded for animal furs. Both China's and, to a greater extent, Russia's relations with the inhabitants of the steppe were shaped not only by encounters with these dispersed and fragmented societies but by their struggle to meet the challenge of an empire formed by the steppe peoples under the leadership of one of their own communities, the Mongols.

The Mongol Empire, the largest and one of the most warlike of all world empires, struck terror into the heart of many peoples including China and Russia, from its inception in the early 1200s to the mid-1300s. The western remnants of this empire, called the Golden Horde, regularly terrorized the people on the southern frontier of Russia, raiding and taking Russians as slaves until Russia fortified its border and expanded southward in the 1700s. To the east, in Mongolia, a more vibrant Mongol state challenged both Russia

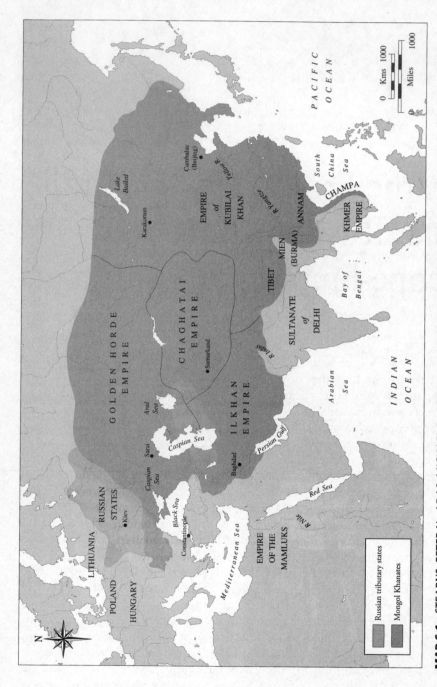

MAP 6.1 STEARNS, PETER N., ADAS, MICHAEL B., SCHWARTZ, STUART B., GILBERT, MARC JASON, World Civilizations: The Global Experience, COMBINED VOLUME 6th Edition, © 2011, p. 244. Reprinted by permission of Pearson Education, Inc., Upper Saddle River, NJ.

and China on their borders and played them off against each other until the Chinese, in a series of military campaigns, destroyed Mongol forces in the 1690s. In the 1600s and 1700s both Russia and China sought to make the peoples on their frontiers swear allegiance to their rulers, the tsar (emperor) of Russia and the Emperor of China. But these frontier peoples resisted mightily so open an acknowledgment of their inferiority and obeisance. In the face of this Russian–Chinese pattern of imperial aggression, there was little room for mutual understanding or the creation of a middle ground as among Europeans and Native Americans (Chapter 4), although it did produce some examples of multiculturalism. In the main, however, this encounter was characterized by warrior ethos and violent clashes on all sides.

THE MONGOLS

In the 1200s, a semi-nomadic steppe people, the Mongols, were united by Genghis (Chinggis) Khan. They lived in an area that today sits north of Beijing in a separate nation called Mongolia. Superb horsemen and feared warriors, the Mongols invaded central Asia, Eastern Europe, and the Middle East on horseback. Their cavalry tactics, military organization, and communications system permitted them to establish the largest land empire in the history of the world, larger than either Alexander the Great's conquests or the Roman Empire, stretching from China, conquered in the east, to Persia (Iran) in the Middle East, and on to the northern most part of India in southern Asia. The Mongol invasion of Eastern Europe stretched all the way from Poland in the north to the Ukraine in the south.

The Mongols were the most powerful and menacing invaders the Russians and Chinese had ever known and struck terror throughout Europe and the Middle East as well as Asia. If leaders insulted Mongol diplomats or resisted their conquest, they were executed by being wrapped in carpets and trampled to death underneath Mongol tents or yurts; the Mongols might then also slaughter the inhabitants of the city-state under the leaders' control. Even after the Mongol Empire collapsed, its remnants remained powerful; in Russia, settlement were heavily taxed or assaulted and Russians were often taken as slaves.

Though known for their ferocity in war, Mongols brought great peace and stability to their vast multicultural empire. They reopened and provided complete security for the legendary Silk Road across central Asia to Europe, which had long before fallen into disuse, though the revived Silk Road's success came at a price: It may have enabled the spread of the Black Plague bacillus from China to Europe.

Though the Mongol Empire was short-lived (it broke up over the quest to find a successor to Chinggis Khan) and its memory has been colored by the terror it inspired, its political and cultural legacy was profound. The steppe peoples inherited Mongol political organization and used the Mongol term "khan" to denote their ruler and "khanate" to describe their polity. They were divided into smaller political units comprised of so-called khanates, which were the divisions created when Genghis Khan divided his western empire into parcels and gave his sons control of them. For a time they held together in a confederation called the Golden Horde. But this soon split apart into rival khanates. Each khanate had its own nobility and local notables led individual villages and clans. The steppe peoples inherited another characteristic from the Mongols. Their societies were organized for war. Warfare and raiding were the methods by which high status was achieved in steppe societies and many people supplemented their herding lifestyle through raiding. To that end, steppe tribes were able to produce large raiding armies. The Kalmyk Khan people—ethnically related to the Mongols—were able to gather an army of 40,000 horsemen and the Crimean Khan twice that number. Therefore, the encounter between steppe peoples and Russians to the north continued to be quite violent and destructive. They also forced Russian villages to pay tribute.

THE RUSSIAN EMPIRE AND THE PEOPLES OF THE STEPPE

In traditional histories of Russian expansion, the peoples the Russians encountered have been rendered nonexistent. They were considered to have no significance because, with the exception of Crimea, they did not possess a centralized state like Russia but rather were nomadic warriors organized by tribe. It was thought these peoples could not engage in historical progress since they had no nation-state and therefore were incapable of change and

MEDIEVAL TARTAR HUTS AND WAGONS.

This sketch shows a Mongol household on the move. The Mongols depended on sheep for food, clothing, and shelter, and they rode both horses and camels. As the drawing shows, they also used oxen to transport their housing for seasonal or longer-term migrations. The Mongols mounted their tents and other goods on enormous wagons so heavy that large teams of oxen were required to pull them. This combination of animal transport and comfortable but moveable shelters made the Mongols one of the most mobile preindustrial societies.   The Granger Collection, NY.

dynamism. In addition, because of their Asian heritage, Russians looked down upon these nomads as primitive. By the end of the 1700s Russia was engaged in a campaign of civilization targeted at frontier peoples no less important than its physical conquest of frontier regions from the mid-1600s to 1700s. In the early period of the encounter in the 1400s to 1500s, however, Russians rarely thought of the conquest or civilization of its southern neighbors.

Who were the steppe peoples and why did they engage in a sustained encounter with Russia over several centuries? The steppe frontier was composed of a patchwork quilt of different peoples many of whom were descendents of Mongols who had conquered this area in the 1200s and then mixed their blood with the conquered peoples. The people of the steppe consisted of larger and smaller political units and a combination of nomadic, semi-nomadic, and urbanized societies. In their great variety and diversity, the steppe tribes were similar to Native American communities of North America (Chapter 4). The Nogays, Kalmyks, and Kazakhs in the western part of the steppe formed successive nomadic confederations in the 1500s to 1700s. These were tribal groups bound by kinship and military alliance. They raised animals on the steppe and moved with the changing pasture land, living on the pasture they raised their horses and cattle upon, thus falling into the category of nomadic peoples. Other peoples of the steppe formed city-states such as Bukhara, Samarkand, Crimea, and Kazan. Samarkand and Bukhara were south of the Kazakh domains, just north of modern-day Iran. The Crimean peoples had a powerful state located on a large peninsula in the Black Sea and spreading north from it toward Moscow. The peninsula was an important trading point on the silk route that brought precious goods from China to Europe. The Genoese and Venetians originally had trading posts here but later on the Ottoman Empire took these over after conquering Constantinople (Istanbul). The peoples of these city-states still practiced nomadic pastoralism at times, although others were merchants and traders.
The Cossacks formed yet another group who were powerful interlopers. While most steppe peoples were unrelated to the Russians ethnically, the Cossacks were Slavic people who lived as independent farmers in the area of modern-day Ukraine and southern Russia. They were fiercely independent and formed an alliance with the Polish-Lithuanian Commonwealth for a short time but later in the 1700s became an important ally of Russia in its drive to conquer the steppe. Excellent horsemen and feared warriors, they served as Russia's frontier militia and struck terror into steppe communities.

Smaller arctic communities fished along the waterways, hunted seals in the Arctic Ocean and bears and moose in the great forests of Siberia, and herded large herds of reindeer. But it was the trapping of fur-bearing animals that attracted the attention of Russia, similar to the interest of Europeans in the beaver fur of North America. These furs became coats, hats, and other valued items in the cold north of Europe. The Samoed, Koda Khanty, Ostiak, Chukchi, and Yukagir peoples spread out across this vast zone of ice, tundra, and forest.

Russia's frontier both shaped Russian politics and society and was shaped by Russia's accelerating expansion into the area. At first in the fifteenth and sixteenth centuries, Russia had to defend its borders from marauding

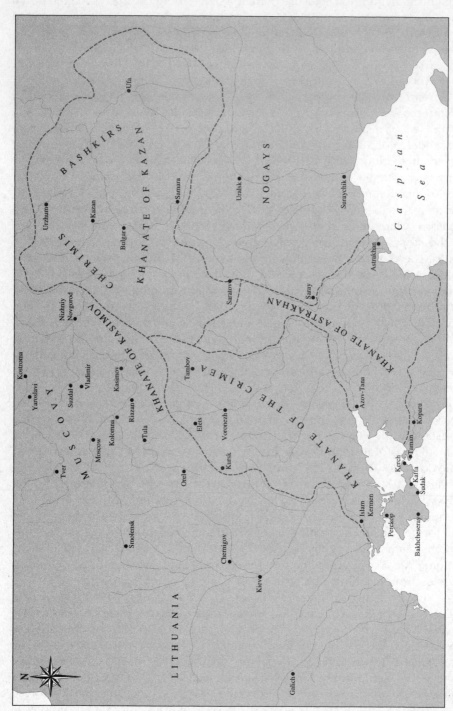

MAP 6.2 Map of Steppe Empires

tribes to the south. Later in the eighteenth century, as Russia consolidated control over its borders, it began to dominate its frontier regions. But given the initial strength of frontier peoples and the weakness of Russia, once mere vassals of the Mongols, they could have easily turned the tables and conquered Russia as they came close to doing in the 1500s. Both sides were fighting for their survival amidst warfare, raiding, and slave-taking and were thus initially open to finding a middle ground or at least copying prevailing steppe custom.

RAIDING AND SLAVES

Raiding represented a kind of guerilla warfare where the steppe tribes rode into villages and towns close to the southern border of Russia and captured supplies, but more importantly rounded up Russian people whom they took back to their homeland to be sold as slaves. The slaves gave steppe peoples a significant source of income. Russian slaves were sold within Ottoman slave markets in Crimea and Safavid (Iranian) slave markets. These slaves were a valuable commodity that fetched a high price. The economic motive for raiding was paramount; some raiders, especially in Crimea, where grazing land was scarce, had no other source of income and faced starvation without the resources gained from raiding.

Raiding was most intense in the 1500s and 1600s. It is estimated that 150,000–200,000 Russians were captured during raiding in the early 1600s. During one campaign in Lithuania, Crimeans captured 50,000 slaves. Russian slaves comprised half of all slaves taken by the Crimeans in 1529. And the slave trade amounted to one-third of all revenues at the Ottoman port of Kaffa in Crimea. In another instance, the Nogays signed a peace treaty with Russia in 1618 and handed back 15,000 Russian captives.

In the 1560s, the Russian state was deeply alarmed over the plight of Russian captives taken by the peoples of the steppe. The Russian state solidified its claim to be the sole leader of Orthodox Christianity with the fall of Constantinople in 1453 (eastern capital of the Roman Empire and seat of Orthodox Christianity) to the Ottoman Empire. Thereafter, the Russians took more responsibility for the welfare of its Orthodox Christian population. Most of the time, the government negotiated a ransom for the release of captives. The scope of the problem is shown by a Russian law that was enforced from 1551 to 1679 requiring a special tax within Russian territory, the proceeds of which were used to ransom the release of Russian captives. As the Russian army became more powerful, Russian leaders threatened the use of force to coerce steppe peoples to release their people. Interestingly, while the Russian government went to great lengths to stop the enslavement of Russian Orthodox Christians, they had no such qualms about western non-Orthodox Christians, whom they sold into slavery regularly.

By the late 1600s the Russians had fortified their southern frontier to stop the raiding and had even begun to penetrate the steppe in campaigns of conquest. Greater access to western firearms greatly aided the Russian conquest of the steppe. As the Russians solidified their hold on the frontier in the late 1700s, the roles of captive and captor became reversed. Russian forces captured prisoners from the tribes of the steppe, and these prisoners who were Muslim were often forced to convert to Orthodox Christianity and integrated into the Empire.

DIPLOMACY AND CONQUEST

A few Russian officials believed that Russia, with its new domains and peoples, should embrace a new identity as a multi-ethnic and a multi-religious empire. However, the bulk of the Russian government and its people continued to think of Russia as an ethnically distinct savior of Orthodox Christianity: The Russian ruler began to insist that he be referred to as tsar after the fall of Constantinople, when he became the sole monarch representing Orthodox Christianity. The tsars thus aspired to be treated as equals to the kings of Europe and the khans of the steppe. This attempt was resisted by both the Pope of the Catholic Church, who had the sole power of crowning kings in Europe, and the Crimean Khan, who was the heir to the Mongols and before this had widely been considered more powerful than the Russian ruler and was sometimes paid obeisance by the Russians.

Another expression of Moscow's search for respect was the custom of removing one's hat in front of the Russian ruler. It was considered a sign of one's political inferiority to the Russian monarchy. Among the Muslim peoples of the steppe, however, covering ones head was seen as a sign of respect. Conflict over these customs ensued as Russians and steppe peoples negotiated over captives, sovereignty, and boundaries. Unlike the situation in the Great Lakes region of North America where a middle ground was created, the resurgent Russians gradually began to seek to define their relations with steppe peoples within their own cultural framework. For instance, they forced Nogay chiefs to remove their hats as a sign of submission to the tsar. In one instance, a compromise was negotiated in which the interpreter of a Kalmyk chieftain was asked to stand and remove his hat instead of the chief himself. Moreover, to buttress his influence, the Russian tsar claimed that he was heir to Genghis Khan (Chinghis Khan), original Mongol ruler. The Nogays, who had become dependent upon the Russian state for protection from other steppe tribes, acknowledged this supposed Mongol-Russian lineage. Though other steppe peoples rejected such a claim, the claim itself demonstrates the continuing influence of the defunct Mongol Empire and the Russian effort to use such "middle ground" tactics as assuming a traditional title or political posture to gain support among its partners in a political encounter.

In other ways, Moscow attempted to build a common vocabulary of diplomacy with steppe peoples. Russian diplomats used the term "shert," which was a Turko-Mongol steppe term that indicated an agreement for peace or a peace treaty, in negotiations of treaties with steppe peoples. However later, leaders of Russia, looking to impose their will upon the steppe peoples, interpreted these agreements as oaths of allegiance to Russia. While these agreements were easily made, they continued to be interpreted differently by Russians and steppe peoples.

Just how different the perceptions of the Russians and the steppe peoples were as they signed these sherts is illuminated by one such agreement made in 1483. In that year when the steppe peoples still had the power to instill fear in the Russians, the Russian military signed a shert with the Khanti and Mansa peoples in the Ural Mountains. Russian diplomats observing the event described the ceremony in an ethnographic manner as follows:

> They [the Khanti] put a bearskin under a thick trunk of a cut pine tree, then they put two sabers with their sharp ends upwards and bread and fish on the bearskin. And we the Russians put a cross atop the pine tree and they put a wooden idol and tie it (sic) below the cross; and they began to walk beneath their idol in the direction of the sun. And one of them standing nearby said "He who will break this Peace, let him be punished by the god of his faith." And they walked about the tree three times and we bowed to the cross, and they bowed to the sun. After all this they drank water from the cup containing a golden nugget and they kept saying: "You, gold, seek the one who betrays."[1]

Later, however, the same event was described in the *Russian Chronicle*, the official history of the nation, as one in which "the local princes swore not to bear any ill will, not to exhibit any violence, and to be loyal to the grand prince of Muscovy." The difference between the two accounts is striking. The first one tells a story of a middle ground encounter where both sides appealed to the cultural framework of the other to establish a way of keeping peace. The first account was a recording of the event by the Russian officials involved in it and has firsthand credibility. The second rendering is the way in which the event was remembered in an official government history of the Russian nation. Its self-serving and nationalist account transformed the event from a middle ground compromise into an expression of submission and loyalty to the Russian tsar.

In another example, the Russians deliberately mistranslated a Kalmyk document that described the tsar as an inferior local ruler into a petition of the local chief to a clearly superior tsar. In yet another case, the peace treaty was written completely in Russian with only Kalmyk signatures, so the Kalmyks did not know exactly what they were signing and were told one thing while the document stated another. Getting local chiefs to sign documents they assumed were trade treaties when they really handed over sovereignty or territory, and creating misleading or false translations were both approaches that Western European imperialists used in Africa in the 1870s to 1890s (Chapter 9). So steppe diplomacy became a conflict over interpretation, not just one of arms or slaves.

Russian translator and diplomat Alexander Tevkelev (originally Mirza Kutlu Mohammad), who was himself a Tatar (people who originated from the northeastern Gobi Desert and were forced westward and subjugated by the Mongols) nobleman from the Crimean steppe, had much experience with the steppe peoples and noted that Kazakh leaders understood Russian intentions and negotiated for peace, not to be treated as inferior subjects of the tsar. According to him, Kazakh elders "advised the Khan to send the envoys only in order to have peace with Russia; they do not wish to be Russian subjects."[2] Tevkelev, who was born and raised on the steppe but had been sent as a hostage to Russia and then adopted into an aristocratic family, understood that steppe peoples had no desire to become subservient to the Russians and he also saw that Russian attempts to force this upon steppe peoples increased their resistance. Instead, he recommended that Russian diplomacy focus on strengthening the khans who ruled the various khanates on the steppe. Establishing sound reliable relations with these leaders would strengthen Russia's hand there. However, the Russians desperately wanted acknowledgment of the superiority of their leader and religion. Therefore, they maintained their interpretation that these agreements represented oaths of allegiance.

Practical issues of power sometimes motivated steppe peoples to seek alliances with the Russians. In 1480 the Russians and the Crimean Khan agreed to an alliance against the Polish-Lithuanian Commonwealth in the west and the remnants of the Mongol Empire to the east. This was an alliance of the vulnerable and those seeking to regain strength. The Russians were vulnerable to the large armies of Poland–Lithuania and to raiding from Mongol warriors from the east and south. The Crimeans sought to regain lands and herds lost in recent wars. This alliance came at a crucial moment in Russian history, allowing the Russians to successfully defend their territory from invasion while also strengthening themselves against traditional foes.

By the 1700s, the Russians no longer hid their sense of superiority and the treaties clearly made steppe kingdoms into protectorates of the Russian state. And the Russians began to demand more from their steppe neighbors. Because the sherts alone did not always guarantee amicable relations, the Russians came to demand hostages to guarantee good behavior. Eventually steppe peoples agreed to submit hostages because the Russians threatened to end trade privileges and the gifts of cash, woolens, and furs they normally bestowed to insure loyalty. Hostage-taking was also practiced on the northern Eurasian frontier in present-day Siberia. Only relatives of leaders were taken as hostages and they were usually released within one year, although if the tribe in question violated its oath to the Russians, the hostage could be turned into a prisoner. On the northern frontier, with precarious economic conditions, unreliable supplies of furs, and natives who were uncooperative, hostage-taking effectively bent the northern tribes to the will of the Russians in most cases. Hostage-taking ended at the end of the 1700s as Russian leaders decided upon a new policy of civilizing the steppe and northern peoples. Sons of the local chiefs were thereafter sent to St. Petersburg to be educated alongside Russian elites. In return Moscow would give presents to local chiefs. These presents were a continuation of long-standing payments of tribute by Russian princes and tsars to the steppe khans. The tribute had begun in the Mongol Empire period in the 1300s when Russian princes paid tribute to keep the Mongols from destroying them and to signal that the Russians were subservient, but it continued into the 1700s. Even after the Russians had become more powerful, they continued to give presents to quell occasional slave raids and promote steppe leaders who were friendly to the Russians.

The encounter between the steppe peoples and Russians was therefore highly dynamic and one in which quite often the Russians had to leverage their limited power and influence with treaties, gifts, and presents. In spite of Russian insistence that the steppe peoples were subject to them, the steppe peoples exercised a great deal of power in the relationship for a considerable time.

In the north at the Siberian frontier, where tribes were smaller and much weaker than on the steppe, Russia pursued many of the same policies as on the steppe, but was able to impose its will more vigorously than on its southern frontier. In the 1600s the Russian government became increasingly interested in collecting taxes there. A tax or the so-called yasak (iasak) was imposed, which amounted to a tax of goods upon the peoples. The northern tribes never possessed great military power and they were forced to trade with the Russian state; they not only had to pay this crushing tax, but were forcibly recruited to fight wars of conquest for the Russians. The Koda Khanty, for example, fought alongside Russian allied Cossacks against the Kalmyks and Crimean Tatars to the south and against the Samoed and Tungus peoples in the north. Russian campaigns of conquest in both the southern and northern frontiers produced cruel forced migrations of defeated steppe peoples and in some cases led to their near extinction.

With newfound stability on its southern frontier in the 1700s, the Russians increased their trade with steppe peoples, giving goods such as leather, furs, and silver in return for horses and goods such as silks and cotton. As Russia expanded southward in the 1600s with fortified towns such as the trading center of Orenburg, located at the southernmost reaches of the Russian Empire, the steppe's great river of human movement upon which the nomads of the steppe sailed increasingly became a Russian-dominated river, and Russian-controlled places such as Orenburg joined Khiva and Bukhara as ports where steppe peoples landed, stopping for supplies and to trade goods and people.

The Russians also became involved in the succession system of steppe leaders, referred to after the Mongol custom as khans. Eventually taking the advice of steppe nobleman-turned Russian diplomat Alexander Tevkelev, Russia sought to confirm or in some cases even confer the title of khan among the tribes. This practice caused as many problems as it solved because the succession process was unruly and violent in many areas of the steppe. In some cases, more than one family claimed title to a khanship and frequently, violent clan wars broke out during the time of succession. Russian officials sometimes took sides in these battles and their interference was resented.

One response to increased Russian influence on the steppe was for Muslim steppe peoples to join together on the basis of their religion to oppose them. Sometimes religion was used strategically to court friends or threaten enemies. Ottoman leader Suleyman the Magnificent attempted to unite the steppe tribes in 1551 by claiming, "we are all Muslims and we should unite against Moscow…"[3] This attempt and others failed because the steppe tribes were fierce rivals of one another and not all of them were Muslim such as the Kalmyks, who were Buddhist. Among steppe peoples, as well as among the Russians and other regional powers, calls for religious unity were often used as a rationale for conquest, but religious diversity and politics hampered these attempts. All of the regional powers, the Russians, the Ottomans, and the Persians contained a variety of religions within their borders including Islam, Buddhism, Christianity, and variations within these and other traditions.

In a complex diplomatic move, Catherine the Great, the first female tsar (tsarina) of Russia, decided in the 1780s to use Islam to try to civilize the Kazakh peoples, whom she believed to be "savage and ignorant."[4] In this case, though, civilization did not mean conversion to Orthodox Christianity, but rather education about Muslim religious traditions. Catherine hired loyal Islamic clerics to educate the Kazakhs about Islam, to create peace and stability, and, most importantly, to ensure loyalty to the Russian state. In 1788 Catherine founded the Muslim Spiritual Assembly in Orenburg to help govern Russia's Muslim subjects. The head of the Assembly was appointed by the Russian government. The *mufti* (Islamic spiritual leaders) served Russia's interests on more than one occasion, and in 1790, the *mufti* traveled to Kazakh territory and successfully convinced local leaders not to rebel against Moscow but rather to agree that the Koran allowed Kazakhs to be subjects of the Russian Empire. The Russian government departed from its fervent Orthodox Christian evangelism under Catherine to reach out to Islamic peoples in the steppe and used Islam to help quell them and subject them to Russian rule.

Once Russia began to conquer the steppe militarily, this new civilizing concept of the relations between Russia and the steppe peoples expanded. While actual interactions were many times still directed by strategic concerns, protection of ones' own peoples, and the reciprocal demands of tribute and presents from both sides, Russian officials and intellectuals began to place steppe peoples within a new framework of primitivity and civilization. The Russians became a civilizing force operating on peoples who were reduced to being viewed as primitive and barbaric. As such, Russians began to think of steppe peoples as "wild, untamed horses."[5] Others described them as "noble savages," in a vein similar to how Europeans described Native Americans in North America (Chapter 4) and Polynesians in the Pacific Ocean (Chapter 5). Historian Michael Khordarkovsky describes the evolution of Russian thinking about steppe peoples this way: "First feared, then despised, and finally pitied, Russia now acquired its version of a 'noble savage.' "[6] Like the American government's approach to Native Americans, the Russian government wanted to convert the steppe peoples to Christianity and make them into farmers.

On the northern frontier, this concern with developing an ideology of civilization took a different form. Unlike on the steppe, where until the 1600s the Russians might have been considered more backward than the steppe peoples they encountered or at least certainly less powerful than them, in the north the Russians had no doubt of their superiority and the primitiveness of these peoples. Out of this conviction grew a fascination with life in the Arctic. In the eighteenth century, Peter the Great demanded artifacts from arctic Siberia and requested that shamans (indigenous doctors) be sent to Moscow for study. He also sent a German scientist to Siberia to study these peoples and their environment. The Russians focused on the superficialities of physical appearance and living of the arctic tribes and found them to be people of "incredible foulness."[7] Just as with the steppe peoples, their goal was to bring these "savages" to civilization.

How did steppe peoples respond to Russia's civilizing mission? Some dismissed it as nonsense that could be ignored. One Kalmyk leader claimed the Russians were "not warriors and military men, rather they were farmers and townsmen" whom he saw as "mice, and he could take them by their ears and give them to the Kazakhs."[8] As the Russians began to exert an overwhelming military force in the steppe, however, it became more difficult to dismiss them so easily.

MISSIONARY ACTIVITY

Converting steppe peoples to Russian Orthodox Christianity was a priority for Russia as their power on the steppe grew. However, the Russians did not send out missionaries to live in steppe communities, but rather forced steppe peoples to move to Russian communities and to convert to Orthodox Christianity. Converts who refused to profess their new faith were put in chains or thrown in jail.

Even though conversion was forced many times, some steppe peoples recognized the benefits of conversion. Steppe leaders who decided to ally themselves with Russia began to convert out of necessity as their people migrated into Russia and they joined Russian leadership circles. When Russia conquered the steppe in the 1700s, steppe peoples who were commoners were forced to migrate out of war zones and many times fled to Russian towns and villages. As fugitives they were sometimes taken captive, forced to convert, and purchased as serfs (virtual slaves bound to the estate of their lord in perpetuity) by the local elites. In a reversal of the earlier situation, steppe leaders, rather than taking Russians captive as in earlier times, now saw Russians taking their people captive and they had to purchase their return in some cases. The Russian government encouraged steppe peoples to flee conflicts emerging from Russian expansionism and settle in Russian lands. This act disrupted and weakened steppe societies and made it easier for Russians to conquer them. And adding people to Russian territory strengthened Russia's economy and military. Eventually, the Russian government authorized the payment of money to the indigenous leaders for the loss of their peoples. Like Native Americans in North America who became dependent upon government payments from land treaties, steppe leaders increasingly depended upon these payments for their sustenance.

Among its large Muslim population, the Russian government pushed people to conversion by destroying mosques and introduced discriminatory legislation and land confiscation. The government gave incentives to converts such as exemption from military service, pardons for criminals, and monetary rewards. Many converted because of these incentives and some found that they could collect rewards more than once by converting more than once, though the government responded by sending these individuals to hard labor in the monasteries. This coercive approach to conversion produced many converts in name only and was criticized by some within Russian leadership circles, not for the cruelty with which conversion sometimes took place, but for the complete absence of religious training. Prince Mikhail Shcherbatov wrote that Orthodox priests did not teach their converts and gave to them only,

> a cross which in their ignorance, they considered some kind of a talisman, and an image of Christ, which they regard as an idol; and forbade them from eating meat on fast days, a prohibition that they did not follow, while priests took bribes from them for overlooking this. Likewise, no attempt was made to translate the Holy Scriptures into their languages, nor to teach these to the priests...[9]

Forced conversion in some cases created resistance and violent uprisings. Rumors of forced conversion also created mass migration away from the Russian frontier. Both the Kalmyk and the Kazakh peoples fled to resist forced conversion. The Kalmyks eventually returned to Mongolia, their original homeland. Russian efforts at Christianization were viewed suspiciously as part of their colonization effort. In the Artic region, many native women were forced to convert to Christianity as a part of liaisons and family formation with male Russian settlers. Russian settlers looked to native women to fulfill their needs because there were so few Russian women on the northern frontier.

CHINA, RUSSIA, AND MONGOLIA

Far to the east on the border of western China and Mongolia, another encounter took place involving China, Mongolia, and Russians. In the 1400s, as the Mongol Empire disintegrated, destroyed by internal rivalries, the Chinese (Ming Dynasty, 1368–1644) initiated successful military campaigns against the remnants of the Mongols. Ming military leaders took advantage of the split among the Mongols into separate and competing khanates, divided into eastern and western Mongols. They became allies with the eastern Mongols, and then broke with them and became allied with western Mongols, and after a military victory over them, once again allied with the eastern Mongols. This strategy of divide and conquer which took place in the early 1400s was successful in controlling the Mongol threat for a short period. This approach would be repeated in the period of the Qing Dynasty (1644–1911) in the late 1600s. Later in the 1400s the situation reversed and the now weakened Ming suffered the humiliating capture of one of their Emperors, the Zhengtong Emperor, during a military campaign against the Mongols in 1449. Eventually he was released and regained the Chinese throne. After the capture of the Emperor, the Chinese strategy toward the Mongols became defensive and the Great Wall of China was expanded and strengthened in the 1500s to attempt to ward off Mongol attacks.

Ming needs for horses complicated the encounter with the Mongols in this period because the Mongols and other frontier nomads supplied many horses for the Ming Empire. The Ming traded tea for horses, and huge amounts of tea were shipped westward in exchange for horses but not enough horses were obtained and their quality was poor. This was part of the reason the Ming military campaigns against the Mongols were generally ineffective. The Ming inability to conquer the Mongols meant that the western borderlands of China were uncontrolled and became a classic frontier arena in the 1500s and 1600s where Chinese soldiers and merchants learned Mongol and other nomadic languages and intermingled freely with these peoples, trading tea for horses.

China went through another conquest, this time by the Manchus, a people to the northeast of their traditional lands, who swept through China in the 1640s and conquered a Ming Dynasty that was in the midst of decline caused by weak leadership, rampant corruption, and widespread poverty. The Manchus, installing themselves under the Chinese dynastic name of Qing, reinvigorated and reorganized the Chinese army which then engaged in imperial expansion that carried it westward into Tibet. Earlier the Manchus had formed an alliance with the eastern Mongols through trade and use of the Mongol writing system. This alliance helped them to conquer China because they did not have to worry about a Mongol attack on them.

In the 1600s, Russian expansion eastward ran up against the Mongols shorn of their empire but still formidable in and around their homelands. Russians also began to approach the limits of the Chinese Empire, thus sandwiching the Mongols between Russia and China.

The Russians, marching eastward, and the Chinese, marching to the west, possessed similar expansionist goals: acquiring wealth derived from trade and tribute and securing their frontiers. The Russians wanted access to Chinese manufactured goods such as silk and porcelain. China sought the animal furs of Siberia for its growing domestic market which proved a lucrative source of revenue for Russia.

Like the Russians, the Chinese wanted the Mongols and other tribes they encountered to pledge allegiance to their ruler, the Emperor of China. But the Chinese did not force the steppe peoples to convert to a new religion as did the Russians. In part this is because the religion of the Mongols, Buddhism, was an accepted and popular religion in China. Tibetan Buddhism had become prominent in western Mongolia in the 1600s with Mongol aristocrats offering their sons to the monasteries in Tibet. In particular, Zayat Pandita, son of western Mongol leader Baibagas, studied at a Tibetan monastery and became a devout Buddhist monk. He also took an important political role as an influential unifier of Mongol tribes in the 1600s. Mongols rallied around his Buddhist religious identity.

The Mongol tribes aimed to play off the various powers against one another in the region and gain the benefits of trade. A Mongol chieftain Gantimur joined Chinese Manchu forces in 1653 and even led them against Russian troops. He eventually allied his community with Russia as they offered superior food, supplies, and military protection. Later, Galdan, another powerful Mongol prince, also attempted to play the Russians and Chinese off against each other. He unified the Mongol peoples into one state, the so-called Zunghar Confederation. Galdan requested that Chinese officials visit his headquarters to collect the tribute he wanted to give China. Galdan even proposed a middle ground approach by offering to use Chinese diplomatic rituals instead of the simple Mongol rites. He also sent lavish tribute gifts to China including 400 horses, 60 camels, 300 sable, and 500 ermine pelts. In this diplomatic exchange, the middle ground approach worked, though only temporarily. In a divide-and-conquer strategy, Chinese diplomats agreed to support Galdan and help him conquer his Mongol rivals. Galdan in return pledged to prevent Mongol raiding parties from attacking the Chinese frontier. Both sides had their own interests in cooperation. Galdan wanted support against Mongol enemies and later played Russia off against the China–Mongol alliance. The Chinese supported Galdan because they preferred to deal with one strong ruler who could provide stability amidst the chaotic atmosphere of rivalry in Mongolia. But both sides understood this middle ground accommodation as a temporary situation, and in a few years the Chinese and Mongols were once again enemies and eventually war broke out.

When the Russians and Chinese gathered at the Russian frontier town of Nerchinsk in 1689, they intended to more clearly demarcate their mutual border. The Mongol leader Galdan was not invited (though a Mongol delegation was there). In the negotiations between Russia and China that followed, the Chinese brought two Jesuit priests who played a crucial role in the negotiations. The Russians wanted the language of negotiations to be in the Mongol language (showing how much influence the Mongols still wielded) but the Chinese refused, instead allowing the Jesuits to insist on Latin for negotiations. The Mongols played no official role in the negotiations but they were the silent third partner since at that point their loyalty to either the Chinese or Russians could swing the balance of power in the region. In the end they agreed to a treaty that had no role for the Mongols and thereby minimized Mongol influence, signaling that the Mongol attempt to play Russians and Chinese off against each other had failed.

The resulting agreement helped free China to focus on destroying Galdan by assuring that the Russians would not give him aid. In the ensuing years, the Chinese army hunted him down. When the Emperor Kangxi finally eliminated Galdan, the Chinese established their power on their western frontier, and like the Russians in central Asia, they abandoned any pretense of establishing a middle ground and instead emphasized Chinese dominance over the Mongols. Like Russia, they also rewrote their official history to emphasize the greatness of their conquest of the Mongols and their Emperor.

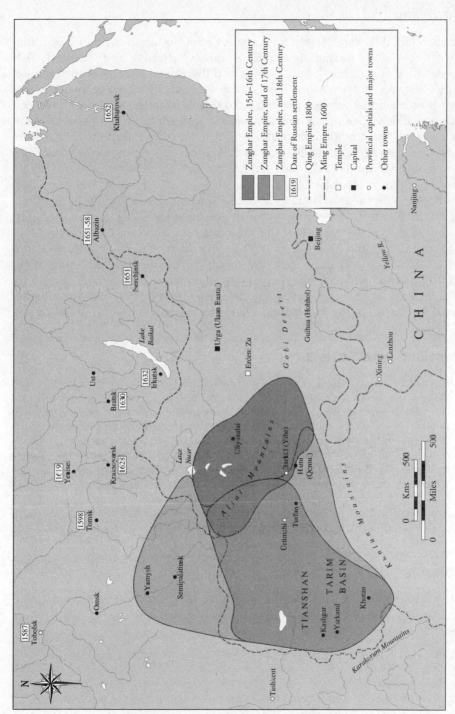

MAP 6.3 Map of Zunghar Empire

Zunghar Empire, 15th–16th Century
Zunghar Empire, end of 17th Century
Zunghar Empire, mid 18th Century
1619 Date of Russian settlement
Qing Empire, 1800
Ming Empre, 1600
Temple
Capital
Provincial capitals and major towns
Other towns

CHINA

Nanjing
Beijing
Yellow R.
Guihua (Hohhot)
Xining
Lanzhou

Goti Desert

Urga (Ulaan Baata)
Erden Zu

Khabarovsk 1652
Albazin 1651-58
Nerchinsk 1651
Lake Baikal
Irkutsk 1632
Bratsk 1630
Ust
Krasnoyarsk 1623
Yenisei 1619
Tomsk 1598
Omsk
Tobolsk 1587

Uliyasulai
Barkol (Yihe)
Hami (Qcmu)
Turfan
Ürümchi
Altai Mountains
Laca Nuar
Yamysh
Semipalatinsk
Kashgar
Yarkand
Khotan
TIANSHAN
TARIM BASIN
Kunlun Mountains
Karakorum Mountains
Tashkent

N

0   500
Kms

0   500
Miles

123

Conclusion

Between the 1400s and 1600s, Russia and China both moved from a position of weakness and vulnerability to one of military strength and conquest. The peoples they encountered, the Mongols and then the remnants of the Mongol Empire, invaded and exploited them in the 1200s to 1500s. When relative parity of power existed between the parties to this encounter, there were attempts to create middle ground accommodation by appealing to the others' cultural assumptions and traditions and allowing for differing interpretations of the same treaties and documents. During this epoch, violence was endemic in these frontier areas as both sides sought to exploit and at times terrorize the other. In addition, forced religious conversion was an important component of the encounter in the Russian case, as in the Spanish conquest of Latin America. But by 1800, with roles reversed, the steppe peoples including the Mongols were now under the control of the Russians and Chinese. Even though the Mongols (1200s) and Manchus (1640s) in an earlier time had conquered and revived the Chinese Empire, in the twentieth century they were seen as alien people by China, to be classified and controlled, while the Russians sought to crush the identity of steppe peoples in the Soviet period (1917–1991), and only after the collapse of the Soviet Union have their identities begun to reemerge.

Questions for Discussion

1. How did Russians and Chinese view the Golden Horde (western tribes) of the Mongol Empire in the early period of this encounter?
2. How did the frontier steppe peoples view and treat the Russians in the early period?
3. What were the goals of the Russian Empire in its encounter with steppe peoples?
4. What did the middle ground between the steppe tribes and Russia consist of? Between China and the Mongol Zunghar state? How successful and long-lasting were these accommodations?
5. What were the new approaches and ways of thinking of frontier peoples as Russia and China became stronger in the later period of contact?
6. How did Russia's emphasis on conversion to Orthodox Christianity operate in practical terms among frontier peoples?

Endnotes

1. Michael Khordakovsky, *Russia's Steppe Frontier: The Making of a Colonial Empire* (Bloomington, IN: Indiana University Press, 2002), p. 54.
2. Ibid., p. 51.
3. Ibid., p. 35.
4. Ibid., p. 39.
5. Ibid., p. 186.
6. Ibid., p. 186.
7. Yuri Slezkine, *Arctic Mirrors: Russia and the Small Peoples of the North* (Ithaca, NY: Cornell University Press, 1994), p. 57.
8. Khordakovsky, *Russia's Steppe Frontier*, p. 187.
9. Ibid., p. 198.

PART D

Imperialism and Nationalism in the Modern World

7

Altered States: British Imperialism and the Rise of Indian Nationalism

Colonialism is often viewed solely in terms of political conquest and exploitation. However, the assertion of power by one people over others who lie beyond one's own frontiers involves much more than the clash of arms or the extraction of resources. It is a struggle over ideas and identities, about the changing cultural attitudes of empire-builders toward their conquered subjects and the multifaceted responses of their "subject-peoples" to subjugation, in cultural as well as political terms. Moreover, long after the battles for and against empire have passed into history, the cultural legacies of former imperial societies linger on, shaping the lives, thoughts, arts, and literatures of both the former colonizer and the colonized. This is particularly true of the nature and legacy of the 400-year long "and counting" encounter between colonial and post-colonial Britain and India.

BRITAIN DISCOVERS INDIA

In 1600, Queen Elizabeth of England granted a royal charter to the Governor and Company of Merchants of London Trading into the East Indies (later known as the East India Company) giving it a monopoly of English trade with India, China, and the then little known lands of Southeast Asia between them. Not long after, she dispatched an Ambassador, Sir Thomas Roe, to the court of India's Mughal Empire, then arguably the greatest Empire of the day, to formally negotiate conditions of trade between England and India.

From this vantage point, Roe learned firsthand how the Mughals, relatively recent invaders from central Asia, had pursued the pattern of all previous intruders dating back at least to the ancient Persians and Greeks. Like their predecessors, the Mughals sought to "indigenize" their rule by engaging in cultural fusion. The Mughal's religious policy was then the world's most tolerant: Some of the highest officers of this Muslim-ruled state were held by Hindus. Mughal art, architecture, music, and even food were a blend of central Asia and South Asian elements. The Mughals hoped to solidify popular support by astute administrative policies, which ranged from a form of checks and balances and separation of powers then unknown in Europe to a progressive taxation system that helped India to achieve the highest gross national product (GNP) in the late medieval and early modern world. Roe was so impressed with the diversity and grandeur of the Mughal Court that he advised his countrymen that if they wished to prosper in India they should respect Mughal authority and seek their profits "at sea and in quiet trade."

The merchants of the East India Company (EIC) initially complied with Roe's admonition, even though it forced them to show subservience to both Muslim officials and Hindu merchants, who regarded them as denizens of an inferior civilization. Muslim distaste for all Europeans was rooted in the long history of cultural as well as military rivalry between Christianity and Islam, especially in the Indian Ocean, which the pioneering Portuguese had entered killing Muslims on sight. Hindus regarded all foreigners as *mlecchas*, so low in the hierarchy of their traditional "caste" system as to be outside of it. Hindus joined with Muslims in finding Europeans literally, as well as morally, unclean. The English rarely bathed as they thought it would induce influenza, and, lacking toilet paper, they thought nothing of wiping their rears with their hands and cleaning their hands off on their clothes. In keeping with Shakespeare's contemporary portrayal of his nation's merchants, the early agents of the EIC were both proud and greedy. They endured their inferior social position in India rather than jeopardize their commerce, which often earned over a 100 percent return on their investment in each ship returning from Asia.

Two factors altered the relative position of the English and their Indian hosts. The first was the slow decline of the central authority of the Mughal Empire. With each passing generation, Mughal emperors slowly abandoned their policy of religious toleration in favor of a more fundamentalist Islamic agenda. They also exhausted the Empire's revenues by profligate monument-building (including the beautiful but budget-busting Taj Mahal) and engaged in many ill-advised wars, including a futile attempt to conquer Afghanistan. Fed up with Mughal maladministration, many Mughal provincial governors and the empire's long-serving Hindu allies sought autonomy within the empire or broke away to establish their own states, which then began to fight among themselves. The collapse of Mughal central authority left the subcontinent vulnerable to foreign invasion and provided a motive, or at least a rationale, for foreign conquest.

Sir Thomas Roe was just one of many supplicants for the favor of
Mughal Emperor Jahangir in 1615. The appearance of European-style
angels adoring the Emperor indicates that the Moghuls sought to
appropriate Western images of grace and power to exalt their own
authority.   The Granger Collection, NY.

The second factor that altered relations between Indians and the
British was the increasing aggressiveness of the EIC associated with a more
bellicose British posture in world affairs. In the mid-1600s, the largely
Protestant English experienced an internationally as well as religiously
colored civil war at home and initiated the brutal subjugation of their Catholic
neighbor, Ireland. These events sharpened deep-rooted prejudices against

non-Protestant and non-Anglo-Saxon peoples and encouraged the recourse to military force wherever it might enrich the British nation. At the same time, Britain had engaged in war with the EIC's chief trade rivals in Asia, including the Dutch, who had largely succeeded in driving English merchants out of Southeast Asia's enormously profitable Spice Islands. Turmoil at home and abroad jeopardized the Company's royally licensed monopoly of trade in India, as Britain's hard-pressed rulers sought to generate more wealth by allowing other British trading companies to compete in the Company's Asian markets. Within India, the decline of the Mughal authority exposed Company merchants to attacks associated with anti-Mughal rebellions and to what the Company deemed harassment by newly emergent Mughal successor states who quite naturally sought to impose their own taxes on European traders.

The combination of Mughal decline, rising British imperial ambitions, rising prejudice against the inhabitants of the world beyond England, and unprecedented commercial competition influenced the EIC directors to take an increasingly bolder stance in the company's relations with Indian rulers. In 1600, Queen Elizabeth had written to the Mughal Court conveying her admiration of its humanity as well as power. By 1754, the English in India felt only contempt for what little remained of Mughal administration and took to boasting that "the country might be conquered and laid under contribution as easily as the Spaniards overwhelmed the naked Indians of America." The decisive opportunity as well as a powerful stimulus to do just that was provided by a fresh round of British wars with its European rivals, this time with France. These conflicts spilled into India (as well as America, where they were known as the French and Indian Wars). The French pursued a strategy in India of playing rival Indian states and their competing internal elites against each other to both gain control over them and use them against the British. Fortunately for British interests, the agents of the EIC were able to turn this strategy against the French, and later used it to seize much of southern India. In 1757, the richest province in India, Bengal, fell victim to the Company's intrigues. Over the next 100 years, Bengal's resources and its European-trained and armed Indian army were used to gain control over much of South Asia. In the process, two fifths of the Indian subcontinent, deemed lacking in commercial value, was left in the hands of politically subordinated Indian princes.

THE ORIENTALISTS

As the EIC's power and influence spread across the subcontinent, so too did its contact with its inhabitants. Warren Hastings (1732–1818), perhaps the EIC official most responsible for setting the tone and pace of the expansion of British authority after its conquest of Bengal, had spent much of his life in India and was impressed by the richness of Indian culture. His interest was shared by a few other EIC key officials in Bengal, particularly William Jones and James Prinsep. Through their collective study of Sanskrit, the ancient Indian sacred language, they helped establish the existence of what thereafter became known as the Indo-European family of languages which included Greek, Latin, Persian, the Germanic and Romance languages (French, Italian, and Spanish), and English.

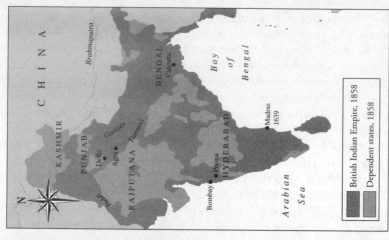

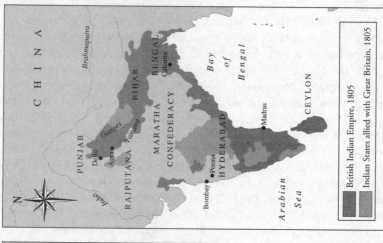

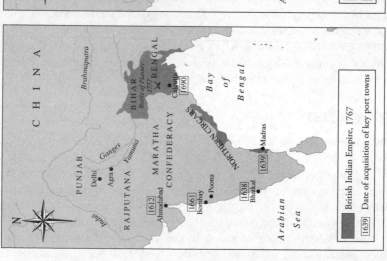

MAP 7.1 Map of British Empire in India

Such work also led to the study of the sacred *Upanishads*, an ancient Indian philosophical treatise dating from the time before the rise of Buddhism. The *Upanishads* suggested that Hinduism possessed an underlying rationalism and a concept of a single divine spiritual consciousness. This idea appealed to Westerners, who had been inclined to reject the ritual sacrifices and polytheism of contemporary Hindu society as morally debased. It now appeared to them that the two civilizations shared a past in which Indians may have once been on a par with the West. These discoveries won the financial backing of wealthy British aristocrats who saw themselves as patrons of the rationalist, scientific, and progressive ideas associated with the European Enlightenment. The Enlightenment, like the European Renaissance before it, had been inspired by Greek and Roman philosophy, which offered tantalizing references to India, with whom the Greeks and Romans had significant cultural as well as commercial contact. British scholars of the Enlightenment were eager to study the culture that was certainly connected to and possibly influenced the Greco-Roman world. Those who pursued this course of study were called Orientalists (a word derived from the Latin word for "East"), which meant students of Eastern knowledge.

Given the decline of centralized Mughal authority and the subsequent political disunity that had permitted the EIC to gain dominion over the subcontinent, most Orientalists regarded their own culture as superior to that of India in its current state. But some Orientalists went further, holding that even if Europeans were presently superior to India materially, Indians were not then, nor were they ever, inferior to Europe spiritually and philosophically. One such thinker was Charles Stuart, a Major-General in the Company's employ. Stuart closely studied and then lived by Hindu customs and manners, earning him the sobriquet, "Hindoo Stuart." He drew attention to what he saw as the parallels between God's taking of human form in the story of Jesus Christ and the life of the popular Hindu avatar of God, Lord Krishna, who was the focus of the most popular piece of sacred Indian literature, the *Bhagavad Gita*. Stuart also drew attention to the great similarities in the divine instructions given by Jesus and Krishna; both stressed love of God as the vehicle of salvation. Stuart published a book (*Vindication of the Hindoos*, 1808) which sought to refute the prevailing criticism of Indians as a debased people. Stuart concluded that "Hinduism little needs the meliorating hand of Christianity to render its votaries a sufficiently correct and moral people for all the useful purposes of a civilized society."[1]

Most of Stuart's colleagues were not prepared to so deeply enter into Indian culture, but had, of necessity, to adapt to Indian conditions. They were dependent on Indians as bankers and brokers who served as middlemen between the British and the Indian producers of high-value commercial products, such as fine cotton textiles and, later, tea and opium. This acculturation took many forms. Europeans in India smoked tobacco in a water pipe (*hookah*) and lived in cottages adapted to the Indian climate called *bungalows*, which, along with other loan words, such as *pajama* and *khaki* (dust colored) passed into the English language.

A few European traders rose above English social prejudices against Hindus and Muslims to develop friendships with Indians. A small number married into the Indian population. Many more took Indian mistresses (*bibis*), whom they provided with homes of their own. These bibigarhs (literally mistresses' houses), along with "nautch" parties featuring Indian dance and musical performances, served as bridges between English and Indian cultures.

Yet another bridge was formed by English tourists who had come to see the Company's achievement. Visiting Britons were deeply moved by the varieties of historical artifacts found in the Indian landscape and its ancient history, a sentiment encouraged by the Romantic Movement then sweeping European salons. Tourists spending an afternoon visiting vine-covered Roman ruins in Italy to experience sentiments of lost glories found that these scenes paled in comparison to nights spent among the palaces of India's many past empires crumbling in tropical heat. This was the view taken by the English painter, William Hodges, who came to India with the idea to make a living selling such exotic scenes to the British public. However, like most Orientalists, Hodges tempered his own sense of wonder at the glories of India's past with a sense of respect for Indians living in the present. Hodges was a frequent visitor to mixed parties of English and Indians in Calcutta, the new capital of British Indian enterprise. There European traders were too busy making money alongside Hindu bankers and merchants to observe the Black Town–White Town division that characterized older Company cities like Madras and Bombay. Hodges remarked that it was "highly entertaining to an inquisitive mind, to associate with a people whose manners are more than 3,000 years old; and to observe in them that attention and polished behavior which usually marks the most highly civilized state of society."[2]

THE BENGAL RENAISSANCE

Indians with inquisitive minds found the British just as interesting. Understandably, most Muslim and Hindu leaders rightly saw the coming of the English as a threat to their traditional political and social dominance. However, elite businessmen, including landlords and merchants, rapidly adjusted to the expanding EIC presence in their society, as they had in the past embraced Greek, Roman, Arab, and Turk as well as Mughal culture and trade. After all, Indian long-distance traders had been among the first to embrace both Buddhism and later Islam and were largely responsible for spreading these faiths through much of the rest of Asia. Some of those Indians benefiting from the wealth generated by commercial relations with the Company became an Indian version of the English Orientalists, in terms of both the depth of their curiosity in foreign ideas and the variety of their responses to them. Ishwar Chandra Vidyāsāgar (1790–1891), a learned Brahmin from western Bengal, first introduced the ideas of Francis Bacon and other British philosophers into the curricula of Calcutta's Sanskrit College (founded in 1824) solely on the basis of what he perceived to be the high quality of their thoughts. Bengali intellectuals, like Ram Mohan Roy (1772–1833), were impressed by the ways in which the West had already achieved cultural innovations, such as women's equality, which they were then seeking in their own society. In Roy's case, this meant a meeting of the two cultures at the same point. Roy, like the Orientalists, viewed the *Upanishads* as proof that the progressive truths of the West were embodied in the sacred texts of Hinduism. He believed that these texts served as evidence that Hindus should reject what he saw as backward Hindu customary beliefs on the grounds that they had no basis in divine scripture. These customary beliefs included the caste system, polygamy, child marriage, and dowry-giving. Roy created a movement called the Brahmo Samaj (a society devoted to the rationally highest form of religious thought), which sought to eliminate such practices.

A similar effort to purify Islamic society, couched in revivalist terms, was adopted by Islamic reform movements such as the Faraizi, Tariquah-i-Muhhamadiyah, Taaiyni, and Ahl-i-Hadith. However, just as Charles Stuart saw Indian society as more advanced in some respects than Western philosophy and religion, a few Indians, drawn together by a charismatic teacher at Calcutta's Hindu College (founded in 1817), Henry Louis Vivian Derozio (1809–1831), rejected Indian traditions and customs wholesale and espoused Western conceptions of rationalism to the point of atheism.

Scholars have since likened this wide-ranging process of cultural reexamination and self-renewal to the European Renaissance, with Bengal serving in the role of Italy and Calcutta as Florence. This parallel was certainly apt in one respect: The Renaissance luminary Galileo suffered for his advanced rationalist views at the hands of religious traditionalists and so did Vidyāsāgar and Derozio—both lost their teaching positions for taking their engagement of Western knowledge a bit too far. But, as was true of the Renaissance, and again of much of Indian history: once the process of self-reflection, adaptation, and cultural renewal had begun, it was impossible to stop. Some scholars today argue that this process was of significance only to Indian elites seeking to find a place in a colonial order; hence they see the first Indian-produced performance of Shakespeare in India in 1852 as a mere effort of Hindu merchants to impress their English masters with their growing European tastes. Others note that Roy's Brahmo Samaj deeply influenced the wider Hindu world through their advocacy of religious and social reforms. Since the spirit of both renewal and hybridity or cultural synthesis was a common theme in Indian culture. It is more likely that Indians were drawn to Shakespeare not out of a desire to endear themselves to their colonial rulers, but because they saw in his works universal themes addressed in their own classical literature.

REMAKING A CIVILIZATION

However, just as the gates of cultural exchange were opening in Calcutta, they were being closed in London. The Company's territorial acquisitions on the subcontinent had attracted the interest of the British Parliament, whose conservative leader, William Pitt (1759–1806), sought compensation in India for the recent loss of its colonies in North America to the American

Revolution, which had won the support of liberals at home. Moreover, Britain had emerged from its wars with monarchical and then revolutionary France as the world's most efficient state and leading military power, but it was greatly divided on social and political issues, divisions Pitt sought to heal. This not only put all of South Asia in Britain's imperial crosshairs, but also enmeshed it within the tumultuous debate in Britain over its emerging national values and imperial culture. To avoid culture war at home, Parliament sought to use India as a distant, and thus safe, socio-political laboratory for addressing ideas such as the relationship between the Western secular state and rising Christian evangelicalism. The EIC had no desire to have its administration and profits in India troubled in this fashion. But the British government gradually transferred to itself the power to do so. In its view, the EIC had never been a "mere association of traders … formed for the extension of British commerce, but in reality a delegation of the whole power and sovereignty of this kingdom sent into the East."[3]

The weight upon India of Parliament's growing influence over Company rule in India was immediately felt. Its society was to be remade in the pursuit of an agenda most clearly expressed by James Mill (1773–1836) in his immensely successful three-volume *History of India* (1818). Mill argued that, rather than studying Indian culture, as the Orientalists urged, the West should be teaching India Western culture. Mill had never visited India, but believed that Indians were barely past what contemporary European philosophers called the "barbarian stage" of human society, and required the "civilizing" hand of efficient British rule. Mill's work captured and reflected the rising cultural confidence that accompanied Britain's newly dominant global role. His much-quoted views on India provided the foundation for later more overtly racist rationales supporting British imperialism, such as social Darwinism.

However, even some among the virtual sea of would-be "Indian reformers" that emerged in Mill's wake, such as Thomas Babington Macaulay (1800–1859), had serious doubts about the morality or appropriateness of surrendering India to Britain's rising imperial impulse. In what became known as the "liberal" school of British thought on India, Macaulay argued that British ideas of commercial profit as well as liberty should rule out any idea of making Indians permanent servants of a British Empire. But even he joined in Mill's attack on traditional Indian culture, declaring that "a single shelf of a good European library was worth the whole native literature of India…"[4]

After his promotion to a high administrative post in India, Macaulay sought to literally "anglicize" it by making English the official language of the higher courts in place of the Persian used by the Mughals, and replacing Sanskrit with English in all higher educational institutions supported by the Company. Macaulay thus discarded the previous policy of indigenization which was long the key to successful foreign rule in India. That mattered little to Macaulay, as he did not expect such changes would reach down to or redeem India's backward masses. His intent was to create an elite hybrid class that would be "Indian in blood, but English in taste and sensibility."[5] Britain's goal in India, according to Macaulay, was to so completely transfer its more efficient way of life to Indians as to ensure that India would eventually become a well-governed independent state, whose masses would be as eager to consume British goods ("wearing our broadcloth working with our cutlery") as its westernized elites, who were already seeking to consume its cultural values.[6]

Liberal reformers forced changes in the Company's charter that included the right of Indians to enter into the government of their own country, but, like British Orientalists before them, they could make little headway against the rising tide of self-interested British imperialism. Most Englishmen believed if India was to be reformed, this would be done via the direct intervention of British administrators and missionaries from "home," not by slow evolutionary exposure to Western political education and by Indians themselves. The color of the rulers of British India was to be white, not brown. A small measure of this change was that once valued and honored officers of the Indian army whose fathers were English and mothers were Indian fell from favor for having the taint of Indian blood. Larger changes soon followed.

Inspired by Mill's condemnation of traditional society in India, British missionaries brought pressure on the British government and the EIC to criminalize or abolish many traditional Indian customs and religious practices. Chief among these was the attempt in 1829 to curtail the rare practice among high-caste Hindus of *sati* (inducing the death of a young widow on her older husband's funeral pyre to prevent any subsequent behavior that might otherwise bring discredit on his name). British evangelical leaders pressed for the EIC to end this practice as a means of soliciting conversions

A "sati" portrayed by an Indian artist as a mark of honor rather than a horror, as usually portrayed by British illustrators.   The Granger Collection, NY.

among living widows, who might more readily accept Christianity if they saw it as a means to escape death or living as outcastes in their own homes, as was the alternative to *sati* in some Hindu families.

Parliament's hand-picked governor-general of the Company's affairs William Bentinck, viewed *sati* as barbaric, as had the Emperor Akbar (1542–1605) and Ram Mohun Roy, who, a decade before Bentinck's legislation, had fought for the abolition of *sati* on the grounds that there was

Indian soldiers, or sepoys, made up a large portion of the rank and-file troops in the armies of British India. Commanded by European officers and armed, uniformed, and drilled according to European standards, troops such as those pictured here were recruited from the colonized peoples and became one of the mainstays of all European colonial regimes. The European colonizers preferred to recruit these soldiers from subject peoples whom they saw as particularly martial. In India, these included the Sikhs (pictured here) and Marattas, as well as Gurkhas recruited from neighboring but independent Nepal.   British Library Board, WD2413.

no justification for the practice in "revealed" Hindu literature. But many Indians—even those who opposed the practice—questioned the right of foreigners to make such decisions. Such was Bentinck's general contempt for Indian culture that he sought no indigenous precedent nor to justify the British right to interfere with Indian customs. As one of his officers told a delegation of Indians complaining about such alleged foreign interference, "You say that it is your custom to burn widows. Very well. We also have a custom: when men burn a woman alive, we tie a rope around their necks and we hang them."[7]

The most fateful of these reforms were those that affected the EIC's army, which was composed of over 350,000 Indian soldiers, many of whom belonged to the highest Indian castes. These reforms included the lifting of the ban on Christian preachers proselytizing among these troops; thereafter soldiers were ordered to stand at attention on parade grounds and compelled to listen to a Christian preacher tell them they were all going to hell unless they converted. A small number of EIC officials who still possessed Orientalist-style "sympathy for the old ways" warned that Indians could not be expected to long endure such treatment. Their warnings went unheeded.

THE WAR OF 1857 AND ITS AFTERMATH

The bloodiest revolt against British rule anywhere in their vast empire the spring and summer of 1857. The British called it "the Great Mutiny" because it was ignited by resistance among Indian soldiers to a procedure that would have them bite the end off newly-issued paper rifle cartridges that would maximize the efficiency of a new rifle being brought into service. The soldiers had come to believe, correctly as it turned out, that the cartridges had been coated with a greasy preservative derived from beef and pork fat. Hindu sepoys feared the loss of caste status associated with eating or touching beef to the lips, while Muslims were prohibited by Koranic injunction from ingesting pork products. The Company's army officers belatedly attempted to address these concerns, but years of thinking themselves superior to Indians so hampered their response that these efforts failed to defuse long-standing Indian discontent that the British meant to degrade their religious practices so as to speed the conversion of the Indian army and the Indian population at large to Christianity. Mass dismissals of Indian troops unwilling to use the new cartridges led to a revolt of soldiers which attracted the support of those most deeply affected by the British rule. These included maltreated Indian princes as well as alienated religious leaders of both major Indian faiths. What began as a revolt over greased cartridges morphed into a more general uprising in which hundreds of resident Company personnel and their families were attacked and often killed with great brutality by Indians not so much seeking to restore their traditional culture, but angered by the increasingly invasive nature of the British *Raj* or rule.

Several factors saved the EIC from being summarily expelled from the subcontinent. Along the coastlines and near major port cities, Indian commercial elites benefiting from the increased access to global markets made possible by British rule remained "loyal," as did many Indian princes who sought to profit from the defeat of traditional enemies who had joined the revolt. More important, no leader emerged to unite Muslim and Hindu soldiery against British rule or to secure and coordinate the participation of the Indian masses. By contrast, British soldiery rallied quickly, backed by recruits drawn from ethnic and religious minorities that had little to gain by any form of Muslim and/or Hindu rule. The British response was not only swift, but accompanied by terrifying reprisals as thousands of captured "mutineers" were lined up and tied with their backs to the mouths of cannons to be dismembered as the guns were fired off one by one. As a result, the Great Mutiny had largely run its course by July 1858, but it permanently darkened Indo-British relations for remainder of British rule on the subcontinent.

Rather than accept responsibility for causing this rupture in relations, the British government blamed the EIC, which it summarily disbanded. They also blamed the Indian people for what they saw as a barbaric betrayal of British trust. The latter view was opposed by British liberals, who forced the government to acknowledge that its exclusion of Indians from the country's administration had blinded it to public opinion there, as well as angering Indians by betraying earlier liberal promises of government employment. Yet, the selective memory of the brutality of the late war, shaped by the spread of wartime photographic images of Indian rather than British atrocities, led to the continued denial of any significant political rights to Indians.

Henceforth, the governing ethos of British rule was that Britain, as was expected of a superior civilization, would strive to advance India's "moral and material" progress through the introduction of British scientific knowledge, industry, and the commercial development of its resources, but in practice such innovations were applied so as to chiefly benefit Britain rather than India. Despite Britain's commitment to "free trade," India's own capacity for industry was throttled back so as not to threaten the progress of Britain's Industrial Revolution, while its environment was plundered for raw materials to feed the needs of British industry. India's people were linked closer together than ever before by modern rail and telegraphic communications, not to aid in their development, but to further assist in India's economic exploitation. India's forests resources were commercially "managed" by removing or criminalizing the activities of the thousands of woodland people who lived in them and depended upon them for their livelihoods. At the same time, a blind eye was turned to the fraudulent recruitment by British agents of thousands of poverty-stricken Indians who were lured by false promises of high wages to labor on railroad building projects and on plantations in Sri Lanka, Fiji, Trinidad, and Eastern Africa where few would ever be allowed to earn even the price of a return ticket. At the same time, relatively high paid British troops were sent to the subcontinent at the Indian taxpayer's expense as a guarantee against any further efforts to throw off the British imperial yoke, while Indian soldiers were deployed in British colonial wars in Afghanistan, Burma, China, Ethiopia, and elsewhere, again often at the expense of the Indian taxpayer.

One of the few lessons of the Great Mutiny accepted by the British was the need to abandon direct interference in Indian religion, but they continued to reshape Indian culture and society, if by less direct means. The Western idea of private ownership of land and the restriction of that right to men alone, first introduced into Bengal in the eighteenth century, was extended across the subcontinent, erasing more flexible and gender neutral traditional community rights and privileges and exposing Indians to market forces beyond their control. British ideas about government noninterference in economic affairs (laissez-faire) were applied to India in so doctrinaire a fashion that millions died in famines in south India from the 1870s to the 1900s because the British government refused on ideological grounds to divert food to the worst affected areas. British rulers, despite the horrific example of the Irish potato famine of the 1840s, still clung to the idea that the relief of famine was best left to the operation of a free market and should not be a government responsibility. As in Ireland, profit-seeking private merchants were expected to bring food to sell in India's famine-stricken areas—unfortunately, the famine was so prolonged that peasants had no money to buy the food they might offer, so merchants enjoying bumper crops in the north of India simply sold their produce at the high prices offered on the international market, which the British did nothing to discourage, let alone divert.

Moreover, as famine mounted, starving peasants were required to walk miles to any relief station as a qualification to receive food rations which some scholars estimate offered a level of nutrition below that given to concentration camp victims in World War II. These policies arose out of the desire of British conservative politicians to send a message to all British subjects that they were not ever to seek nor expect to receive a free lunch from their government.

Almost invisible, but just as deadly in the long term, was the equally doctrinaire introduction of the machinery of the modern state without consideration for Indian circumstances, best exemplified by the rigid application in India of the modern British census system. As employed in India, the census acted to fix with the force of modern law what had been a more fluid caste hierarchy. The census thus served to reduce caste mobility and harden both caste identity and caste competition. The census also hardened divisions between Hindus and Muslims. Moreover, British census categories and related population studies were based upon short-lived and now discredited European pseudo-scientific ideas, such as phrenology, in which human intelligence and behavior was believed to be determinable by an examination of the shape of the human skull.

OIL AND WATER

The latest such European novelties in racial theories were used not only in applying the census, but also to keep Indians in their place, which became a major post-Mutiny concern. This racism had many roots. Some were old and similar to the prejudice against Britain's Irish subjects; some accompanied the initial effort to "Anglicize" Indians; still others arose from the writings of men such as James Mill and the appeal of social Darwinism that was spurred by conceptions of national pride and power engendered by the Industrial Revolution. The British response to the Great Mutiny also played a role: Seeking greater security, British officials and their families increasingly lived apart from Indian communities in self-contained enclaves called "civil lines" adjoining Indian cities and military cantonments. This insularity was encouraged by the opening of the Suez Canal and arrival of steam travel in the Red Sea and Indian Ocean in the 1860s, which meant that officials could go "home" on leave more frequently. These improved means of travel also accelerated the arrival of British women, who were expected to bring British domesticity to the subcontinent and thus reenforce the growing conception that Britons in service to India sacrificially bound themselves to exile in a savage land in the dim hope of bringing civilization to the heathen. Both factors contributed to near-apartheid social relations between Britons and Indians that to some degree persisted until the granting of independence. These conditions sickened even so committed an imperial handyman as Charles "Chinese" Gordon (1833–1885), whose exposure to Anglo-Indian society moved him to make the following remark about British officials in India:

> To me they are utterly wrong about the government of the subject races. They know nothing of the hearts of those peoples and oil and water would sooner mix as these two races. Men may argue as they like, but our tenure of India is very little greater than it was a hundred years ago. The people's interest not having been...involved in our prosperity or disaster they are equally indifferent to either, in fact, they may hope to gain more from our disasters than our prosperity.[8]

Gordon's comments proved prophetic: Every major step taken by British Indian administrators in the aftermath of the War of 1857, from initially crushing traditional elites to the enshrinement of racist policies that assumed Indian inferiority, served to undermine British authority. Their assault on tradition helped clear the way for, and their racism helped inspire, a new generation of progressive Indian leaders emerging from the Bengal Renaissance. These included Swami Vivekananda (1863–1902), who electrified attendees of the 1893 World Council of Religions meeting in Chicago with a lecture that left its audience in no doubt that India was the home of great religious and philosophical traditions. Muslim intellectual Syed Ahmed Khan's 1858 pamphlet, *Asbab-e-Bhaghawath-e-Hind* (*The Causes of the Indian Revolt*), boldly attributed the "Mutiny" to unethical British policy, and Muslim thinkers in central India and elsewhere began to formulate ideas embraced by today's Islamicist movements by arguing that the power of Western civilization was based on its secularism and that it was up to the Muslim world to defend God's cause by rising to that challenge, even by using the West's own ill-begotten tools against them.

Whether by seeking accommodation with the West or rejecting its values, South Asians began to believe that they were the moral, intellectual, and cultural equals of their British rulers and Western culture at large. This sense of growing confidence was expressed both culturally and politically. The subject of perhaps the first modern Indian historical novel, *Anandamath* (*The Abbey of Bliss*, 1882), by Bankim Chandra Chattopadhyay (1838–1894) took the theme of expelling foreign rulers as a prelude to self-rule. It inspired *Vande Matram*, later the national anthem of the independent Republic of India. A leading Indian political economist, Dadabhai Naoroji (1825–1917), set the base line for all intellectual critiques of empire by arguing that the growing wealth and power of the West was made possible by "draining" wealth from its colonies. In 1913, Bengali poet and philosopher Rabindranath Tagore (1861–1941) became the first Asian to receive a Nobel Prize. The significance of this award, for Literature, was magnified in the minds of Indians as it honored a collection of visionary poetry, *Gitanjali*, that expressed the inner spirit of Indian people, a spirit even British rule could not stifle ("They come with their laws and their codes to bind me fast; but I evade them ever, for I am only waiting for love to give myself up at last into his hands").[9]

This self-confidence encouraged a belief among many Western-educated Indians that the achievement of a modern national identity, such as that enjoyed by their colonial masters, was within their reach. This outlook was reenforced by their growing command of British political ideals and also by contemporary European developments such as the rise to nationhood of Italy (1815–1871), whose diverse modern population had not possessed a common identity until its people joined together to throw off their foreign masters. Indians were well aware that their own leaders were members of a Western-educated elite vulnerable to using their mastery of the modern state apparatus to benefit themselves only, but this elite struggled with this problem perhaps more honestly than the British upper classes dealt with their own lower classes. They also had to confront the traditional divisions among Indians—by region as well as religion and ethnicity—which the British had exacerbated by taking no deliberate steps to unify the people they had conquered piecemeal. Those who spoke for India's freedom also had to face challenges from both Hindu and Muslim fundamentalists and by many oppressed minority groups who saw little future in a secular state decided by "one man, one vote," in which the majority always ruled.

India's answer to these difficulties was ultimately to be found in the eclectic political philosophy of the man who more than any other single figure guided South Asia on its path to independence, Mohandas Karamchand Gandhi (1869–1948). Like other many nationalist leaders, Gandhi was a British-trained lawyer who had admired as well resented British rule from childhood and had become as well-versed in the work of Western political theorists as in the texts of the classical Indian political tradition. However, unlike most of his contemporaries, he most closely identified with those

Indians of the past, such as Ram Mohun Roy, who sought to build a bridge between tradition and modernity. While a law student in London, he had been surprised and delighted to find himself welcomed into the homes of English men and women, a gesture that in British India would have been the subject of hostile comment. His experience of the kindness of Britons who had no direct stake in empire helped Gandhi toward the realization that the moral faults that produced the suffering of colonized people at the hands of their colonizers lay not in a clash of civilizations, but was a result of a political relationship—the domination of one people over another—which varied in strength and could, like most human hatred, be dissolved by the force of compassion. Gandhi sought to accomplish this through means by which

In 1931, Mahatma Gandhi returned to Great Britain for the first time since his student days in 1915. Though his attempts to negotiate with British leaders came to little, he was a great hit with the British public, in part because of his sly sense of humor. When asked if he was embarrassed to meet King George V in the scant khadi-cloth apparel he wears in this photo, Gandhi quipped that the King Emperor had on enough clothes for the both of them.   Ullstein Bild/The Granger Collection, NY.

the oppressor could regain their sense of humanity and allow the oppressed to embrace them as friends. The means Gandhi developed to achieve these ends was, he hoped, the answer not merely to colonial oppression, but to all division and oppression, of rich over poor, of high caste over low, and even of husband over wife. That answer was formed from many sources, which included nearly equal parts of the call of the textual centerpiece of modern Hinduism, the *Bhagavad Gita*, for self-less action in pursuit of righteousness, the Sermon on the Mount's evocation of the transformative power of love, American philosopher Henry David Thoreau's (1817–1862) practice of civil disobedience against government-sponsored injustice, and the Jain-Buddhist philosophy of *ahimsa* (nonviolence) that had permeated Gandhi's childhood environment in western India. Through a synthesis of these ideas he called *satyagraha* (holding fast to the truth), Gandhi created a vehicle for disciplined, but nonviolent political action designed to persuade the oppressor to accept the "truth" of the near-universal religious dictum that injustice was the denial to others of that which one desires for one's self. In Gandhi's view, violence against the oppressor merely enabled him or her to justify their own violent behavior. Nonviolent resistance not only removed this path of escape, but offered open arms to the oppressor, thus creating space for reconciliation.

Gandhi's appeal attracted the support of liberals in Britain and the world over, and succeeded in fatally undermining British resolve to remain in India, a resolve already weakened by two world wars and the Great Depression. However, the machinations of imperial-minded British politicians like Winston Churchill (who voiced racially colored arguments that chiefly focused on holding onto India for its economic value) complicated the conditions of the British exit from India. By playing Hindu against Muslims and aristocratic princes against mass politicians to the very end, the last generation of British rulers in India helped produce a catastrophic partition of the subcontinent along religious lines that lead to unprecedented conflict and left South Asia more divided than when the British began to assert its political authority more than 200 years earlier.

The British people often regard their empire in India as having an important role in the growth of the British state and in the shaping of the British national identity. It is even regarded by some with nostalgia as a marker for the high-watermark of British national power. Many see their impact on the subcontinent as beneficial, citing the region's political and social integration driven by British-introduced transportation and communication networks (rail and telegraph). They also boast that British rule introduced parliamentary democracy and modern industry into India as well as capitalist commercial and financial institutions. The recent purchase by India's Tata Industries of one of Britain's biggest steelmakers, as well as the emblematically British Rover and Jaguar car companies, the evolution of Britain's national food from roast beef to an Indian dish, chicken tikka masala, and the frequent winning by Indians of the Man Booker Prize given annually in Britain to the finest novel in English (past winners include V. S. Naipaul and Salman Rushdie) are viewed by many Britons as illustrations of their Indian empire's ultimately positive role in the process of globalization.

Conclusion

There is no doubt that Indians value the British-inspired constitutional frame-work that supports their political systems. They are especially devoted to one of its corollaries, an independent judiciary. But while they appreciate the value of these "gifts," they argue that such things were already inherent in their own traditions or could have been acquired without their political sub-jugation. They despair of the *Raj*'s more troublesome legacies. Britain's hasty exit, leading to the partition of the subcontinent, not only cost the lives of millions through religious violence, but left its successor states with festering border conflicts that have taken thousands of more lives since independence. That Indians win prizes for their novels in English in Britain is a reminder of the cost as well as benefits of globalization, so much so that extreme Indian nationalists at one time urged Indians to throw their English typewriters and keyboards into the Indian Ocean.

Some Indian scholars have recently laid stress on the residual evil of "post-coloniality," wherein former colonial populations remain wedded to colonial-era models of thought and socio-political and economic practice, as well as language. This includes the British model of the census that still serves to divide Indians, if no longer by measuring people's skulls. The Cambridge University–educated first Prime Minister of India, Jawaharlal Nehru saw Western-style factories as "temples" of progress. His successors have perpetuated the colonial-era emphasis on "development" that lacks sufficient attention to its environmental or human cost. This tendency aided in the recent triumph of neo-liberalism or free-market capitalist ideas in India over Gandhian concepts of devotion to the collective good, while generating vast profits for India's economic elite.

While Indians take great pride in their current rivalry with China in their bid to become the world's largest economy, they see their growing status in the world as evidence of the strength of their traditions, not mere borrowing from others. They remind those who regard the legions of rising Indian software engineers as an emblem of Western achievement that Indians were the originators of the numerical ("Arab" numerals) and the binomial system (based on one and zeroes, zero being an Indian invention) that undergirds all computer programming. However, much as their colonized ancestors embraced Shakespeare, Indians today remain open to that which they deem valuable in global culture, whatever its source.

Questions for Discussion

1. What was the nature of the initial encounter between Indians and the British? How did they first view each other and what factors led to a change in their relations between 1600 and 1757?
2. What aspects of cultural exchange can be seen in British "Orientalist" thought and in the ideas associated with the Bengal Renaissance?

3. What were some similarities and differences between the views of India found in the ideas of James Mill and Thomas Babington Macaulay?
4. In what ways did Gandhi embody as well as address the encounter between Indians and the British? Between Indians and the world?
5. Why and in what ways does the colonial experience continue to affect British and Indian culture and society?

Endnotes

1. Charles Stuart, *Vindication of the Hindoos...by a Bengal officer* (London: J.W. Morris, Dunstable, Black Kingsbury, 1808).
2. William Hodges, *Travels in India: During the Years 1780, 1781, 1782, & 1783* (London: Printed for the author, and sold by J. Edwards, Pall-Mall, 1793), pp. 59–60.
3. Quoted in William Wilson Hunter, *A History of British India*, Vol. 2 (London: Longmans, Green and Company, 1900), p. 7.
4. Thomas Babington Macaulay, "Minute of 2 February 1835 on Indian Education," *Macaulay, Prose and Poetry*, selected by George Malcolm Young (Cambridge, MA: Harvard University Press, 1957), pp. 721–724, 729.
5. Thomas Babington Macaulay, "Speech in Parliament on the Government of India Bill, 10 July 1833," in George Malcolm Young (ed.), *Macaulay, Prose and Poetry* (Cambridge, MA: Harvard University Press, 1957), pp. 716–718. Macaulay remarked, "I feel that, for the good of India itself, the admission of natives to high office must be effected by slow degrees. But that, when the fullness of time is come, when the interest of India requires the change, we ought to refuse to make that change lest we should endanger our own power, this is a doctrine of which I cannot think without indignation...It would be, on the most selfish view of the case, far better for us that the people of India were well governed and independent of us, than ill governed and subject to us; that they were ruled by their own kings, but wearing our broadcloth, and working with our cutlery, than that they were performing their salams to English collectors and English magistrates, but were too ignorant to value, or too poor to buy, English manufactures...[that] would keep a hundred millions of men from being our customers in order that they might continue to be our slaves...Are we to keep the people of India ignorant in order that we may keep them submissive? Or do we think that we can give them knowledge without awakening ambition? Or do we mean to awaken ambition and to provide it with no legitimate vent? Who will answer any of these questions in the affirmative?"
6. Ibid.
7. See John Rosselli, *Lord William Bentinck: The Making of a Liberal Imperialist, 1774–1839* (Berkeley, CA: University of California, 1974).
8. Charles Gordon to Florence Nightingale, April 25, 1881, British Library Additional Manuscript 45806, ff. 136–137.
9. Rabindranath Tagore, *Gitanjali: Song Offerings, a Collection of Prose Translations Made by the Author from the Original Bengali. With an introduction by W. B. Yeats to William Rothenstein* (London: India Society, 1913), p. 10.

The Japanese in East Asia: A Non-Western Empire and Nationalist Reactions

Japan built a large empire before World War II consisting of Taiwan, Korea, and eventually Manchuria (Manchukuo), the eastern parts of China and islands in the central Pacific. After the bombing of Pearl Harbor, the Japanese expanded their empire to include much of Southeast Asia. From the perspective of its militarists, Japan's colonial possessions provided for Japan's national security and brought in crucial resources for Japan's economy. But the Japanese also claimed their empire brought progress and modernization to its colonies outside the negative influence of western imperialism. They saw themselves as bringing enlightenment to its subject peoples much as did western empire-builders in Africa and India (Chapters 7 and 9), and their attitude of superiority similar to that of Europeans tainted Japanese encounters within what Japanese came to call the "Greater East Asia Co-Prosperity Sphere." Much like the course of the colonial policies of European powers, Japan's self-interest and sense of superiority overwhelmed its Pan-Asian civilizing mission.

The Japanese islands represent a unique situation in the history of cross-cultural encounters because before 1853, the Japanese government, led by the Tokugawa shogun, pursued a strict policy of isolation from much of the rest of the world. From 1640 onward, when this policy was implemented, Japanese officials closed the border to all westerners except for one Dutch ship per year, which could land at the southern port of Nagasaki, but only at an artificial island (in the harbor of Nagasaki) called Deshima, specially built by the Japanese to allow the Dutch to bring in their trade goods without actually having contact with the Japanese. Therefore, the Japanese were one of few nations in the early modern period that sought to greatly limit cross-cultural encounters.

The threat of western conquest led Japan to close its borders in the 1600s, but in the late 1800s, the western threat reemerged in the unequal treaties, accompanied by growing trade imbalances and growing monetary debts. Japan's isolation was broken only occasionally by a few shipwrecked sailors, some of whom settled in Japan and became successful farmers or merchants. In 1853, the United States sent a fleet of warships to Japan to force open its trade and commerce and the era of isolation ended. Japan signed its first commercial treaty with the United States in 1858, allowing western trade and intercourse in selected ports. This so-called unequal treaty was modeled on several other treaties forced upon non-western countries in the 1800s, as far-flung as Egypt and China. The treaty was called unequal because the privileges granted favored the foreign powers. Treaty ports were opened up and foreign merchants and others arrived and took up residence there. The Japanese were forced to grant rights of extra-territoriality to these residents, which allowed foreigners in Japan to possess the same legal rights as if they were in their home country and included the right to trial in a consular court at their own embassy, not a Japanese court if the foreigner was charged with a crime. Further, the tariff structure in unequal treaties allowed for high tariffs (or taxes) on goods going from Japan to the West and low tariffs on goods shipped from the United States to Japan, which allowed the foreign country to make immense profits on their trade. The unequal treaties gave western powers like the United States, Great Britain, France, Russia, and other western nations an unfair advantage in trade and commerce. Westerners turned this unfair advantage into greater control over non-western nations until they dominated through spheres of influence without even having to conquer them. This was the case in China in the nineteenth century.

Japan responded with an aggressive campaign of self-strengthening (modernization), eventually canceling the unequal treaties, building its own industries, creating a modern army to protect against invasion, and building an empire to protect itself from its neighbors. The empire allowed Japan to gain access to raw materials, to demonstrate its strength and protect itself, and, according to Japanese nationalists, to bring progress and enlightenment to the rest of Asia outside of western imperialism. Japan's imperialism invited an encounter with other Asians.

ACQUIRING AN EMPIRE

Japan's empire began with the takeover of the Ryukku Islands in the 1870s from China. It accelerated when Japan fought and won two wars on the Asian continent, the Sino-Japanese War in 1894–1895, which led to its control

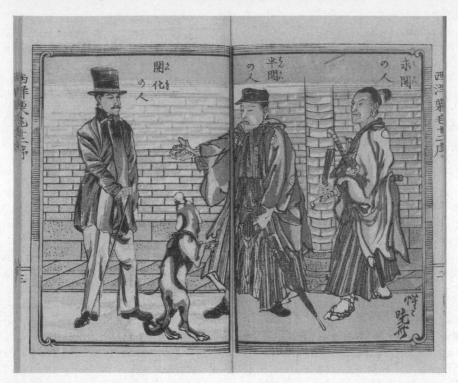

This Japanese woodblock demonstrates their awareness of the transforming modernization taking place in Japanese society at the end of the nineteenth century.   Trustees of the British Museum.

over Taiwan, and the Russo-Japanese War in 1904–1905, which allowed the Japanese to take over Korea and eventually annex it to their empire in 1910. Thereafter, the Japanese continually encroached farther into Manchuria, which is located in northeastern China.

Japan's encounter with the rest of Asia came at a time when loyalty to the nation and nationalist ideologies became very powerful worldwide. Strong nationalism had the tendency to distinguish those who belonged to the nation from those who were perceived to not belong. The basis of nationalism in the 1800s and 1900s was ethnic and linguistic unity. In Europe, this led to the unification of German-speaking and Italian-speaking peoples and the creation of the modern German and Italian nations. And it excluded from full citizenship those with different languages or ethnic backgrounds; the excluded populations often faced severe discrimination. A similar situation developed in the Japanese Empire. Because of Japan's very homogeneous ethnic makeup, ethnic purity was emphasized within its empire and Japanese nationalism allowed the Japanese to think of themselves as superior to their colonial subjects.

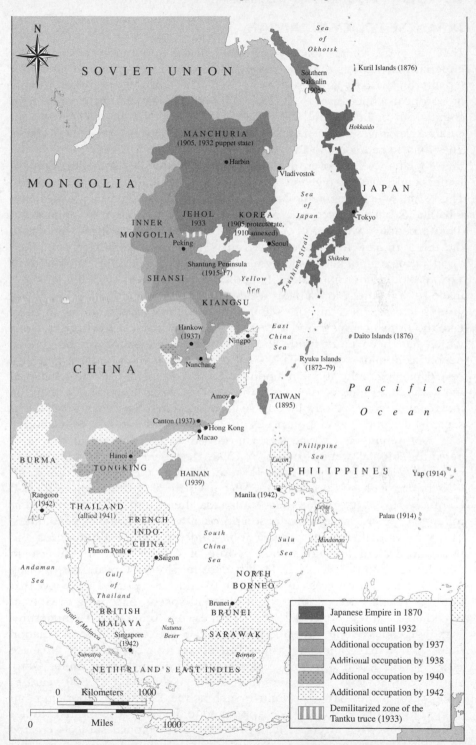

N

Sea of Okhotsk

Kuril Islands (1876)

SOVIET UNION

Southern Sakhalin (1905)

Hokkaido

MANCHURIA
(1905, 1932 puppet state)

•Harbin

•Vladivostok

J A P A N

MONGOLIA

INNER MONGOLIA

JEHOL
1933

KOREA
(1905, protectorate, 1910 annexed)

Sea of Japan

•Tokyo

•Peking

•Seoul

Shikoku

Shantung Peninsula
(1915–17)

Yellow Sea

SHANSI

KIANGSU

Hankow
(1937)

Ningpo

East China Sea

Daito Islands (1876)

Ryuku Islands
(1872–79)

P a c i f i c

C H I N A

Nanchang

Amoy•

TAIWAN
(1895)

O c e a n

Canton (1937)•

•Hong Kong
Macao

Philippine Sea

BURMA

Hanoi •

TONGKING

HAINAN
(1939)

Luzon

P H I L I P P I N E S

Yap (1914)

Rangoon
(1942)

THAILAND
(allied 1941)

FRENCH INDO-CHINA

Manila (1942)

Leyte

Palau (1914)

Phnom Penh •

•Saigon

South China Sea

Sulu Sea

Mindanao

Andaman Sea

Gulf of Thailand

NORTH BORNEO

BRITISH MALAYA

Natuna Beser

Brunei •

BRUNEI

SARAWAK

Strait of Malacca

Singapore
(1942)

Sumatra

Borneo

NETHERLANDS EAST INDIES

	Japanese Empire in 1870
	Acquisitions until 1932
	Additional occupation by 1937
	Additional occupation by 1938
	Additional occupation by 1940
	Additional occupation by 1942
	Demilitarized zone of the Tantku truce (1933)

0   Kilometers   1000

0   Miles   1000

MAP 8.1 Map of Japanese Empire to World War II *Source:* Wikicommons, public domain

JAPANESE POLICY IN TAIWAN

The first place where Japanese officials had the opportunity to implement imperial policies was the new colony of Taiwan, received from China after Japan won the Sino-Japanese war in 1895. The Japanese used the example of European imperialism to develop colonial theories and justify their own colonialism in Taiwan and elsewhere. Taiwan was the site of centuries of cultural exchanges between the Chinese and the indigenous people of Taiwan. The Chinese had come to Taiwan as rulers and to do business there. By the time of Japanese takeover, the island was composed of 2 million Chinese settlers and 150,000 indigenous people sometimes referred to as "aborigines." The term, which originally came from Roman mythology, indicates first inhabitants but was used in a pejorative manner in modern imperialism to denote peoples who were considered primitive and uncivilized, similar to the term "Indian" for Native Americans. The Japanese military embarked upon a campaign of pacification which resulted in the deaths of thousands of Taiwan's indigenous population. In addition, from 1898 to 1903, the Japanese made several population surveys which placed native and Chinese immigrant groups into separate categories and imposed ethnic classifications on each. Like the British census in India, these surveys tended to sharpen distinctions which had been more fluid. The Japanese categorization of indigenous people as primitive was, similar to that of North American Native Americans, very damaging to the aboriginal population in Taiwan. The Japanese believed the immigrant Chinese community to be much closer to modernity than the indigenous people of Taiwan, and so they separated these two groups into separate categories for the purposes of education and cultural assimilation.

Goto Shimpei, a young German-trained doctor, was put in charge of Taiwan's colonial administration in 1898. He led research surveys of the population in Taiwan and later in Manchuria as the head of the South Manchurian Railway Corporation (SMR), a Japanese government–controlled company in charge of Japanese railroads there, and thus became very influential in shaping the Japanese approach to these colonial encounters. The surveys gathered data that emphasized the cultural uniqueness and backwardness of the indigenous people of Taiwan and the Chinese in Manchuria. Goto believed that the Japanese mission in Taiwan was to bring the Taiwanese to progress and modernity and he endorsed the view that different peoples became modern at different speeds. According to Goto, it would take 100 years to civilize the Taiwanese and bring them to modernity, with indigenous people expected to take longer than the Chinese population there. Nitobe Inazo, a brilliant young bureaucrat from the northern Japanese island of Hokkaido who joined the colonial administration under Goto, shared Goto's views, but believed it could take as long as 800 years to bring peoples they saw as primitive such as the Taiwanese "aborigines" to modernity. Nitobe eventually was appointed to the Chair for Colonial Studies at Tokyo Imperial University. Japan's views of its colonial subjects created an "Orientalist" framework—similar to European colonial Orientalism—that defined them as backward and in need of civilization.

（臺下学校と台平公）　苗栗街公學校人番高士苗栗，総勤の蕃スウイメ

Sopou, Kuoioeaet, Savage School Children.

This photo and its caption reflect Japan's belief that its aboriginal Taiwanese subjects were primitive and in need of its civilizing influence.   Lafayette College Art Collection.

Although these views were similar to Europeans' concerning colonialism, one major difference existed. While European racism often conceived that an unbridgeable gap existed between themselves and their African and Asian colonial subjects, the Japanese believed that, with the right kind of education and inculcation of loyalty to the Japanese Emperor, all their colonial peoples could eventually become full Japanese subjects of the empire. This came to be expressed through Pan Asianism expressed in slogans like "Asia for Asians." Okakura Tenshin, an early advocate of Pan-Asianism stated, "Asia is one."

Known as the policy of gradualism, this approach dictated that the inhabitants of Taiwan should be educated in the same way as Japanese in the home islands. Goto was a strong proponent of gradualism and believed that education was one of the keys to assimilating and modernizing the

Taiwanese people. In Taiwan, he chose an open and progressive model, opening up Japanese language schools for Taiwanese to learn Japanese and other schools for Japanese settlers in Taiwan to learn the language and culture of Taiwan. But this early educational system did not include the indigenous people of Taiwan and was never fully realized. Instead, the goal of assimilation dropped away and the Japanese set up separate schools for the children of Japanese settlers, Taiwanese of Chinese origin, and "aborigines." Given the Japanese attitude of superiority toward the Taiwanese, it is easy to see why they gave up on this goal early and designed only basic educational offerings for Taiwanese children. Rather, Japanese officials in Taiwan applied a more superficial assimilation by requiring Taiwanese to dress like Japanese, live in Japanese-style houses, and learn Japanese. Only in the 1920s as the Japanese Empire grew, their notion of Pan-Asianism solidified, and their rule in Taiwan consolidated did deeper assimilationist approaches to education reemerge. By then, middle and upper class Taiwanese began to adapt to Japanese rule and culture. With the onset of World War II these schools were integrated and made open to any ethnicity.

JAPANESE ENCOUNTER WITH INDIGENOUS PEOPLES

The indigenous peoples the Japanese encountered in Taiwan had been forced to adapt to the rule of outsiders over a long period of time. China had controlled Taiwan for several centuries before the Japanese conquest. Chinese merchants and commercial agents reached out to the indigenous Taiwanese population and intermarried with their women in order to do commerce with them. In times of scarcity, they sold their daughters to Chinese merchants for scarce money and to cement trade relationships. Likewise, young Chinese women were lured into the mountains and married indigenous men. While some Chinese parents objected, the indigenous families could make enormous profits from the trade that was initiated through the daughter's marriage. This practice is similar to that of Native Americans who allowed their females to marry white European fur trappers and traders.

When the Japanese arrived to take control of Taiwan in 1895, they encountered these indigenous peoples—who lived in the central mountainous region—and announced their new rule in Taiwan and the changed status of the indigenous as subjects of the Emperor. Some resisted Japanese rule and indigenous rebellions were suppressed with armed force. While some regions remained very dangerous and one trade expedition of 14 Japanese was ambushed when they traveled outside of the area the Japanese military had secured, Japan succeeded in making many areas safe for commerce relatively quickly.

Japanese merchants in Taiwan immediately picked up where Chinese merchants had left off in marrying indigenous women to cement trade agreements as several Japanese–indigenous Taiwanese unions took place. This form of marriage was fairly typical in cross-cultural encounters ranging from Native Americans and traders in North America to Polynesians in the Pacific Ocean (Chapters 4 and 5). But the Japanese males involved were quite ignorant of indigenous custom and offended them. For instance, one Japanese government official agreed to marry the daughter of a high chief of the Wushe (Musha) peoples. But he allowed several men from a rival tribe to collect the gifts given at the wedding and later gave gifts to other tribesmen. This violated the chief's prerogative of deciding who ought to receive gifts and angered him enough that he came to the Japanese official's home and fired a weapon at his gate.

The Japanese colonial government began to regulate interethnic marriage after the Russo-Japanese War in 1904–1905. Japanese government officials noted that the unions between Japanese merchants and aboriginal women caused distress among indigenous Taiwanese men because sometimes Japanese men abandoned indigenous women after their marriage and this limited the available women for indigenous men. Officials recommended state support for the abandoned women, because their association with Japanese men made it impossible for them to find new mates. Japanese marriage practices in Taiwan eventually went beyond trade and commerce. There were even a few instances of Japanese "going native" to gain status in indigenous society. When one tribe lacked a successor to its chieftainship, a Japanese male married into the tribe with the understanding that by joining the female's household, after the wedding he would become the new chief of the tribe.

The colonial government encouraged Japanese to marry into the tribes to gain control of the mountainous territory the indigenous Taiwanese inhabited. After gaining entrée into the tribes, these Japanese then manipulated them into attacking their rivals and weakening them to the point that the Japanese could move troops and weapons in and take over mountain passes and exert formal control over the situation. In October 1903, male Wushe villagers became caught in a bloody trap. Lacking salt and firearms, they agreed to a meeting with their rivals, the Gantaban men, to help supply them. After serving the Wushe men large quantities of alcohol, the Gantaban struck, killing 95 of the 100 men at the meeting. The Gantaban brought 27 of the killed men's heads to the local Japanese official, indicating possible prior Japanese involvement in the event. The Gantaban might have been promised rewards by Japanese officials to attack the Wushe. In the aftermath, the Wushe tribe, which had previously resisted Japanese calls for cooperation and alliance, became much more cooperative. While the Japanese official role is not completely revealed, they seemed unsurprised by the outcome, and there was no punishment forthcoming for the Gantaban men. There is also some evidence that an indigenous woman named Iwan Robau who had married a Japanese pioneer Kondo Katsusaburo was involved in the initial invitation to the Wushe people to parley and could have been the go-between for negotiations with the Gantaban. At any rate, the Japanese colonial government benefited greatly from the massacre, gaining more control over the area.

Another example of Japanese behind-the-scenes manipulation of indigenous Taiwanese took place in 1909. Kondo Katsusaburo through his marriage to Iwan Robau had close relations with the Wushe. However, he then divorced Iwan at the request of the Wushe headmen and married into another family to cement a Japanese-Wushe alliance. Kondo then organized Wushe warriors into a war party and attacked a rival section of the Wushe community, successfully leading Wushe warriors alongside Japanese troops in a campaign that subdued their now common enemy. The resulting military victory allowed the Japanese government to control of commanding heights in the mountains of northern Taiwan where they eventually mounted artillery pieces permitting them to command the entire region. It would appear that interethnic marriage between Taiwanese aboriginals and Japanese was productive for both sides, cementing alliances and profiting merchants and chiefs in commerce early on and later allowing the Japanese to gain control of more upland aboriginal territory in Taiwan. Over time these encounters enhanced Japan's colonial power in Taiwan and eventually resulted in complete Japanese subjugation of the indigenous people there.

JAPAN IN KOREA

Japan's entrance into Korea occurred in a much different context than in Taiwan and also came with a much greater expectation of change. Korea had been on Japan's imperial radar screen since the 1590s when the Koreans had defeated the warlord Toyotomi Hideyoshi's armies who were bent on conquest of the Korean Peninsula. In the modern period, characterized by East Asia ringed with treaty ports and criss-crossed by foreign railway concessions, Field Marshall Yamagata Aritomo, the architect of the modern Japanese army, subscribed to the theory that Korea was a threat to Japanese security, a "dagger pointing at the heart of Japan." Korea was very close in geographical proximity to Japan but traditionally aligned with China. Korea was also home to an ancient civilization and a proud dynasty; the well-educated Yangban class practiced Confucian ethics more carefully than did China, home of Confucianism. In the 1880s, a split arose among Korea's intellectuals between the traditionalists who adhered to traditional Confucian ideas and the modernists who rejected the Korean Emperor and desired a republican form of government. Japan supported the modernists while the traditionalists found support in China leading to increasing tension between Japan and China.

Japan fought two wars to decide Korea's fate, the first Sino-Japanese War of 1894–1895 and the Russo-Japanese War of 1904–1905. The Sino-Japanese War was fought on Korean territory and pitted the traditionalists against the modernists within Korea. In the later war, the Japanese battled the Russians in northern Korea and Manchuria; in a decisive victory, they won control over Korea. In 1907, Japanese Governor General Ito Hirobumi extended Japanese control over the Korean government by arranging for Japanese to serve in important positions within the government. He also disbanded the

Korean army. Finally, in 1910, after Ito was assassinated by a Korean patriot on a trip to Manchuria, the Japanese government annexed Korea.

Japan envisioned its role in Korea as a constructive one, stabilizing and securing northeast Asia while bringing progress and modernity to Korea outside of western imperialism. Ebina Danjo, a Japanese Christian leader who traveled to Korea in 1914 on a mission trip, described his perception of the situation there prior to Japanese arrival and the impact of Japanese influence:

> Previously Korea was everywhere thoroughly decaying. The mountains, rivers, and vegetation were covered with the scars of that ruined country. From the ruling family to the lowliest laborer, no one owned private property...But the Japanese people grafted a completely different system onto this situation. The progress created by the Japanese advanced leaps and bounds...Vegetable oil [lamps] were replaced by electric lights, the sedan chair became the automobile. In truth, outside of wonder and admiration there is no response. The Japanese, without going to confront, made radical progress. This peninsula accepted various things and today it has good harbors, steamships, and trains...[1]

Ironically, it was Japan's conflict in Korea, the Russo-Japanese War, that likely caused the scars to which he referred. Nonetheless, Ebina saw Koreans as a backward people—corrupt and indolent—and thus in great need of Japanese enlightenment. Like missionaries elsewhere (Chapters 5–7 and 9), Ebina and many other Japanese Christians endorsed Japanese control over Korea because they believed it would do no harm and was likely to bring progress to the colony. The Koreans, however, saw Japanese annexation of Korea quite differently.

Koreans had nurtured powerful memories of Hideyoshi's destructive invasion and resisted Japanese rule from the outset. Private schools all over the country displayed nationalist slogans such as "Independence to Great Korea" and "Restoration of the State." Japanese control was greeted with rioting by Koreans, with almost 3,000 skirmishes taking place between Korean patriots and Japanese police and troops between 1907 and 1910. In the end these protests were savagely repressed by the Japanese.

Christian Koreans became some of the fiercest leaders of the independence movement. Many of these Koreans came from the elite Yangban (literati or scholarly) class. This was the most educated class in Korea and also the most disposed toward nationalistic thinking. As early as 1906, Korean Christians expressed their resentment about the Japanese consolidation of control in Korea. A prominent Korean Christian who had served as a minister of state remarked that his people would approach the Japanese with toleration, but were fearful that their new Japanese masters would seek to affect the complete absorption of Korea into the Japanese Empire.

The Korean YMCA became a forum for the rising nationalist aspirations of Korean Christian patriots. American YMCA missionaries had established the YMCA in Korea in the 1890s. The American YMCA missionary movement was the result of a strong Christian revivalist movement spearheaded by the YMCA (Young Men's Christian Association) in the 1870s to 1890s that also committed itself to spreading the Christian gospel around the world. The YMCA missionaries who came to Korea were recruited at the best American universities, such as Yale and other east coast institutions. The Japanese government took a hands-off approach to the missionaries because of their links to the western powers. But the American missionaries threw their support behind these young Korean Christians in their quest for freedom from Japanese rule. YMCA Summer Schools and a YMCA-sponsored lecture series in Korea became forums for nationalist rhetoric and action. In short, both the American missionaries and Koreans used the YMCA organization to agitate for Korean independence.

Tensions between the Korean YMCA and the Japanese reached a breaking point after the annexation of Korea by Japan in 1910. Thereafter, Japanese police began to round up Korean YMCA leaders. They were subsequently accused of a conspiracy to assassinate the Japanese governor general, General Terauchi Masatake, a plot which alleged was hatched at the YMCA summer school in 1911. Yun Ch'i-ho, a leading member of the Korean YMCA in Seoul, was jailed and accused of being a ringleader in the plot. Syngman Rhee, who had been an associate secretary in the Korean YMCA and was to become the first president of South Korea after World War II, was also under suspicion. Rhee was saved only through the intervention of John R. Mott, head of American YMCA who happened to be on a tour of the Far East. He convinced the Japanese authorities that Rhee was so well known in the United States (he was a friend of soon to-be President Woodrow Wilson) that arresting him would only serve to damage relations between the two countries. A short trial was held for those arrested and over 100 were found guilty, after which the supposed ringleaders of the plot were given 10 years prison sentences, which on appeal were reduced to six years. After further protests were lodged by the United States, all the prisoners were released in February 1915. Because no convincing evidence was ever found against these men, it is probable that the crimes with which they had been charged had been concocted by the Japanese government in Korea to discredit the activities of these Christian nationalists.

March 1, 1919, saw the most powerful Korean anti-Japanese resistance effort prior to World War II. In honor of the death of Korean King Kojong, a "declaration of independence" was read in Seoul on March 1. On that day, peaceful demonstrations were held all over the country which included thousands of Korean Christians, and female students from Ewha University led demonstrations on their own campus in Seoul. However, in response, Japanese police and soldiers attacked the protesters and engaged in a more savage repression of Christianity in Korea than that which occurred at the time of the alleged conspiracy to assassinate General Terauchi Masatake.

Japanese Machine-gunners in front of Chosen Bank in Korea during Korean rebellion.   Lafayette College Art Collection.

Over the next few months, 2,000 Koreans were killed, 20,000 arrested, 3,500 Christians rounded up, 41 Presbyterian leaders shot, and 12 Presbyterian churches destroyed.

In the aftermath of this incident, which was condemned by world leaders and even Japanese Christians, the Japanese government in Tokyo replaced their governor general in Korea, who was seen as ineffectual and brutal. They also instituted reforms that gave the Koreans more autonomy: Japanese military police were replaced by civilian police, limited freedom of press was instituted, and women were allowed to have their voices heard through print media.

However, this more open policy came to an end in the 1930s after the repression of another round of protests and the Japanese military embarked upon expansion into Manchuria and northern China by force, compelling them to strengthen their hold over nearby Korea. A new policy of forced assimilation to Japanese culture was introduced which sought to erase the Korean people's sense of their own cultural heritage.

As part of this new policy, Korea's anti-Japanese newspapers were closed and replaced by Japanese government–sponsored Korean language newspapers. In the schools, the teaching of the Japanese language was made a required subject while Korean was reduced to a mere elective. Korean history was removed from the curriculum and Korean history books were seized and destroyed. In its place Korean students were forced to study the history of the Japanese Empire and were expected to bow before portraits of the Japanese Emperor in Japanese schools. Korean families were also required to worship at Japanese Shinto shrines. Public monuments devoted to Korean subjects were altered, while Korean songs were rewritten to praise Japan. The colonial government even encouraged Koreans to change their family names to Japanese names. Assimilationist policies in Korea became the most strictly enforced within Japan's empire in part because of the ferocity of Koreans' resistance to Japanese rule.

During World War II, Koreans experienced even greater acts of submission and cruelty at the hands of the Japanese. They were conscripted into the Japanese army and shipped in large numbers to Japan to be conscripted into the Japanese labor force. Korean women were forcibly conscripted into military brothels for use by the Japanese army. Many Koreans along with prisoners of war of many nations died from medical experiments conducted by the Japanese in their infamous Unit 731 located in Manchuria. These experiments included collected data on human responses to extreme cold. Thousands of Koreans forced to work in Japanese factories in Hiroshima and Nagasaki were killed in the atomic bombings of those cities.

Most Koreans responded to the assimilation policy and the wartime repression with renewed nationalism. Linguistic scholars standardized the Korean writing system in the 1930s as a way of supporting the Korean language. Underground history texts focusing on Korean historical figures were widely circulated. Korean elites sponsored newspapers and associations in the United States to spread anti-Japanese propaganda and drew attention from their increasingly sympathetic audience. However, not all Koreans were opposed to Japanese colonial rule. A few elites collaborated with the Japanese and these pro-Japanese Koreans received jobs within the Japanese colonial government and other preferential treatment. Some even changed their family names so as to be written in Japanese characters. However, with the end of Japanese rule in 1945, Korean collaborators became ostracized within Korea. Called Chinilpa (literally people friendly to Japan), these Koreans were prosecuted between 1945 and 1950 as war criminals and a few were sentenced to death, though their sentences were not carried out, presumably because of the fresh turmoil produced by the outbreak of the Korean War in 1950. However, investigations of the Chinilpa and their families have resumed in Korea since 2002. The Korean government has passed laws supporting the public naming of Chinilpa and directing the confiscation of their substantial property holdings.

JAPAN IN MANCHURIA AND CHINA

In 1931, Japan expanded its empire from Korea to include Manchuria in the aftermath of the so-called Manchurian Incident. The Japanese army in Manchuria covertly blew up a small portion of the railroad they controlled there and blamed it on Chinese bandits. They used this manufactured outrage as an excuse to launch a full-scale invasion of Manchuria and northern China. Manchuria was proclaimed an independent country and renamed Manchukuo though in reality it was little more than a Japanese colony.

Japan's attitude toward China had been shaped over the centuries by both respect and fear of China's civilization. Japan had adopted the Chinese writing system and China's Confucian ethics, and even the city design of China's ancient capital Xian had influenced the layout of the imperial capital of Kyoto in broad straight streets set on a grid. In the modern period however, China became weakened and dominated by western interests. Japanese success in its own colonial expansion led them to see themselves as replacing China at the head of a modern Asian civilization; the Japanese dismissed China by referring to it as the derogatory "shina," which was a derivation of the western word "China," rather than the laudatory "Middle Kingdom," by which it had been traditionally and far more respectfully known. China was to become the centerpiece of Japan's civilization project aimed to bring Asia out of its weakness and backwardness and turn it into a civilization that was modern, powerful, and free of western hegemony.

In Manchuria, the Japanese encountered a wide variety of peoples, including aristocratic, anti-communist, and other Russian refugees from the Russian Revolution, Manchu farmers and herders, and over 29 million Chinese who comprised the vast majority of the population. Japanese settlers came in greater numbers to Manchuria after the Manchurian Incident because the Japanese government sponsored a program of emigration to Manchuria, highlighting its large, bountiful land areas and great resources. However, while the government envisaged millions of Japanese settlers coming to dominate Manchuria, only 200,000 actually came. The Japanese also had to deal with thousands of Koreans who had settled in Manchuria close to the border with Korea. This variety had drawn American YMCA missionaries to Manchuria as well, beginning in the Russo-Japanese War. The YMCA posed no immediate threat as they had established several local YMCAs there to serve Japanese troops and Korean immigrants, and had built a large comfort station and a YMCA English language training institute for children of Russian refugees in the Manchurian city of Harbin, thus relieving the Japanese of this responsibility.

The encounter in Manchuria between the Japanese and these various ethnic groups revolved around increasing Japanese hegemony over the area. First, the Japanese set up the South Manchuria Railway Company (SMR) after the Russo-Japanese War to operate the rail lines it took over from the Russians. But the company was also there to expand Japan's interests. It built many factories and buildings in Manchuria under the auspices of modernizing the region but also with the intention of expanding Japanese control there. Later, the Japanese found it necessary to move troops into Manchuria to protect the SMR and Japanese settlers. In the aftermath of the Manchurian Incident, Japanese administrators moved quickly to set up the puppet state of Manchukuo and took steps to place all nongovernmental organizations under their control. For example, the YMCAs in Manchuria, which had been under American and Chinese control, increasingly became targets of a Japanese takeover. By the time of the Sino-Japanese War in 1937, all of the YMCAs in Manchuria were under the control of the Japanese.

South of Manchuria, in China's Shantung Province, the Japanese and Chinese had been locked in tensions since World War I. The Japanese had invaded this territory at the outset of World War I in 1914 and wrested it from German control. Like Koreans in Korea, the Chinese protested against the Japanese presence which was eventually expressed in the May Fourth Movement of 1919, which began when a group of 3,000 Chinese university students marched through Peking in protest of the Paris Peace Conference decision to allow Japan to continue to occupy the former German holdings in the Shantung Peninsula. Twenty students were arrested, but when more tried to be arrested the government released all of the students and issued an apology. Later the students and a few of their professors issued a manifesto for change advocating morality in politics, democratic governance, social reform, political activism, modern education systems, and women's rights. Many university students turned against Confucianism and took their inspiration from western philosophers and intellectuals including Karl Marx. A communist party was established in China during the midst of the revolutionary social and political ferment brought about by the Japanese occupation of Shantung. Students held demonstrations in the Shantung provincial capital of Qingdao (Tsingtao). As in Korea, the Japanese military repressed the demonstrations, though not as savagely. Chinese leaders quietly supported the demonstrations and, like Koreans, sponsored newspapers and associations in the United States to spread anti-Japanese propaganda.

FAR EASTERN GAMES

The tensions between Japan and China were also expressed through sports. In particular, the Far Eastern Olympic Games originated in 1913 through the work of one Elwood S. Brown, who was the Physical Director of the YMCA in Manila, Philippines, and the president of the Philippine Athletic Association and Manila Carnival Games. The YMCA had become involved in sports and physical training as a part of their emphasis on training the body and the mind for Christian spirituality. Brown and other YMCA leaders believed that the creation of an Olympic-style Far Eastern Games could strengthen the bonds of friendship between Asian countries. "The plan to bring the races of the orient—the yellow man, the brown man, and the omnipresent white man—together in friendly athletic rivalry through recurring Oriental Olympics has not merely an athletic but also an ethical and international aspect."[2]

Despite these admirable intentions, the planning of events and organizing of the Games took place against the background of deteriorating relations between Japan and China in the 1920s. The headquarters of the Games had been moved to Tokyo for the 1917 Games, which was held there. In an attempt to control the games the Japanese put forward a motion in 1921 before the Shanghai Games to permanently locate the head office of the games in Tokyo. The Chinese objected to the motion and eventually the Japanese dropped the idea. At a subsequent meeting, each country sent three representatives. The Chinese sent two Americans and one Chinese representative, which irritated the Japanese, who according to the Games' coordinator Franklin Brown, "naturally looked with suspicion upon whatever looks like American domination of things Chinese."

Sino-Japanese tensions were evident at the Shanghai Games themselves. No Chinese officials came to meet the Japanese athletes at the docks on their arrival. There was also a bitter row over the movie rights to the Games in Shanghai, which had been granted to a local Chinese firm. The Japanese representatives recognized that the filming was a form of propaganda about East Asia and if they didn't control it, they might end up suffering damage of their image abroad. The Japanese also believed that the local YMCA secretary in Shanghai, Dr. Gray, who organized the Games, had profited unfairly at them. Stories circulated among the Japanese of Gray asking the crowd to make more room so that he could sell more seats.

The situation worsened as the Games appeared very disorganized. There were not enough seats for the number of spectators who attended, not enough baseballs were brought to allow the teams to change balls during rainy games, and during the track and field competition the cartridges were of the wrong size for the starter's pistol. One judge, a Chinese man, made the wrong ruling on a Japanese competitor's throws in the discus trials. And he missed another of the Japanese athletes' names on the roster; the athlete missed his turns at the discus throw. In another incident, another Chinese judge asked that the coaches for the Japanese volleyball team leave the field while the Filipino team coaches against whom they were playing were allowed to stay.

The end result was that the Games were turned into a venue for the expression of growing tensions between the Japanese and Chinese governments, instead of an event that could bring the sides together and strengthen bonds.

THE SINO-JAPANESE WAR AND THE RAPE OF NANJING

In 1937, the Japanese army penetrated into North China and drew close to Peking, the capital of China, which led to a full-scale war. The fierce resistance of the Chinese army at Shanghai in October of that year, the evacuation of Nanjing by the Chinese government to the city of Chongqing far to the west out of the reach of the Japanese, and the generally strong feeling in the Japanese army against the Chinese people led to widespread crimes against humanity when Japanese forces entered Nanjing. One can also argue that the Japanese ideology of Pan-Asianism, which maintained that the Japanese and Chinese shared a common Asian foundation, raised expectations within the Japanese army of a warmer welcome in China, when in reality Sino-Japanese tensions had been widespread for two decades. As a result, the resistance of the Chinese to the Japanese military advance in 1937 outraged the Japanese, who had expressed their relationship to the Chinese as one of love for a wayward brother. One Japanese leader proclaimed, "We are fighting in China because we love China."[3] Now the ones they loved had turned against them and their sense of betrayal helped unleash a murderous campaign against the Chinese in Nanjing.

The Japanese entered Nanjing on December 13th and the atrocities that followed are to this day known as the Rape of Nanking and included the mass rape of Chinese women, the summary killing of Chinese civilians, and a reign of terror against the Chinese population. Although these crimes were most intense in the six-week period from the middle of December through the end of January, the atrocities continued at a high level until June 1938, according to the eye-witness account of Miner Searle Bates.

Bates, an American missionary who taught history at Nanjing University, was on the scene when the Japanese entered Nanjing and became the chair of the Emergency Committee of the University of Nanking. About 170,000 Chinese fled to the University of Nanjing, which was part of the Safety Zone for the protection of civilians from the Japanese army. It was set up by a volunteer International Committee of 20 Europeans and American doctors, missionaries, and businessmen of whom Bates was a member.

As Chinese resistance to Japanese invasion in 1937 and 1938 stiffened, the invading armies resorted to random, mass executions to cow Chinese soldiers and civilians into submission.   Ullstein Bild/ The Granger Collection, NY.

Bates wrote several letters of complaint to the Japanese Embassy in Nanjing, which was located near the University of Nanjing. His first letter of December 16th described the rape of several female students and the disappearance of others. The rest of the letters detailed similar outrages. "In our Agricultural Economics Compound (Hsiao T'ao Yuan) more than thirty women were raped last night by soldiers who came repeatedly and in large numbers. I have investigated this matter thoroughly, and am certain of the correctness of the statement."[4] Bates also pointed out that the Japanese army had lost an opportunity to show that it was a better organized and more disciplined organization than the disorderly retreating Chinese army. Bates later gave eye-witness testimony of the Nanjing atrocities to the Tokyo War Crimes Tribunal in 1946.

Historical writing about the Rape of Nanjing has recently become a flashpoint of tensions in East Asia. Historian Iris Chang dramatized Japanese atrocities in her book *The Rape of Nanking: The Forgotten Holocaust of World War II*, published in 1997. In it she exposed Japanese atrocities and argued that they produced over 1 million deaths, while on the other hand Japanese right-wing revisionist historians have argued that the Nanjing Massacre never happened and was concocted by Chinese and westerners to discredit Japan. Although Chang's numbers are likely too high (200,000–300,000 civilian deaths is a more reliable estimate), her book offers strong evidence of Japanese rape and murder and has become very influential; Japanese revisionists have little credibility and a very small reading audience. However, the Japanese government has tried to downplay the incident. Government-approved school textbooks refuse to acknowledge the full extent of the atrocities and refer to it as the "Nanjing Incident" to neutralize its significance. Chang's book and the Japanese government's stance, in addition to Japan's half-hearted apologies to the victims of its empire-building (horrific treatment of prisoners of war and exploitation of laborers from Indonesia and elsewhere), have inflamed public opinion in Asia and produced massive protests in China and elsewhere in the postwar period. Japan's aggression during World War II has generally made relations with other Asian nations of China, Korea, the Philippines, Malaysia, and Indonesia more difficult.

Conclusion

The Japanese encounter with other Asians as they expanded their empire was wide-ranging and various. The Japanese tended to mimic European imperialism in seeing other Asians as less civilized, less rational, more primitive, and in need of Japanese enlightenment. In the encounter in Taiwan, there was some openness in areas where the Japanese exerted less control over the situation on the ground, with Japanese interacting openly and intermarrying with Taiwanese indigenous peoples. However, this was possible only in the early period of Japanese colonialism; thereafter the openness disappeared. Rather, many encounters within the Japanese Empire were shaped by Japan's assumption that these people were primitive and inferior and needed to be brought to modernity under Japanese guidance and control by any means including coercion by Japan's military power. These convictions were quite similar to those of western empire-builders with whom the Japanese claimed to liberate from alien rule. The Japanese ideology of Pan-Asianism played a prominent role in encouraging expectations among the Japanese themselves, but also among relatively few non-Japanese, that other Asians should be assimilated into the Japanese Empire and would readily accept this approach. But Koreans, Chinese, and other Asians often responded by resisting Japanese rule in a variety of ways, from the writing of underground histories to student protest movements to officials ruling against the Japanese in the Far Eastern Games. The Japanese response to this seeming betrayal was brutal as exemplified by the Rape of Nanjing. By punishing those who refused to surrender to Japanese cultural hegemony and accept that resistance to their rule was futile, the Japanese encounter with the rest of Asia in the early twentieth century has left bitter memories in Asian countries formerly occupied by Japan.

Questions for Discussion

1. What were Japanese assumptions about the peoples who lived in Japan's expanding empire before World War II?
2. How did these assumptions influence Japan's treatment of its subject people?
3. What role did education play in Japan's attempts to integrate its colonies into the larger empire?
4. What was the purpose of Japanese intermarriage with aboriginal Taiwanese in colonial Taiwan?
5. What was the role of Korean Christians in the development of Korea as a Japanese colony?
6. How did the tensions in the Far Eastern Games parallel the geo-political tensions in East Asia at that time?
7. Why is the Rape of Nanjing still considered a controversial subject today?

Endnotes

1. Ebina Danjô, "Kakuseishi kureru shin nihon" (The Coming Awakening of a New Japan [in Korea]), *Kaitakusha*, Vol. IX, No. 8 (August 1914), p. 53.
2. "Editorial Comment," *Physical Training* (Published by the Physical Director's Society of the YMCA, New York), Vol. 10, No. 6 (April 1913), p. 172.
3. Takeuchi Tatsuji, "The Background of the Sino-Japanese War," *Amerasia*, Vol. 2, No. 4 (June 1938), p. 183.
4. Letter, Miner Searle Bates to Japanese Embassy, December 16, 1937, Miner Searle Bates Papers, Yale Divinity School Library Special Collections, 1.

Mapping Africa: European Perceptions and African Realities

Africa, the second largest continent in the world with 800 million people, is characterized by diversity similar to that of the Native Americans of North America. Historically, the continent experienced cultural exchanges with places as remote as Southeast Asia and the Pacific, from where it received bananas, and as close as the Arabian Peninsula, from where some of the world's first Muslims migrated to Ethiopia. Since Roman times, Africans participated in trade in gold, ivory, salt, slaves, and teak that connected them with the Middle East, Europe, and Asia.

Modern Europeans, however, initially had little contact with Africa save via the Atlantic slave trade with its coastal communities. Thereafter, they characterized Africa as a dark and mysterious continent stuck in a primitive state and unconnected to the rest of world. This view was shaped by growing European racial and cultural prejudices against nonwhites which by the nineteenth century had become a self-serving justification for seizing the lands and resources of others around the world.

European contact with Africa slowly intensified after the abolition of the slave trade in the early decades of 1800s. Missionaries led the way but Europeans were susceptible to malaria and over half of them died in their first years in Africa. In the 1840s, after the discovery of the medicine quinine, made from the bark of a cinchona tree, Europeans came to Africa in ever larger numbers. Pressed by rising trade barriers and growing industrial competition in Europe and with the United States, European explorers and adventurers sought markets and resources within the African interior. These

The size of African cities and the power of African rulers often impressed European observers. Here the city of Loango, capital of a kingdom on the Kongo coast, is depicted as a bustling urban center. At this time it was a major port in the slave trade.   The Granger Collection, NY.

lands, unknown to Europeans, were mapped by European explorers and adventurers in the 1860s to 1870s, drawing boundaries to suit European national spheres of influence rather than African political realities. Eventually existing African states and empires were reduced to possessions of the great powers of Europe. African resistance to this process was relentless and took a variety of forms ranging from outright rebellion to accommodation strategies, including attempts to play one European power off against another. Many Africans, overmatched by superior European technology in the form of steam gunboats, machine guns, and railway building, came to accept the reality of European rule in the short term, accepting conversion to European faiths, western education, and even service in European armies in Africa and abroad.

Thus, while the political encounter with Europeans was characterized by inequality and the oppression of Africans, other encounters took place. African Christians were brought into closer contact with Muslim Africans; Africans who belonged to one community encountered Africans of more distant origin. And large portions of Africa were relatively untouched by the encounter with Europeans. Some of these encounters were benign; some were positive in encouraging regional or African identities that served to strengthen African resistance. Other encounters proved disastrous. To cut costs, Europeans often employed a form of "indirect rule" which placed one segment of their African colonial population (for example, educated

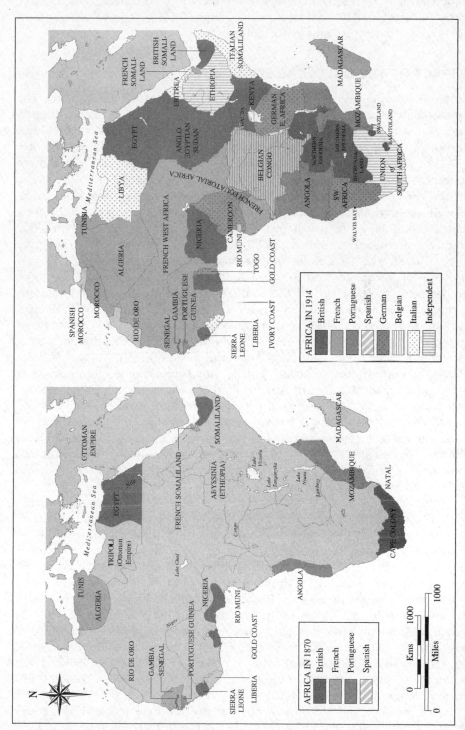

MAP 9.1 Map of European Imperialism in Africa

settled farmers) under the control of another (less educated semi-nomadic cattle herders), or Muslims over non-Muslims. These steps would produce post-colonial civil wars and genocidal conflict.

IMPACT OF THE COLONIAL ENCOUNTER

Colonialism operated in Africa with great effectiveness and speed. The Industrial Revolution had made available to Europeans the tools they used to dominate Africa such as tropical medicine, machine guns, and steam ships. European control over Africa came very quickly and very completely after 1870 with only Ethiopia remaining independent at the turn of the twentieth century. The British took over Egypt, Sudan, Kenya, Zanzibar, and Uganda in East Africa along with Nigeria, Ghana, and other areas in western Africa, as well as South Africa and Rhodesia (Zimbabwe) to its north and Southwest Africa (Namibia) to its northwest. The German state claimed Tanganyika, although after Germany's defeat in World War I, Tanganyika was turned over to the British as a League of Nations mandate. The French controlled vast stretches of North and West Africa including much of the Sahara Desert and the island of Madagascar off the southeastern coast of Africa. The Italians conquered Libya and attempted unsuccessfully in 1896 to take over Ethiopia, although they eventually did conquer Ethiopia in 1935 using tanks and airpower. The older imperial regime of Portugal, which dated from before the Atlantic slave trade, controlled Angola in the southwestern part of Africa and Mozambique in the southeast. Finally King Leopold of Belgium took over the central equatorial area of Africa called the Congo as his private estate, which became the most violent, brutal regime of European exploitation and forced labor in all of Africa. His rule ended when the Belgian government took control after crusading European journalists exposed Leopold as a merciless tyrant in 1908. Leopold's army committed cold-blooded murder, took hostages, forced labor upon the Africans, making them into virtual slaves, and took land for themselves.

Because Europeans initially knew little about Africa, they were driven by national rivalries for territory, and their control was so complete, they redrew the boundaries of Africa without consulting their African subjects, in the process creating new states and nations where none had existed before and in some cases dividing states that had previously existed, leaving one part of a former African state in one European colony and another part in a colony administered by another European state. This changed the nature of the encounter in Africa drastically. The new and old political units did not match up in many cases, not only cutting up into pieces peoples and tribes who had existed as one polity for long periods, but also putting together in the same political unit political rivals in other cases. Traditional cultural and political identification became disconnected within these new colonies and created dangerous situations that still play out today.

For instance, the Somali people were divided into new colonies under the rule of three different Europeans powers, the British, the Italians, and the French. These divisions among the Somali people persisted when Somalia was

PUNCH, OR THE LONDON CHARIVARI—November 28, 1906.

IN THE RUBBER COILS.

Scene—*The Congo "Free" State.*

As this political cartoon of a vicious snake with Leopold II's head squeezing the life out of a defenseless African villager illustrates, an international campaign developed in the 1890s in opposition to the brutal forced-labor regime in what had become the Belgian king's personal fiefdom in the Congo after 1885. The much publicized scandal compelled the Belgian government to take over the administration of the colony in 1908.   Mary Evans Picture Library/Alamy.

unified and became independent in 1960 and as a result, civil war ensued. The northern part made war against the central government of Somalia after it seemed that the north was losing power to the southern part of Somalia. Somalia today still suffers from the political fractures resulting from European rule there as attempts at unifying the former colonies into a coherent nation and cohesive government have so far failed. Somalia is a chaotic brew of competing interests that has allowed terrorist cells and pirates to flourish in their midst. In addition, the creation of the nation of Somalia from its different colonies produced a regional rivalry with Ethiopia that has resulted in almost constant warfare. In another example, the Mandinka and Hausa people of West Africa were divided between French and British territories while the British colony of Nigeria was composed of at least three different religio-ethnic groups, whose struggles have led to warfare there, a conflict which currently threatens some of the world's oil supply. In Rwanda, first German and then Belgian rulers sided with the semi-nomadic Tutsi tribe against the settled Hutu people until they became bitter rivals. The Belgians also issued racial identity cards for the Tutsi and Hutu in 1933, which racialized the distinction between them. In the colonial period this divide—the pre-colonial period was class-based with the Tutsi as the upper class and the Hutu as the lower class— was transformed into an ethnic rivalry. The Rwandan massacre that resulted from Hutu turning on Tutsi in 1994 killed almost 1 million Tutsi.

In governance, the European encounter with Africa produced governments with very few European officials at the top and mostly poorly trained African underlings running day-to-day governance. Africans served as interpreters, policemen, and servants and in local leadership such as traditional chiefs, who kept order in localities, but always from a position of inferiority as Europeans organized such relationships with a clear sense of their own racial superiority and the belief that western civilization was superior to African civilization. This attitude made it impossible for Africans to climb into positions of leadership within European colonial governments. For instance, it was not until 1942, near the end of colonial rule, that two Africans were appointed assistant district officers in Ghana.

The few Europeans who came to Africa other than the colonial officials were businessmen who came to profit from the natural riches of Africa and settled mostly in eastern and southern Africa. Europeans settlers, farmers of coffee, sugar, cocoa, and tobacco plantations, took the most fertile land and the Africans were sometimes forced out of these areas in the process. This happened in Kenya and also in South Africa, where 90 percent of the land came to be owned by Europeans, who were only 10 percent of the population. Even though the Europeans hired Africans to work for them on their farms, the overall profits from these ventures went back to Europe. Sometimes Africans were forced to move to plantation areas to work on farms to pay off colonial taxes designed to force them to work on European-owned plantations. This was often done by taxing in full each of the "huts" of Africans who had many separate houses for family members at one site, and forcing payment only in European cash, which Africans could only obtain by working for European establishments. The resentments that this system of agriculture caused still are present today. In early-twentieth-century South Africa, British rulers goaded on by Dutch "Boer" or white settlers there instituted strict racial policies that forced anyone who was not white to carry racial identity papers, took land and gave it to white settlers, and enforced racial separation ultimately known there as *apartheid*. Later after the end of colonialism, the resentment spawned by these land grabs created a backlash against European farmers in southern Africa with deadly consequences. Zimbabwe's post-colonial government took land from Europeans farmers in the 1990s and gave it to Africans. Land reform in Zimbabwe turned violent as Africans murdered some farm families to free up farms and intimidated others to flee.

Europeans also came to mine gold, diamonds, and other ores under the ground of Africa. Africa's immense mineral wealth was a spectacle to

Europeans such as Cecil Rhodes, a young man who came to Africa to get rich by finding gold and instead bought a plot of land that turned out to be littered with diamonds. Rhodes became immensely rich, took his fortune back to Europe, and then returned to Africa to become colonial governor of South Africa and eventually conquered the interior of southern Africa to the north of today's South Africa, an area that became known as Northern and Southern Rhodesia (today Zambia and Zimbabwe, respectively). In part to support solidarity among whites in English-speaking nations, Rhodes also founded the Rhodes scholarship, a prestigious scholarship that allows American college students to study in England.

Other non-European migrants came in large numbers as contract laborers to certain parts of Africa. They came under deliberately obscure contracts that appeared to offer them wealth after labor required for a set number of years for their employer. But upon arrival, they found that wages and other economic realities meant that they could never earn enough money for a return passage, let alone live more comfortable lives. Under such circumstances, many Indians from British-controlled India came to East Africa to work on the railroads being built there and came to South Africa to work on sugar plantations. Indians encountered racism similar to Africans under the apartheid system.

Africans responded to the European intrusion in a variety of ways. Africans generally welcomed the innovations of technology and the economy that helped them to be more efficient. Overall they welcomed more modern ways of doing things. For example, the introduction of European forms of currency was a big improvement over barter trade and the use of heavy iron bars as currency, and it helped facilitate trade and commerce. And Africans welcomed the opportunity to give their children more education wherever European rulers implemented educational systems and European missionaries set up schools. However, modernization did not always benefit Africans. More modern weaponry such as the machine gun, which was used in the European conquest of Africa, killed many Africans. The Industrial Revolution and modernization gave Europeans more power than Africans possessed and they used it to dominate Africans. Thus Africans responded to the innovations of modernization in complex ways with appreciation for the things that helped them and with fear and loathing for the oppression and terror that imperialism wrought on their lives.

EUROPEAN PERCEPTIONS

European perceptions shaped the colonial encounter in important ways. In late-nineteenth-century literature, Europeans referred to Africa as the "dark continent." It was said to be in darkness because Europeans believed its inhabitants to be uncivilized people incapable of modern progress. Henry Stanley, who became famous for his exploration of Africa in the 1870s and later infamous for his brutal treatment of Africans in the Congo, used the word "dark" in two of the bestselling books he wrote about his exploration: *Through the Dark Continent* (1878) and *In Darkest Africa* (1890). In his first

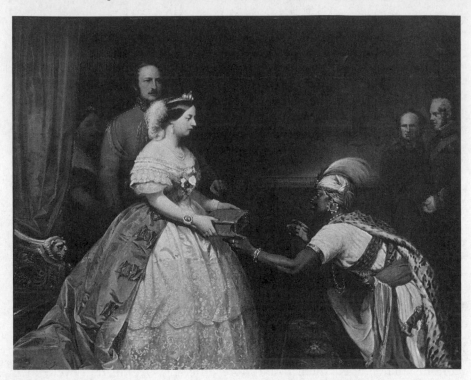

Like the missionaries the ruling classes of Europe believed that the Christianization of Africans would make them easier to rule over.   The Granger Collection, NY.

book, he describes the alleged wonderment of the Africans at the technology of the steam-powered riverboat, which demonstrated to Stanley their lack of civilization and savagery. As well, Stanley expressed a deep suspicion and almost loathing for the Congo River, which he traveled upon in his exploration of Africa. Europeans who came to Africa sometimes described it as a wasteland, which is almost unbelievable given the great natural beauty of Africa, but is also ironic given that the Europeans, once in control, dramatically altered Africa's environment in some cases turning it into a wasteland. This distaste for the African environment might have been an expression of early explorers' inability to control the environment and a projection from Africans' supposed barbarism wherein the environment was seen as savage and hostile as the Africans themselves. Stanley and many other Europeans came to Africa with curiosity but eventually turned against the Africans who could not be made to fit into European categories of civilization and therefore were seen as either harmless or truly dangerous and bloodthirsty savages. This feeling was aided and abetted by biological theories of racism prevalent in Europe. They were described as intellectually inferior and capable of monstrous acts. In reality, this was a projection, since it was the European colonial powers which wrecked devastation upon Africa, as in the case of King Leopold's Congo.

CHRISTIANITY IN AFRICA

The perception of darkness also guided European missionaries who came to Africa. Missionaries began arriving in the 1810s mostly from Great Britain and established a significant presence by the 1840s in western and southern Africa. When combined with the landscape of Africa which was stunningly different from England, the perception of darkness was relied upon to define Africa. One missionary who went on a trip up the Heart River in southern Africa described the river this way: "…a river never before seen by a white man's eye, so you may easily conjecture the dreadful state of dark heathenism in which they [the bushmen] must be involved."[1] Without the civilizing and christianizing influence of white men, Africans must surely have lived in darkness, according to this view. Another missionary relates his impressions of the African landscape: "We traveled through a barren and desolate land, in which we saw no living creature beside our party, except when the quagga or zebra passed; reminding us, in their lonely way of some impressive imagery of the Hebrew prophet."[2] This description of the landscape demonstrates the European view of Africa as a waste land. Nonetheless, a stark image of the African landscape was connected by missionaries to the biblical idea of the wilderness. Clearly the missionaries saw themselves as the prophets of biblical times wandering through the wilderness on a sacred journey. This negative image of the African "other" was likely a reflection of the missionaries' early uncertain status in Africa. Similar to the Jesuits in East Asia (Chapter 2) or the colonists who sailed to North America (Chapter 4), they were outsiders with little power or influence.

AFRICAN PERCEPTIONS

How did Africans respond to the missionaries' relative vulnerability? African leaders used what they knew of other Europeans in forming their opinions of the missionaries. Other white Europeans—mainly traders laden with goods to trade and soldiers with firearms—had arrived even earlier than missionaries. They were immediately given great respect because of their firearms and trade goods. African leaders assumed that missionaries would have these same powerful tools. In their interactions, therefore, the missionaries were given high status in the eyes of the Africans. But the missionaries had other powers that the Africans soon came to know. One was the written word. Most non-Muslim Africans did not have systems of writing. Others, Muslim and non-Muslim, did have writing, but in all cases, European books and letters were objects of fascination for them. This respect for the written word meshed with the European goal of teaching Africans to read and write for it was in reading and writing that Africans would be able to read the word of their god and go forward to convert their own people to Christianity. But reading and writing also allowed African Christians to become more independent from European missionaries. This led to the indigenization or Africanization of Christianity and it gained more steam in the twentieth century. Like Polynesians in the Pacific Ocean, African Christians eventually rejected missionary influence and created churches independent of Europeans.

The location of the Christian mission many times became a struggle between African rulers and missionaries in the early days. The place of the mission after all would determine what status the missionaries were to have in African society. While the missionaries were attractive because they had tools and goods at their disposal that could improve African existence, they were alien people who, as some African chiefs recognized, could fundamentally reconfigure or even destroy the communities they ruled. Danger was present alongside the power they represented. The chiefs generally preferred that missionaries be located as far from the capital of the tribe as possible but the missionaries wanted just the opposite, to be as near to the capital as possible or even to reside inside the capital. For them, central residence meant strong influence and the potential to convert tribal leaders. In one case in South Africa, the ruler of the Tswana people relented only after the head missionary gave him his gun. It was a symbolic victory for the chief; the thing which gave the white man his preeminent power was handed over to the Africans.

In addition, Africans rejected the missionary belief, similar to that of the colonists in North America, that turning the Africans into agriculturalists would put them on the path to civilization and godliness. While the missionaries made a point to show the Africans how they farmed using animal husbandry and European scientific methods, Africans, on the other hand, were embarrassed that male missionaries were engaged in farming, something they saw as women's work.

In the contest to place the mission at the center of African life, the missionaries eventually won out. White men's skills and the power of the weapons they brought with them were too attractive and dangerous to dismiss. When the missionaries proceeded to build their churches, they used the physical construction of the mission church to demonstrate missionary superiority with a building that towered over the settlement. This was true not only in Africa but also in Latin America, where the Spanish conquistadors generally chose the highest ground possible to build large European-style cathedrals, such as in San Cristóbal de las Casas in Mexico and in Quetzaltenango in Guatemala. In these places, Catholic cathedrals were located strategically to demonstrate the power of the Catholic Church.

The Africans and missionaries also negotiated access to water, a precious asset on the dry African steppe in southern Africa. As with the location of the mission, the encounter was more contest than conversation. In one well-known instance, both the missionaries and the Africans needed access to water and sometimes the water flowed across mission-controlled land to get to African villages. At one point the missionaries made a dam in a creek to divert more water to the mission; African women in the nearby village, who needed the water as badly as the missionaries, took matters into their own hands and destroyed the dam to restore the original flow of the creek.

The Africans and missionaries also clashed over traditional cultural practices such as the African ritual for rainmaking. Here as elsewhere, the debate between missionaries and Africans was more complex and contradictory than the crystallized perceptions of the Europeans. The following is a quote from a discussion of David Livingstone with a rain doctor about medicine and rainmaking, in which Livingstone questioned the legitimacy of the rainmaker's task of bringing rain. Livingstone, who is most famous for his exploration of Central Africa in today's Republic of Congo, first came as a missionary doctor to southern Africa.[3] Earlier, when Livingstone worked as a missionary, he challenged the rainmaker to justify his belief in rainmaking, and the rain doctor replied to Livingstone that:

> I use my medicines and you employ yours; we are both doctors, and doctors are not deceivers. You give a patient medicine. Sometimes God is pleased to heal him by means of your medicine; sometimes not—he dies. When he is cured, you take the credit of what God does. I do the same. Sometimes God grants us rain sometimes not. When he does, we take the credit of the charm. When a patient dies, you don't give up trust in your medicine, neither do I when rain fails. If you wish me to leave off my medicines, why continue your own?[4]

The rainmaker's argument neutralized Europeans' assumption of the superiority of European ways and the Africans' supposed lack of civilization by turning the discussion into a matter of faith and cultural context (notably not claiming the superiority of his own culture in the discussion). In another arena, that of missionary proselytization, Africans again used this strategy, pointing out to the missionaries that their own African religions were more than adequate. But the missionaries persisted and the Africans became more and more disenchanted with the missionaries and their preaching. While the missionaries were attractive to Africans for the reasons mentioned above, their efforts to change Africans' way of life from root to stem were met with resistance and skepticism.

This reaction can be seen as nearly universal among the encounters explored in this volume. Indeed, from Taino to Maya to Aztec, converts to Spanish Catholicism were unwilling and had to be forced to adopt European faiths, sometimes upon pain of death. In Japan and China, missionaries were tolerated and even occasionally venerated, not for their preaching or their Christian message, but for the ways in which they were useful to or fit into Chinese or Japanese ideas and plans. Even those who converted took what they saw as useful to their own way of life from the missionaries but were highly selective and eclectic in their choosing. Although their lives were changed sometimes in dramatic ways, they did not adopt wholesale the culture and ways of the missionary interloper. This fact led to a constant and growing frustration of the missionaries who sought to see themselves as making progress by spreading Christianity and civilization.

CHRISTIANITY AND CONQUEST

While there were not many new converts until Christianity became more independent of colonialism, even in small numbers they contributed to change in African society and politics. As more Africans converted to Christianity, they began to undermine the traditional political leadership in their own communities. The broad social changes sought by missionaries impinged foremost upon chiefs' role in religious rituals and as possessors of executive power. In this regard, the new African converts played a pivotal role. These converts led the way in rejecting traditional forms of authority. Many new converts were from lower status groups or lacked wealth and had fewer stakes in the existing social and political status quo than did the leaders. So the new converts engaged in contests over various kinds of power: from the concrete power of chieftainship to the power of judicial punishment to the social power of defining collective social norms. In one case, the brother of a chief who converted to Christianity disobeyed his brother and then broke completely with him and set up his own chieftainship. In an ironic twist, as the Christian chief gained more power, he then also broke with the missionaries and became completely independent. So even though the missionaries had vowed to stay out of secular affairs, the broad sweep of their goals and the development of indigenous converts who carried out these goals enmeshed them sometimes quite directly in political affairs. In this manner, they operated unintentionally as agents of their home governments in destabilizing and weakening the political situation in Africa and ultimately laying the groundwork for imperial takeover.

However, it is important to point out that many missionaries resisted the role of imperialist agent. Many missionaries disdained secular authority in general. In addition, they became very enamored of their converts. So even though they might have unwittingly paved the way for European conquest in the late nineteenth century and sought to quell African rebellions against European authority, their loyalties pushed them toward their converts. This is a situation similar to that of modern East Asia (Chapter 8) where we saw YMCA missionaries develop a strong affinity toward peoples in the countries they served. In Africa, Dr. Livingstone presents a similar case; his loyalty and admiration for African culture and community was clear. Livingstone even traveled to England to raise money for his African Tswana community although he unwittingly stimulated British imperialism by referring to Africa's s great natural resources in his speeches. He was even accused of illegal gun-running for Africans. In response, he denied any wrongdoing, in colorful language stating instead that he believed British and Dutch colonists were responsible for all gun-running in Africa for the simple reason that they could not resist the great profits. With a final shot at colonial authorities, he claimed that anyone who thought it possible to stop the European gun-running "might as well have bolted his castle [door shut] with a boiled carrot."[5]

Not all missionaries ended up opposed to colonial government. Two missionaries who served later in the century, John MacKenzie and John Moffat, actually became agents for the British government in South Africa. Mackenzie was appointed Deputy Commissioner of Bechuanaland after the British took the territory as a protectorate in 1884 and Moffat took several positions, the last as Bechuanaland Assistant Commissioner in 1887. Mackenzie saw his position as trying to bring the interests of the African peoples to the attention of the British government in South Africa, but the British appointed him to manage disputes between settlers and the tribes. Mackenzie did not last long because he saw quickly that the British government cared more about the expanding European settlements than the welfare of the tribes. Moffat was more amenable to British interests and negotiated treaties which allowed the British to take more land, this time in Zimbabwe. Eventually, both came to recognize that British imperialism was more about settlement and conquest of new territory than help for Africans. Moffat was eventually moved out of his Assistant Commissioner position by Cecil Rhodes—governor general of South Africa and the chief architect of British expansionism there— because of Moffat's outspoken condemnation of land grabs in South Africa as "wholesale robbery." Thereafter, he served as a preacher to prisoners and became a champion of rights for South Africans. Mackenzie campaigned against white attacks and land grabs against northern tribes in South Africa. He even formed a support committee for South Africans, the South African Committee. In both cases, these missionaries' influence within and outside of the colonial government were quite limited, and Rhodes mostly ignored their pleas. McKenzie and Moffat were clearly imperialists; however, they condemned the most crude and exploitative aspects of imperialism, especially the physical and social dislocations that accompanied it. In their role as middlemen, they introduced the Africans to a world Africans themselves did not create nor could control, and however unwittingly, these missionaries helped to open Africa up for plunder. Whether the missionaries resisted or supported the colonial government, they became conduits for the dramatic changes that made Africa more conducive to conquest.

ISLAM IN AFRICA

While Christianity became the dominant European religion to be transmitted to South Africa, many Islamic Asians from Dutch East Indies came as slaves and political prisoners of the Dutch Boer ("farmer") state in South Africa. The Dutch saw Islam as a false religion and dangerous to the state. Until 1804, it was illegal to practice Islam in public. Shortly thereafter, the first mosque was founded in South Africa and in 1912 the first madrasa (Islamic school of theology) was founded there. Muslims in South Africa were slow to resist apartheid (legal racial segregation), but after 1983 when the government proposed a new parliamentary system that was clearly designed to divide blacks against mixed race and Asian peoples, Muslims united with other anti-apartheid groups to oppose it and it was finally overthrown in 1994 with the first fully democratic elections.

While Muslims comprised a small minority in South Africa, Islam had long been the preeminent religion of the northern part of Africa, an extension of the spread of the first Arab and then the Islamic Ottoman empires into Egypt, Sudan, and other parts of the Mediterranean coast of Africa. Islam even spread across the Sahara Desert into northern Nigeria and other areas of the west coast of Africa. Timbuktu, located in an area which was once at the western edge of the Sahara Desert but is now overtaken by desert, was a great center for Islamic learning with mosques and madrasas and Muslim scholars and teachers. The encounter of Islam with Africa thus took place over a very long time and is still continuing.

Driven by religious differences, the encounter of Muslims and Christians in Africa in the period of European colonialism was characterized by tension and open conflict. In Sudan, which was under the control of the Ottoman Empire in the 1800s, a popular Islamic rebellion broke out in the 1880s led by a Mahdi (Holy Warrior) named Muhammad Ahmad, whose supporters were closely engaged in slave trading. Because of the proximity of Sudan to Egypt, which had recently come under the control of the British, the British invaded Sudan in the name of anti-slavery to put down the rebellion which threatened their authority in Egypt. After a combined British and Egyptian force was defeated by the Mahdi, the British sought to remove Egyptian officials and subjects from the region. They entrusted this mission to Charles "Chinese" Gordon ("Chinese" because he had served the Chinese Qing government in putting down the Taiping Rebellion in the 1850s). Gordon had earlier been governor general of Sudan under the Egyptian Khedive who had been under the suzerainty of the Ottoman Empire. When Gordon returned to Sudan to evacuate the area of British and Egyptian subjects, he found that task impossible. He sought to offer the Mahdi the governorship of part of the Sudan and contemplated allowing slavery in the hope of saving Egyptian and African lives, but he became trapped in Khartoum due to the advance of the Mahdi's forces and British dithering. He was killed defending the city in 1885 mere hours before a belatedly sent relief force arrived. He was seen as a martyr to the cause of civilization in Great Britain and his death helped fuel the British takeover of Sudan in the 1890s on terms that Gordon—a defender of oppressed Irish and Indian colonial subjects—would likely have deplored.

In the southern part of Sudan, Christianity dating to ancient times reemerged under British tutelage at mission settlements and schools. In the north, Islam held sway. After the British withdrew from Sudan in the 1950s, conflict between the two developed almost immediately as the majority Muslim northern population took the reins of government and the southern Christian population began to suffer from a new internal Islamic colonialism by the north that replaced British colonialism. Civil war broke out and only in the last few years has an uneasy peace been brokered and a referendum held in 2011 in which a huge majority of southerners voted to approve semi-autonomy for the Christian southern part of Sudan.

From 1885 to the present, Christian southerners and Arab Islamic northerners in Sudan encountered one another not only on the battlefield but also in the classroom. The British goals for educating the Sudanese were to create bureaucrats capable of running the British Empire in the Sudan and to give them the gift of western civilization. Shortly after takeover, the British established several schools including Gordon College named after Charles Gordon. Gordon College's curriculum and activities offered a western-style education: The College occupied a beautiful spot on the Nile River in Khartoum and had excellent facilities. Sports were emphasized in the activities of the school because the British believed that sports would build the character of the Sudanese people as they believed it had built their own. The British catered to northern Arab students whose families were wealthy and influential in government rather than to southern mostly Christian "blacks" (of Nubian descent and with darker skin color) to the consternation of Christians and missionary societies from Great Britain. The lower status "blacks" were funneled into trade and vocational schools, similar to white American attempts to funnel American blacks into vocational training after the Civil War. Very few southerners made it into Gordon College and they were generally stigmatized if they did, as were students from the Darfur region or the very eastern part of Sudan on the Red Sea where Muslim nomadic peoples called the Beja lived.

British bureaucrats who worked in Sudan sometimes sought to exploit such ethnic and religious divides to dampen proto-Sudanese nationalism as it began to arise in the pre–World War II period. In one case a Gordon College graduate took a job in the Financial Secretary's Office in Khartoum. Khidir Hamad, a young Arab stenographer, was interrogated by a British inspector in the office about his nationality and he replied that he was "Sudanese." The inspector responded by referring to his "tribe" at which point Hamad retorted that he refused to recognize "these tribalisms." The British inspector then baited him saying, "Did Gordon College teach you to deny your nationalities [tribal identity]?"[6] He replied that Gordon College had nothing to do with tribes. Hamad clearly possessed ideas of Sudanese nationalism and independence. Later, as he reflected on his interrogation he remarked that "People take the term Sudanese for granted now, for indeed it became a term of pride but once upon a time it was attacked from every direction…"[7] Educating Sudanese for bureaucratic roles had given them a vocabulary that included independence, freedom, nationalism, and other terms that provoked fear among the British. So the British walked a tightrope of offering a liberal western-style educational training while trying to discourage ideas of self-rule and independence. As in India, this effort to preach freedom as an ideal but deny it in practice was doomed. It only served to promote independence movements throughout the British Empire.

By the 1920s to 1930s Gordon College graduates had become radicalized enough to start an independence movement, in part through the influence of Egyptian students who attended Gordon College and tended to be nationalistic and anti-British (eventually the British barred Egyptians altogether from attending the College). In the early 1920s the White Flag League, an organization committed to Sudanese independence, was founded by graduates of Gordon College, many of whom had become lower level employees in the colonial bureaucracy. These Gordon College graduates had been trained to assume leadership positions, but the British had placed them in menial positions within the bureaucracy such as in the Postal and Telegraph Service or in doing stenography. And then in 1923, independence ideas and anti-British feelings boiled over into a series of protests and demonstrations. There were protests in the major cities of the north. One event, the celebration of the Prophet Muhammad's birthday at Omdurman, the second largest city in the Sudan, became a subtle protest against the British when several poets, all graduates of Gordon College, took the podium and read verses in Arabic celebrating Muslim heroes from the past and crying out for freedom. This took place right under the noses of British officials, who sat in the front row in the audience but did not understand Arabic. The poets had to feel some satisfaction about this subterfuge. But the protests themselves died down quickly and there were few arrests. They did, however, set the stage for the movement which culminated in Sudan receiving its independence in 1956.

British and Sudanese encounters were mostly structured by school or workplace. There were very few social encounters. The British had their own clubs from which the Sudanese were barred. This division between the British and Sudanese, a reflection of the British sense of superiority, was part racial, part social, and part political. There was also a dress code at Gordon College that emphasized traditional dress. The diversity of traditional tribal dress was less threatening to British rulers than the modern garb of western suits, which seemed to suggest that Sudan was becoming united and building the capacity to be an independent nation. Part of the threat to British overlords was cultural; a British subject would always feel himself superior to a person identified as tribal but these new ideas of nationhood threatened not only the colonial political system but also the British sense of superiority.

RISE OF NATIONALISM AND DECOLONIZATION

As the Sudan example illustrates, a new sense of nationalism appeared in Africa in the early twentieth century and impacted how Africans interacted with European rulers. Africans began to assert their desire for independence from their colonial overlords. World Wars I and II significantly eroded the European concept of superiority. Were Europeans, who killed one another in such vast numbers and committed genocide, really superior to Africans? Africans served in both wars and saw firsthand the brutality of Europeans. In addition, Africans shed their blood on the battlefields of the wars and began to believe that their sacrifice entitled them to a greater say in their own governance. In 1922 in Egypt, the British allowed Egyptians to organize political parties and hold elections. To their surprise the independence-minded party, the Wafd Party, won the elections and began to rule in Egypt. However, the British government still controlled Egypt's foreign policy and the Suez Canal and exerted strong influence over the politics of Egypt.

In Somalia, Sayyid Hasan and his so-called "Dervish Army" began a long struggle for independence from not one but three different foreign powers—the British, the Italians, and the Ethiopians. Abd al-Krim began a war of independence against the Spanish in northern Morocco. He created a republic in the mountains of Morocco and envisioned uniting Berber-speaking clans into a nation where equality would reign and modern education and other services would be available to the people. In South Africa, African farmers and others who found themselves disenfranchised by apartheid organized the African National Congress (ANC), an organization based upon the Indian National Congress from the time of India's independence movement earlier in the century. In West Africa, nationalists united to form the West African Students Union, led by Kwame Nkrumah and others. Nkrumah became a famous Pan-Africanist, arguing for regional cooperation in West Africa against the colonial powers. He became the first president of newly independent Ghana in 1960. The *African Morning Post*, a Pan-African newspaper, was founded in Nigeria in 1934 by Benjamin Azikiwe. Azikiwe went onto become the first president of Nigeria in 1963.

In a different kind of encounter outside of colonialism, both Nkrumah and Azikiwe studied in the United States as college students in the 1930s to 1940s. Both received bachelor's degrees at Lincoln University in Pennsylvania and master's degrees at the University of Pennsylvania. Azikiwe even became

Kwame Nkrumah became an important nationalist leader in Africa but brought significant ideas about Pan-Africanism from his education in the United States. Everett Collection.

an instructor for a short period at Lincoln University. In their time in the United States, Nkrumah and Azikiwe were deeply influenced by the ideas of Marcus Garvey and W.E.B. Dubois, champions of African pride and unity across the world, and generally soaked in the intellectual atmosphere of Pan-Africanism, an argument that Africans everywhere should be free from colonial domination and that Africans should have the right to determine their own future. Their encounter with Americans, especially Garvey and Dubois, profoundly influenced their thinking about colonialism and independence for their homelands. They and others helped to found Pan-African organizations such as the Pan-African Congress.

These political elites were part of a small group of Africans who became well educated and interacted closely with westerners. Because Africa had few educational institutions, many elites had to travel to Europe or the United States to receive education. They became well acquainted with their hosts and imbibed western political theory and economics, including concepts of sovereignty and nationhood. Like Mohandas Gandhi, they came to appreciate western political ideas of freedom and liberty, and upon their return to Africa, they sought to apply these ideas in the colonial context by resisting European domination and arguing for independence. Their encounter with westerners and western ideas created a unique synthesis of western and non-western influences, and this experience allowed these elites to become effective independence leaders back in their homes. They understood the language, politics, and culture of their homeland and they also understood the West and how to deal with western imperialists. So it is no surprise that Nkrumah and Azikiwe went from Africa to Pennsylvania and then back to Africa to lead anti-colonial revolutions. It was through encounter with others, including these westerners, that some of the future leadership of Africa came to maturity and eventually took the reigns of power.

Conclusion

The nineteenth- and twentieth-century European encounters on the continent of Africa deeply influenced the situation in Africa today. The legacy of unequal power in many of the encounters during the period of western imperialism has left parts of Africa in jeopardy today. And former colonial powers such as the British, French, and Belgians have continued to exert influence after giving their colonies independence through control of resources or other forms of economic control in a process called neo-colonialism. But Africa has survived, and the activism and agency of Africans themselves in these encounters opened Africa to change. Africa went from being dominated by Europeans to the status of an independent continent. By using European liberalism against Europe, Africans freed themselves from European control. When they became strong enough, Africans also built their own institutions through these encounters. By embracing the encounters of many different peoples and ideas in the last two centuries, Africa is building its own future today.

Questions for Discussion

1. Explain why colonialism in Africa happened with such speed and completeness.
2. Describe how Europeans viewed Africa in the nineteenth century.
3. Explain why the physical location of the missionary settlement was so important to both missionaries and African rulers.
4. How did Africans view missionaries and how did these views impact the missionaries' prospects for gaining converts to Christianity?
5. Explain the sources of conflict between Muslims and Christians in the Sudan?
6. Why did the British tend to emphasize tribal and religious forms of identity in the Sudan?
7. How did the Sudanese establish their own evolving identities and goals of independence within British rule?
8. Describe the ways Africans asserted their independence from Europeans? How did Africans develop the ideas and skills to play a leadership role in decolonization? How did they push forward their ideas and plans?

Endnotes

1. John Campbell, Klaarwater Letter, July 26, 1813 Found in Council of World Missions, London Missionary Society Incoming Letters (South Africa), 5-2-D.
2. Samuel Broadbent, *A Narrative of the First Introduction of Christianity amongst the Barolong Tribe of the Bechuanas, South Africa* (London: Wesleyan Mission House, 1865), p. 2.
3. Henry Stanley, another famous explorer later in the century, was paid to find the allegedly lost Livingstone as a publicity stunt meant to sell newspapers (Livingstone was not actually lost!). When he encountered Livingstone living in an African village, Stanley was said to exclaim, "Dr. Livingstone, I presume."
4. David Livingstone, *Livingstone's Private Journals, 1851–1853*, edited by Isaac Schapera (Berkeley and Los Angeles: University of California Press, 1960), p. 239f.
5. David Livingstone, *David Livingstone: South African Papers, 1849–1853*, edited by Isaac Schapera (Cape Town, South Africa: The Van Riebeeck Society, 1974), p. 14.
6. Heather Sharkey, *Nationalism and Culture in the Anglo-Egyptian Sudan* (Berkeley and Los Angeles: University of California Press, 2003), p. 33.
7. Ibid.

Twentieth Century Challenges

Testing the Limits of Multiculturalism: Immigration into Europe in the Twentieth and Twenty-First Century

Western Europe is in the midst of a multicultural revolution. Immigrants from all over the globe have flooded that subcontinent since World War II. Their arrival has been perceived as so explosive that it has produced counter movements expressed by the need on the part of many peoples, indigenous and immigrant, to reaffirm their cultural identities and the cultural boundaries that set them apart from other cultures and nations. The tension between a multicultural world community and movements to assert essential cultural values has turned Western Europe into a contested ground that suggests the conflicts and compromises that will become increasingly prevalent throughout the globalizing world.

Western Europe is experiencing tremendous immigration from areas that surround it, mainly from North Africa, the Balkans, Turkey, Eastern Europe, and Russia. This influx is at historically high levels. About 2 million immigrants have entered Europe annually since 2003. Berlin now has the third largest Turkish population in the world. This immigration started in the post–World War II economic boom when European leaders invited immigrants to settle in Europe and fill out the labor pool. After the recession in the 1970s, many European countries had decided to stop actively bringing in new immigrants. But by that time, the flow of immigrants, who were attracted to the higher standard of living in Europe and came from countries unstable politically

Two girls, Irish and Bengali, stop for a rest during playtime at Kingsmead School. Kingsmead is one of the most diverse and impoverished areas of London. Photographer Gidoen Mendel gave the schoolchildren there cameras to record events in their lives. The result is a stunning visual display of Britain's multiculturalism.   Gideon Mendel/In Pictures/Corbis.

and embroiled in violence, became much stronger. As a result, the number of immigrants has increased dramatically in more recent decades.

Single men predominated in the migrant labor pool before the 1970s and they many times came temporarily, eventually returning home with earned wages in their pockets. More recently entire families have come to Europe to settle permanently. Immigrants from the same country tend to settle close to one another and they have retained their connections to their home countries, sometimes returning for vacations, sending money back home, or even living part of the year in their home countries and part of the year in Europe. Many immigrants are impoverished in Europe, but in their home countries where their European wages go much further, they are thought to be wealthy and successful. Some immigrants will go far to impress family back home. For example, some Turkish immigrants in Belgium will borrow money to buy an expensive car to drive back to Turkey to impress their relatives with their success and riches and then sell the car when they return to Europe.

In Europe, which has some of the lowest birthrates in the world, immigration is an important solution to the dwindling labor pool. Spain, Italy, and Greece are all below 1.5 births per female. Because it takes 2.1 children to maintain the current population level, the number of young people in Europe has fallen and the population of Europe is shrinking and aging rapidly. It is estimated that 500,000 new immigrants per year will be needed in Germany to maintain the age balance there. Since Europe needs more people to fill out its workforce, one might assume that Europeans would welcome these new immigrants with open arms, since they are filling the population void. But the reality of the immigration scene in Europe is much more complicated. Immigrants who cannot find jobs have become a burden on Europe's welfare system. In addition, with immigrants has come the fear on the part of Western Europeans of being overwhelmed by them, especially of being taken over by Muslims, people with a religion (Islam) and way of life which is perceived as alien to European traditions.

In the earlier single-male immigration, the cultural values of the immigrants were not an issue, but today, the permanent residence of immigrant families who are still very attached culturally to their home countries has created a clash of cultural values and practices between Europeans and immigrant communities which has become a flashpoint, drawing much attention in the world's media. To argue that this is a clash between East and West or between Christian and Muslim civilizations (as Samuel Huntington does in his work *The Clash of Civilizations*) oversimplifies what is happening in Europe. The much greater complexity of these encounters needs to be analyzed more closely to fully understand the situation. For example newspaper headlines have focused on Muslim immigration, which leads one to conclude that the immigration to Europe is mostly from Islamic countries.

Young German skinheads give a Nazi salute at a right-wing demonstration. Youths like these form the vanguard of the anti-immigrant movement. Reuters/Corbis.

Yet less than 50 percent of the immigrants to Europe in the postwar period are Muslim. The rest offer a diversity of backgrounds and experiences that have added greatly to the complexity of immigration. In Spain, where one would assume that most immigrants would come from Muslim Morocco or other neighboring Islamic countries, the largest group of immigrants are Catholics from Latin America. This is a result of deliberate Spanish government policy that invites Latin Americans to emigrate because of their fluency in the Spanish language and their cultural background, which is similar to Spanish culture. This policy is an attempt to limit the number of Muslim immigrants because they are seen as culturally alien. Ironically, the Spanish who once conquered much of Latin America now have invited Latin Americans to come to Spain, and possibly one day if the numbers of Latin immigrants become high enough, they will in turn come to dominate Spain.

Some Europeans have come to see the new immigrants as undesirable and have campaigned for stricter immigration controls. Governments have also attempted to discourage immigration in a variety of ways. In 2007, the Spanish government took out advertisements in northwest Africa describing how illegal immigrants would be caught and deported and those who stayed would be miserable in Spain to discourage potential immigrants from Morocco and other African countries. The concept of multiculturalism has been directly questioned by the leaders of France, Germany, and the United Kingdom (Great Britain). In 2011, David Cameron, prime minister of the United Kingdom, reversed some aspects of the official British policy of toleration and multiculturalism, which has allowed all immigrants to live according to their own cultural values in separate communities. Cameron argued that Europe had made a mistake in not fostering a common spirit of western liberal values of human rights, democracy, and equality before the law and needed to take action to assimilate the immigrants to these values. The subtext for Cameron's announcement was pressure by the United States for Cameron to reign in Muslim radicals in the United Kingdom who had denounced the West and were thought to promote terrorist activities with their speech.

CONFLICTS

Europeans debating the relative value of immigration face two major issues: the assimilation or lack thereof of immigrants into European culture and Europe's tolerance or intolerance of them. Cultural conservatives question the relatively open immigration policies of Europe because in their view the policies threaten to destroy Europe's cultural heritage and replace it with an alien religion and culture. Liberals and radicals on the other hand defend immigration and the immigrants fiercely, arguing that immigration is needed in Europe to buoy the economy and is good for the immigrants because it raises their standard of living and offers them a civil democratic political system. At one extreme, a few pro-immigrant Europeans display contempt for European culture and religion and point to twentieth-century European

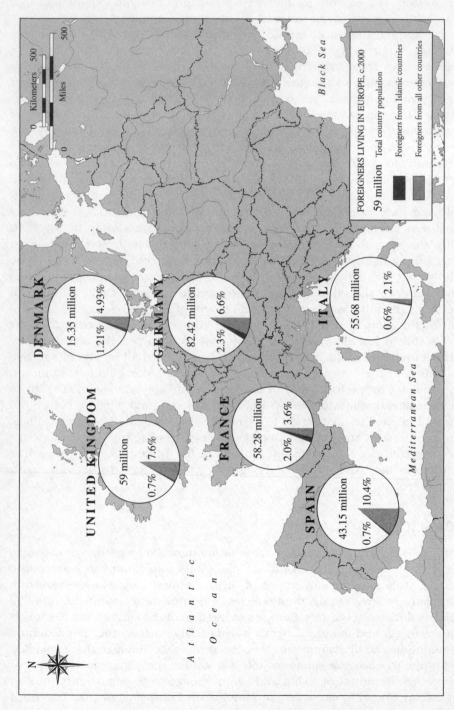

FOREIGNERS LIVING IN EUROPE, c.2000

59 million   Total country population

■ Foreigners from Islamic countries

▨ Foreigners from all other countries

UNITED KINGDOM
59 million
0.7%   7.6%

DENMARK
15.35 million
1.21%   4.93%

GERMANY
82.42 million
2.3%   6.6%

FRANCE
58.28 million
2.0%   3.6%

SPAIN
43.15 million
0.7%   10.4%

ITALY
55.68 million
0.6%   2.1%

Atlantic Ocean

Mediterranean Sea

Black Sea

N

Kilometers   0   500
Miles   0   500

MAP 10.1   Map of Postwar Immigration into Europe, 2000

190

wars and the Holocaust to show that the European cultural heritage doesn't deserve to be protected. At the other end of the spectrum, anti-immigrant groups have used violence to attack immigrants and their cultures.

The encounter between Islam and Europe involves many particular points of conflict. Languages, cultural assumptions, and the question of assimilation or acculturation are all sources of tension between Muslims and Europeans. While Europeans want the new immigrants to learn their language, many times the immigrants refuse as a statement of defiance against European culture. In the Parisian ghettos of Montfermeil and Goutte d'Ore, French is missing from the languages spoken; instead a great variety of African languages and Arabic are heard.

But not all of the points of contact have been points of conflict. Both sides have had to accommodate the other. For instance, Ford Motor Company in Cologne, Germany, has created prayer areas for Muslims so that they can pray during the work-day; its factory lunchrooms observe Muslim dietary requirements and serve meals after sundown during the month of Ramadan. (Ramadan is a Muslim religious holiday in which fasting is observed during the daylight hours. Muslims eat and drink once the sun has gone down.) The Austrian military provides special foods for Muslim soldiers and areas for prayer; Muslim clerics are appointed chaplains to serve them. In turn, these Muslim soldiers who had refused to salute the Austrian flag were given permission by their chaplain to do so. So the possibility of middle ground accommodation exists although there may be more glaring examples of conflict than cooperation.

LAW AND SEX

Another point of conflict is Islamic law or Shariah and the European legal system. The two systems are incompatible in many different ways, with different rules about sex, exposure of the female body in public, treatment of women in general, food, even the use of money for investment. Therefore sex, gender, and dress have become matters of heightened cultural debate in the encounter.

It has been said that there is no better example of the conflict than differences over sex. Europeans who have become more and more committed to sexual liberation in the twentieth century confront a religion in Islam that has an age-old commitment to control sexuality, especially female sexuality. Islam requires females to be covered at all times in public, including their heads and in some cases faces. Some Muslim cultures practice female mutilation, sometimes referred to as female circumcision, in which the clitoris is removed in childhood and/or the vagina is sewn shut. While scholars of the Koran have found no text stipulating this practice, nonetheless Islamic cultures in North and East Africa continue this practice and various Islamic immigrants have brought the practice with them to Europe. Female liberation in Europe confronts an archaic Puritanism in Islam in Europe. It is no surprise, therefore, that this is an area where there has been an immense amount of controversy.

It would seem that in this situation, there is very little room for adaptation or accommodation. However, adaptation has taken place in between the cracks in culture and one can see a slight movement toward a middle ground. Whether it is a temporary or permanent trend is unclear. For Muslims, female chastity before marriage is paramount. Any evidence that a woman has engaged in premarital sex can be devastating for the woman's prospects for marriage and family and can result in even worse consequences such as beatings, organized rape, or even murder at the hands of her family. In Europe, where gynecological surgery is a ready option, a few Muslims have taken to covering up the evidence of premarital sex with surgery. They have had their daughters undertake a gynecological procedure called hymenoplasty to create a new hymen and in a few cases even embedded a capsule with blood-like substance in the newly constructed hymen. On the surface, this might seem like a ridiculous and expensive concealment of the truth. However, it does show that some Muslims are beginning to attempt to adapt to the realities of living in the cultural context of Europe, where premarital sex is common and widely accepted, but where Muslims rules about chastity still apply. Surgery allows young females to participate in both cultures, albeit by participating in a hoax. As more and more Muslims engage in premarital sex and more surgeries are done, at some point it might become clear to Muslim communities that premarital female chastity is no longer worth going to such great lengths to protect. Of course there is no guarantee that this will happen, but this is the nature of middle ground accommodation. It is tenuous and temporary but it has the potential to lead to permanent cultural shifts and new cultural formations. The other point to be made is that there are many Muslim leaders who have spoken out against clitoris removal so we should be careful not to assume that all Muslims think and act alike.

A closely related issue is Islamic practice concerning marriage and divorce and its relation to the European political state. Currently, marriage and divorce proceedings for Muslims in Europe are done many times at the mosque by Muslim clerics. While this seems to work within the European system, some Europeans fear that eventually governments will sanction these proceedings. Interestingly, the British government put in place a mechanism in the eighteenth century to allow for minority communities to adjudicate their own marriages and divorces by allowing for the creation of rabbinical courts to exist and negotiate these proceedings. In a technical sense, the courts do not have the power of state law so they are more like arbitrations than legal judgments, but nonetheless a way was found to accommodate a disparate community's need to keep its own culture within an alien legal framework. Muslims have the same recourse within Britain to have clerics arbitrate divorce.

Arranged marriages represent another point of conflict between European and Muslim sensibilities. Among many Muslims in Europe, finding a marriage partner among the European population is considered unacceptable. Only 1 percent of Pakistanis and Bangladeshis in Great Britain have chosen a white European partner. In addition, more than half of immigrant marriages are with spouses born abroad. After new restrictions on immigration were put into place in the 1980s, many of the recent immigrants have come as brides to be married to someone already living in Europe. And among this group arranged marriages are quite common. This would seem to be an area where there is very little middle ground accommodation to be made. Some Europeans have even suggested that arranged marriage is illegal in Europe. However, an experimental new marriage law in Denmark demonstrates that given the right circumstances, cross-cultural marriages are a viable option. The law, which requires that Danish citizens who want to marry non-EU spouses have to be at least 24 years old, forces young immigrants to either wait or marry a Danish citizen. The law has dramatically lowered the number of marriages between non-western Danes and nonciti-zens from 63 percent in 2002 to 38 percent in 2005. Non-western Danes now have to choose whether they want to stay in Denmark and marry and if so, they are compelled to look for a partner among European Danes by virtue of the small number of non-western females residing in Denmark. While the law is distasteful to many Europeans for its coercive approach, some supporters claim that it is working to help integrate non-Danes into Danish society. "There is a completely different tendency now amongst younger groups of immigrants and their children to instead look for a partner here in Denmark or in Europe," said Zubair Butt Hussain, spokesperson for the organization Muslims in Dialogue.[1] The result from the encounter is likely to be a cultural change and hybridity over a longer period. In other news that suggests movement toward cross-cultural mixing, a recent study in England found that interethnic unions and mixed race children have increased by 20 percent over the last 10 years, even though Muslims in England are still mostly marrying within their own ethnic and religious groups. This is another positive sign for cultural change in the encounter but must be measured against evidence that Muslim communities in Europe are still highly segregated.

Another area where women are disproportionately impacted is the controversies over the wearing of the headscarf by Muslim women. The Koran stipulates modesty for women and this has translated into a variety of headscarves in Islamic culture ranging from a simple scarf that Turkish women wear to the hijab, which covers the hair completely, to the niqab, worn in Saudi Arabia, which covers hair and the whole face with eye slits to see out of, to the burqa, which covers the whole body and is worn in Afghanistan. Such a dramatically visible and distinctive cultural practice was bound to create clashes and controversies in Europe, especially in a prevailing climate of female liberation. Like the other cultural practices mentioned above, the headscarf looks like a big step backward in the view of European feminists. The conflict has been strongest in the schools where native European students and teachers are confronted up close with this visible display of cultural difference. France has responded most aggressively, instituting a ban on the wearing of any religious symbols in schools in 2003 that included large crosses and headscarves. While the French law was deemed constitutional because it did not discriminate between Christian and Muslim religious symbols, no one was able to explain exactly what a "large cross" meant and so Christians who wanted to wear a cross around their neck were allowed to do so. It was apparent to everyone including the Muslim community in France that the law was aimed at the headscarf. The law, effective in keeping the headscarf out of schools, further alienated Muslims from mainstream French society.

EXTREMES: ISLAMOPHOBIA AND ANTI-SEMITISM

The immigration debate has produced some extreme responses on both sides. Anti-immigrant political parties exist in every European country. The most prominent of these parties, the French Front National led by Jean Marie Le Pen in the 1990s to 2000s, won the first round in the presidential election in 2002. The British and the Germans have the smallest, weakest anti-immigrant parties but both countries have the strongest most violent anti-immigrant gangs. The neo-Nazi groups and skinheads from Germany and England, respectively, roam the streets looking for immigrants to beat up or worse. It could be that the prominence of extremely violent groups in both countries is the result of the weakness of the political actors on the right wing of the immigrant debate. Anti-immigrant rhetoric is taken up by the well-organized and powerful French Front National in France and therefore its extremely violent groups are smaller.

Debates over the building of mosques have produced extreme responses as well. In Switzerland recently a national referendum banning the building of minarets on mosques passed by a 57.5 percent majority. The Swiss anti-immigrant political party, the Swiss Peoples Party, led the campaign and those who voted in favor of it expressed the fear (cultivated by the Peoples Party) that Muslims would take over the government and establish Muslim law of Shariah. This attitude is prevalent in a country where Muslims make up only 5 percent of the population as of 2009.

In northern Italy, the Lega Party, a right-wing anti-immigrant political party, has fought the building of a mosque in Lodi for several years. In 2000, Lega supporters marched to the site of the mosque and dumped pig urine all over it. (Muslims consider pigs to be unclean and do not eat pork.) Then the Party invited a priest to say a mass on the same ground, further desecrating it in the eyes of Muslims. Muslim leaders were appalled by these acts but Lega's actions have prevented the mosque from being built there. Illustrating further strong anti-Muslim feelings in Italy, an Italian politician from the conservative political party Forza Italia (the former party of Silvio Berlusconi, the Italian prime minister) stated, "In a few years, Muslim immigrants will make up 10 to 15 percent of the population, thus putting in danger the purity of our values. They aim to marry our women, to convert them to Islam, and to bring down our society's structure from the inside."[2] Italy's Muslim population made up only 1.4 percent of the total in 2009. This paranoid response has found a hearing in Italy, especially in northern Italy, where the anti-immigrant sentiment is strong. But this sentiment is not universal. Romano Prodi, the last president of the European Commission, officially inaugurated a religious building in the city of Novellara in Emilia-Romagna. The opening celebrated freedom of religion and diversity. In this case, however, the structure was a Sikh Hindu Temple, not a Muslim mosque. Thus, Italians have exaggerated the dangers of Islam while also in certain cases embracing some kinds of diversity. Extremists have played upon irrational fears of domination in many of the debates over Islam.

In Germany the debate over immigration has become polarized between the xenophobic and violent neo-Nazis and the strongly pro-immigrant and anti-racist movement. The strongly pro-immigrant movement is an interesting phenomenon there. This movement has grown strong in post–World War II Germany because the memory of the Nazis and the Jewish Holocaust in wartime Germany has had a profound impact on the collective psyche of the German people. The politics of national guilt over the Nazi past and the Holocaust has fed the development of the anti-racist movement and political parties in Germany. These groups despise the German past and support immigration and the immigrants very strongly. In addition, the political left in Europe has felt guilt over the legacy of European imperialism and has responded by embracing immigration from former colonies.

Among immigrants themselves the same extremes can be found, ranging from harsh criticism of Islamic culture, Shariah law, and Muslim immigrants' treatment of women to ethnocentrism against European culture, and virulent anti-Semitism. Ayaan Hirsi Ali, a Somali woman who immigrated to the Netherlands, has been outspoken in favor of Muslim women's rights and a sharp critic of Shariah law and Islamic fundamentalism. She has condemned female circumcision practiced in her home country. She fears Muslim immigrants' rapidly increasing numbers will someday impose Shariah law in the cities of Europe. While her support of Muslim women is admirable, she has invoked the same fears about Muslim domination as many among the political right in Europe.

Muslim immigrants' anti-Semitism has also emerged in Europe. In the aftermath of the second Palestinian uprising against Israeli rule in 2000 and the 9/11 attacks, Europe experienced an increase in anti-Semitic acts among Muslim immigrants. In France, Muslim students poured ridicule on teachers giving lectures on the Holocaust. Anti-Semitic violence in France increased dramatically after the 9/11 attacks, giving rise to the assumption that the World Trade Center attacks had emboldened radical elements among European Muslims. Jewish schools were firebombed, synagogues and cemeteries desecrated, and Jewish people assaulted.

In another example of extremism, the debate surrounding a newspaper-sponsored cartoon contest in which political cartoons were drawn about the Muslim Prophet Muhammad in Denmark in 2005 produced violence and death. In a tragic irony, the original intent of the cartoon contest was multicultural education. A Danish children's book writer was writing a book about Islam with the intention of educating Europeans and encouraging multiculturalism and wanted to include an image of the prophet of Islam. He could find no one to do the illustration because Muslims disapprove of images of him and artists were afraid of violence that might be directed against them. A Danish newspaper editor took up the author's cause and decided to combat what he saw as self-censorship by holding a cartoon contest and commissioning a dozen cartoons depicting the Prophet Muhammad to be published in his newspaper, *Jyllands-Posten*. The published images were unflattering to Islam—the cartoonists were accused of being anti-Islamic by Muslims—and included one cartoon with the image of an Arab with a stick of dynamite in his turban. Kurt Westergaard, who drew the turban image, is a secularist who was motivated by his disgust with religious extremism. He explained that he intended his illustration to critique radical Islamists' use of religion to justify violence. But his extreme attempt to discredit extremism simply provoked more extremism. The cartoons stirred up outrage among the Muslim community in Denmark and a price was put on the head of the *Jyllands-Posten* editor, Flemming Rose, by a radical Pakistani political party. Then some Danish Muslim clerics traveled to the Middle East and showed the cartoons there. The situation exploded into an anti-Danish, anti-European rampage. Europeans were attacked and several were killed amid Nigerian protests and Middle Eastern countries started a boycott against Danish products such as Legos and Bang & Olufson. In 2008 a plot to assassinate Westergaard was uncovered and three people were arrested. More recently, an assailant broke into Westergaard's home and attempted to kill him. Westergaard barricaded himself in a specially built panic room that likely saved his life. What had started as an attempt to bridge the cultural gap between Europe and Islam had turned into an attack on Islam in the cartoons and then an Islamic attack on Europeans. That the encounter could so easily and quickly turn from multiculturalism into stereotypes and violence reminds us of the volatility of the situation in Europe. However, the absolutism of extremists on all sides belies the inevitable changes taking place in Europe as Europeans and immigrants change in response to each other.

NON-MUSLIM IMMIGRANT EXPERIENCES

Immigrants from Eastern Europe and the Caribbean have had quite different experiences in Europe than Muslim immigrants. Away from the debates, controversies, and absolutisms of the Islam-in-Europe equation, many other immigrants are encountering Europe for the first time. These immigrants have become much more integrated into European society than Muslims, and Europeans have been more open to the changes these immigrants have brought. Exploring the experiences of the non-Muslim immigrants is easier to do because researchers have studied them and done oral interviews with them. These immigrants have experienced a range of cultural responses including assimilation, acculturation, and even creation of a hybrid culture as in Creole Amsterdam. But the persistence of the home culture of these immigrants is also on display throughout Europe. Of course, generalizations about their experience are hazardous and have the same limitation of any generalization. But in general, the immigrants express a two-sided view on the encounter. Those who are successful emphasize the risks and personal struggle and pain of leaving their homes and home country and then their happiness at having become successful in their new adopted country. On the other hand, among Eastern Europeans such as Bulgarians, there is a strong sense that they don't quite fit in or haven't fully adapted to European culture even after several years. One Dutch woman stated of her husband who immigrated from Bulgaria to Amsterdam and has became a successful psychotherapist,

> And my Dutch friends, they think that Andreas can be quite difficult. It's so funny, to them, I have to keep explaining: he's from Bulgaria, he's used to other ways of being in relationship, of treating women, and he does think about it, he does his best. But it's the upbringing and a socialization that you just can't flatten out or erase.[3]

Immigrants from the Caribbean to Europe have also brought their home culture to Europe. For instance, immigrants to Amsterdam arrived from the former Dutch Caribbean colonies of Curacao, Aruba, Bonaire, St. Eustatius, Saba, St. Maarten, and also Suriname in northern South America. Together with Sub-Saharan Africans, they make Amsterdam the largest black immigrant city in Europe, comprising over 7 percent of its population in 2000. But the word "black" does not describe these immigrants very well, especially those from Suriname. Known for its interesting ethnic mix, Suriname was an early plantation colony of the Dutch in South America where African slaves were brought in to do the labor. Due the brutal conditions on the plantations, slaves many times escaped into the jungle, formed communities with Native South Americans, and had offspring with them; they were referred to as Maroons. The Maroons were very successful and became a threat to the plantations, raiding, plundering, and freeing slaves. Soon Suriname became even more ethnically mixed. After the end of slavery, Asians from Dutch colonies in the East Indies and elsewhere in Asia were brought in to work on the plantations. Javanese from Indonesia, Chinese, Indians, and even some Arabs migrated to Suriname as laborers. In the process, Suriname became one of the most ethnically and culturally diverse places in the world. African-European, African-Native American, and African-Asian mixed peoples, sometimes referred to as Creoles, then migrated to Amsterdam starting in the 1970s.

Unlike Eastern Europeans who more often have been able to get good jobs and become economically independent, immigrants from the Caribbean and Suriname have remained at the margins of the Dutch economy, unemployed and living off of welfare checks or doing wage labor. But in their social life, Creoles have created a strong public presence in Amsterdam with a Creole musical style, unique dress, and a party circuit. The parties can happen in public places such as clubs or in the immigrants' homes as in family parties. The music and parties provide a place where the Surinamese, who otherwise feel quite alien in Europe, can express themselves. Creoles state that Amsterdam is the only city in which they feel at home because of its large Creole population. Like African-American subculture in the United States, Creole subculture in Amsterdam has had a strong influence on the dominant culture there. Dutch young people can be found playing Creole music and going to Surinamese clubs. This cultural infusion in the Netherlands will continue because in the case of Suriname, these immigrants are already Dutch citizens (Surinamese were offered Dutch citizenship when Suriname became an independent country; 40 percent took the offer and became Dutch citizens). They can return to Suriname whenever they please and then come back to Amsterdam again, bringing the culture of Suriname with them, demonstrating the power and stubborn persistence of cultural habits.

Conclusion

The twenty-first-century encounter of Europeans and immigrants has produced a great variety of cultural formations and responses, from the cultural hybrid of Creole Amsterdam to the cultural extremes of the debate over Islam in Europe. It has created a real dilemma in Europe among those who worry about preserving European heritage and real opportunities for the immigrants themselves. Part of the reason the debate continues is that there seem to be few answers to the question of how Europe will remain Europe within its new strongly multicultural model. Journalist Christopher Caldwell argues that the American model of a melting pot (which isn't even a very accurate description of immigration in the history of the United States) is not the right model for Europe, because in an age of globalization, immigrants can bring and keep their cultural identities because the links to their home countries remain strong and vibrant, unlike an earlier time when immigrants had little choice but to adapt to the culture of the host country. In addition, the rise in the twentieth century of the concepts of cultural relativism and multiculturalism has made the host country a more tolerant place for immigrants than previously, but the European example seems to suggest that tensions surrounding encounters of different peoples are getting worse, not better. Certainly the rise of nationalism in the eighteenth century and of religious extremism in the late twentieth century have forced encounters into more narrow absolutist pathways with less room for negotiation or middle ground accommodation.

Caldwell suggests that the Ottoman model of toleration of minorities on its lands is one that might work for Europe. Certainly the Ottoman model is worth examining. The Ottoman rulers' willingness to attract and then provide toleration for Orthodox Christians and Sephardic Jews from Spain and Portugal is a remarkable example. Even there, however, much intolerance was produced alongside official tolerance. But overall it was a very successful encounter. Not only did the Ottoman government provide official toleration but at the level of individual communities the characteristics of positive encounters were evident: cultural hybridity in the fused language of the Salonica business community, middle ground accommodation in some cultural practices, acculturation in the changing cultural habits of Jews there, and cultural persistence in the cultural autonomy that allowed Jews and other minorities to practice their own religion and culture with government protection. Will it work in the globalized and yet fractious world of the twenty-first century? In some ways the Ottoman model is working already, because one can find all of these characteristics in the European encounter with its new immigrants. On the other hand, Europeans have grave concerns about the lack of assimilation among immigrants, especially Muslims, but also the Romany people, often called gypsies. Recently France has begun expelling Romany people over concerns that they bring in crime and corruption. David Cameron, prime minister of the United Kingdom, has argued that the British policy of allowing separate communities has gone too far and is allowing the promotion of anti-western ideas that encourage terrorism there.

The answer might lie in the history of encounters themselves and the evidence of tolerance and creativity that sits alongside evidence of intolerance and extremism in almost every encounter studied in this volume. European intellectual historian Mark Lilla wrote in 2007,

> It is an unfortunate situation, but we have made our bed, Muslims and non-Muslims alike. Accommodation and mutual respect can help...Western countries have adopted different strategies for coping, some forbidding religious symbols like the head scarf in schools, others permitting them. But we need to recognize that coping is the order of the day, and that our expectations should remain low.[4]

The potential of encounters to open up the cracks in societies and nations and create new cultural, social, and even political formations should not be underestimated. But neither can the heavy toll of the human record of intolerance toward cultural difference be ignored. This duality is the true legacy of cross-cultural encounters.

Questions for Discussion

1. With huge numbers of immigrants flooding in Europe, what are the various ways Europeans have responded to the new immigrants?
2. Outline the debate among Europeans about immigration?
3. Why is the encounter between Islamic immigrants and Europe so troublesome?
4. Describe the role of sex and assumptions about female sexuality in the immigration debate.
5. Explain the rise of extremism in the debate over immigration? How has the existence of extremism in responses to immigrants and Europeans alike affected attitudes about immigration?
6. What are some of the characteristics of non-Muslim immigrants to Europe?
7. How can Europeans change the nature of their encounter with immigrants?

Endnotes

1. Quoted from http://islamineurope.blogspot.com/2006/10/denmark-marriage-immigration-drops.html, Wednesday October 26, 2006, Found on February 3, 2011.
2. Lisa Hanley, et al., ed. *Immigration and Integration in Urban Communities: Renegotiating the City* (Washington, DC: Woodrow Wilson Center Press, 2008), pp. 105–106.
3. Luisa Passerini, et al., ed. *Women Migrants from East to West: Gender, Mobility and Belonging in Contemporary Europe* (New York: Berghahn Books, 2007), p. 170.
4. Christopher Caldwell, *Reflections on the Revolution in Europe: Immigration, Islam, and the West* (New York: Anchor books, 2009), p. 281.

INDEX